Contents

About the authors vi
How to use this series vii
Introduction ix

UNIT 1 BEING A SCIENTIST IN THE MYP   1

Introduction 2
    Investigation 1.1: Understanding how pendulums swing 4
How does science work? 5
Care with scientific claims 6
Being a brilliant MYP scientist 7
    Investigation 1.2: A practice investigation: the gummy bear challenge 8
What makes MYP Science special? 14
Becoming great learners 21
Unit questions 22

UNIT 2 CLASSIFYING THE NATURAL WORLD   23

Introduction 24
Sorting things 24
Sorting and grouping the natural world 26
Classifying the living world 28
Living kingdoms 30
Dichotomous keys 31
The six kingdoms 32
    Investigation 2.1: Living lunch 35
A timeline of classification 37
Seven levels of classification 39
Linnaeus' naming system 39
Species 40
Unit questions 43

UNIT 3 LIVING IN A MANGROVE SWAMP   45

Introduction 46
Life on the coast 46
    Investigation 3.1: How much salt is too much? 48
A mangrove feast 50
    Experiment 3.1: It's all in the beak 51
Interactions in a mangrove swamp 53
Ecosystems 56
Unit questions 60

UNIT 4 EVERYDAY ACIDS AND BASES — 61

Introduction 62
Acids 63
Bases 65
Measuring acids and bases 66
    Experiment 4.1: Making an indicator 68
Concentrated or dilute? 72
Neutralisation 74
    Experiment 4.2: Baking soda and vinegar reaction 74
    Investigation 4.1: Treatment of acid lakes 75
How to use a Bunsen burner 76
Unit questions 78

UNIT 5 SOLIDS, LIQUIDS AND GASES — 79

Introduction 80
The four states of matter 80
Moving particle theory 82
    Experiment 5.1: Free space in solids, liquids and gases 83
Change of state 84
    Experiment 5.2: Changes of state 85
    Experiment 5.3: Evaporation rates under different conditions 87
    Investigation 5.1: The best drying conditions for clothes 87
Changes of state and the weather 89
Expansion 90
    Experiment 5.4: Demonstrating expansion 93
Temperature and the moving particle theory 94
Diffusion: let's spread out! 95
    Experiment 5.5: Diffusion 96
Air pressure 96
Unit questions 98

UNIT 6 FORCES AND SAFETY — 99

Introduction 100
    Investigation 6.1: The use and design of safety helmets for cyclists .. 100
Forces 101
    Experiment 6.1: Mass and weight 103
    Experiment 6.2: Ramps and gravity 105
    Investigation 6.2: How much friction? 108
    Experiment 6.3: It's a drag! 113
Balanced and unbalanced forces 114
Calculating speed 118
Unit questions 120

Rick **Armstrong** | Jennifer **Barnett** | Gareth **Jones** | Elani **McDonald** |

Science
1
for the international student

NELSON
CENGAGE Learning

Australia • Brazil • Japan • Korea • Mexico • Singapore • Spain • United Kingdom • United States

NELSON
CENGAGE Learning

Science 1 for the International Student
2nd Edition
Rick Armstrong
Jennifer Barnett
Gareth Jones
Elani McDonald
Jenny Sharwood

Publishing editor: Sarah Craig
Editor: Catherine Greenwood
Proofreader: Stephanie Ayres
Cover design: Aisling Gallagher
Cover image: Stocksy United Photography/Marcel
Text design: Aisling Gallagher
Permissions researcher: Sian Bradfield
Production controller: Emma Roberts
Typeset by: Macmillan Publishing Solutions

Any URLs contained in this publication were checked for currency during the production process. Note, however, that the publisher cannot vouch for the ongoing currency of URLs.

© 2016 Cengage Learning Australia Pty Limited

Copyright Notice
This Work is copyright. No part of this Work may be reproduced, stored in a retrieval system, or transmitted in any form or by any means without prior written permission of the Publisher. Except as permitted under the *Copyright Act 1968*, for example any fair dealing for the purposes of private study, research, criticism or review, subject to certain limitations. These limitations include: Restricting the copying to a maximum of one chapter or 10% of this book, whichever is greater; providing an appropriate notice and warning with the copies of the Work disseminated; taking all reasonable steps to limit access to these copies to people authorised to receive these copies; ensuring you hold the appropriate Licences issued by the Copyright Agency Limited ("CAL"), supply a remuneration notice to CAL and pay any required fees. For details of CAL licences and remuneration notices please contact CAL at Level 15, 233 Castlereagh Street, Sydney NSW 2000, Tel: (02) 9394 7600, Fax: (02) 9394 7601
Email: info@copyright.com.au
Website: www.copyright.com.au

For product information and technology assistance,
in Australia call **1300 790 853**;
in New Zealand call **0800 449 725**

For permission to use material from this text or product, please email
aust.permissions@cengage.com

National Library of Australia Cataloguing-in-Publication Data
Armstrong, Rick, author, editor.
Science 1 for the international student / Rick Armstrong, Jennifer Barnett,
Gareth Jones, Elani McDonald, Jenny Sharwood.
   2nd edition.
   9780170353403 (paperback)
   Science for the international student.
   Includes index.
   Series editor: Rick Armstrong.
   For secondary school age.
Science--Textbooks.
Science--Study and teaching (Secondary)--Australia.
International baccalaureate--Study guides.

Barnett, Jennifer, author.
Jones Gareth, author.
McDonald, Elani, author.
Sharwood, Jenny, author.

500

Cengage Learning Australia
Level 7, 80 Dorcas Street
South Melbourne, Victoria Australia 3205

Cengage Learning New Zealand
Unit 4B Rosedale Office Park
331 Rosedale Road, Albany, North Shore 0632, NZ

For learning solutions, visit **cengage.com.au**

Printed in Singapore by 1010 Printing International Limited.
1 2 3 4 5 6 7 20 19 18 17 16

UNIT 7 MAGNETISM AND ELECTRICITY 121

Introduction 122
Electricity..122
Creating electricity 123
     Experiment 7.1: Can you feel electrons? 123
Electrical circuits and currents 124
Series and parallel circuits 126
     Experiment 7.2: Measuring current in series and parallel circuits 128
Voltage (potential difference) 129
     Experiment 7.3: Measuring voltages (potential differences) 131
Magnets 132
     Experiment 7.4: Magnetic poles and fields..135
Magnets can be permanent or temporary 137
     Investigation 7.1: Electromagnets..139
Future of magnets 141
Unit questions 142

UNIT 8 OUR DYNAMIC EARTH 143

Introduction 144
From the beginning 146
The changing Earth 146
Structure of Earth 149
Plate tectonics: a theory is born 150
Tectonic plates and their movement 151
The rock cycle...155
Weathering: breaking down or dissolving rocks 157
     Experiment 8.1: When rocks freeze...158
     Investigation 8.1: Investigating chemical weathering of a variety of rocks 159
Erosion..160
     Investigation 8.2: How do river rocks become round? 162
Unit questions 163

Appendix 1: Approaches to Learning (ATL) framework in MYP Sciences.........................165
Appendix 2: MYP Science 1 assessment criteria..167
Appendix 3: Guidance on carrying out and writing up MYP 1 scientific investigations (criteria B and C) 169
Appendix 4: Articulating the conceptual framework in MYP Sciences 171
Glossary 175
Index 180

About the authors

Authors

Rick Armstrong (series editor)
Rick Armstrong has been involved with MYP sciences guide writing since 1994. He has experience with leading sciences workshops in all International Baccalaureate regions, moderation, school visits and authorisations, as an Approaches to Learning workshop leader, and as DP examiner. Rick is currently a freelance educational consultant in Madrid, Spain.

Jennifer Barnett
Jennifer Barnett has been involved with the MYP since 2005 and is a Sciences workshop leader and school authorisation team member. Recently, Jennifer was chosen to be part of the International Baccalaureate service, 'Building Quality Curriculum' to evaluate teachers' unit plans for school authorisation. She has also led a number of local and state workshops on incorporating technology in the Science classroom and differentiating Science for exceptional students. She currently teaches Integrated Sciences to MYP Years 1-3 in Austin, Texas.

Gareth Jones
Gareth Jones has taught the MYP for the last eight years. He has experience across a range of subjects teaching Science, Mathematics and Physical Health Education. This experience across the disciplines led him to be an examiner for the MYP Interdisciplinary eAssessment. He is currently an MYP and DP science teacher and Student Wellbeing leader at Halcyon London International School.

Elani McDonald
Elani McDonald has dedicated her entire teaching career to working in IB schools. She is a workshop leader and a MYP visiting team member. She has been involved in monitoring and moderation of assessment and was involved in writing the Science and Personal Project 2014 guides, as well as the 2014 Teacher Support Material for Physics. Elani is dedicated to making learning relevant and engaging and was shortlisted for the TES Maths teacher of the year 2014/15 award. Elani is teaching Mathematics and Sciences full-time and doing consultancy work part-time.

How to use this series

The *Science for the international student* series provides students with a variety of engaging and stimulating formats for learning, understanding and immersion in both the Middle Years Programme (MYP) philosophy of the International Baccalaureate (IB) and the science content. The features of the student book have been specifically designed to support this and to deliver exciting content in a variety of ways.

Specific MYP features

Each unit begins with a unit opening page that specifies:
- the key concept that is covered in the unit
- the related concepts that are covered in the unit
- the Global Context of the unit
- the Statement of Inquiry
- inquiry questions, divided into factual, conceptual and debatable questions.

Key and related concepts

Each unit is based around one *key concept* of an enduring transdisciplinary nature and a small number of *related concepts* designed to help frame the unit in the minds of the students.

Global Context

Students will be encouraged to see science in the *global context* of its ability to provide a basis for creative inventions that are capable of enriching our lives in areas such as space, materials, sports and medicines.

Statement of Inquiry

The *Statement of Inquiry* drives the unit and is strongly related to the units' concepts and context.

The inquiry questions are divided into factual, conceptual and debatable questions. Factual questions are related to the unit content, conceptual questions are related to the unit concepts and debatable questions are related to both and designed to stimulate deeper thinking.

Performance assessment tasks

Opportunities for assessment tasks occur throughout each unit and these are each identified by a *performance assessment task* icon.

The *summative performance assessment task* associated with the Statement of Inquiry is identified at the beginning of each unit. The criteria assessed by the assessment task are also identified.

Approaches to Learning

Opportunities to develop and apply *Approaches to Learning* skills are identified by an 'ATL' icon. Teachers can use these prompts to discuss and reinforce learning strategies.

Investigation

Investigations challenge students to design and perform their own experiments either individually or in groups. Investigations are designed to satisfy criteria B and C.

Experiments

Experiments provide students with the opportunity to develop and practise their skills, by following processes and procedures, to discover information for themselves and to build a greater understanding of, and interest in, scientific concepts. Experiments are designed to satisfy criterion C.

Taking action

Taking action suggestions are identified by a 'TA' icon and are designed to satisfy the MYP requirements for service as action.

Other features

Review

Review boxes contain questions and break the content into smaller sections, allowing students to review what they have learnt so far.

Activity

Activity boxes reinforce or develop concepts and skills through short, fun and hands-on activities.

Weblinks

Weblinks are identified by an icon and direct students to exciting websites to further explore the world of science.

Unit questions

Unit questions conclude each unit. They include review questions sorted under the MYP assessment criterion A, levels 1–8. Reflection questions are included to review the concepts underpinning the unit, to encourage further consideration of the debatable inquiry questions, and at times to consider further lines of inquiry.

NelsonNetBook

The *Science for the international student* NelsonNetBook is an interactive ebook that can be used online or offline. It is compatible with interactive whiteboards, computers and tablets, with optional Web 2.0 functionality for class groups. Students can add highlights, annotations, audio and video clips, and weblinks, and teachers can use it to share their personalised version with the class.

Visit the NelsonNet portal at www.nelsonnet.com.au to find out more, register or log in if already registered.

NelsonNet teacher website

The NelsonNet teacher website contains further valuable advice, including draft MYP unit plans covering the first two pages of the revised MYP planner, and a curriculum overview as required by the IB. Other resources include blackline masters (BLMs) containing possible further experimental work and classroom activities, ideas for further resources, and further advice relating to teaching in a conceptual way and for the use of the Approaches to Learning framework. Answers are also provided for all questions, as well as a list of extra resources for each unit.

Contact your sales representative for information about access codes.

Introduction

To the student

We hope you will enjoy using this exciting student book, which has been designed to provide an up-to-date science experience around the principles of the new enriched Middle Years Programme (MYP) offered by the International Baccalaureate (IB). You are likely to already be an experienced IB student, proud of being an *internationally minded* student, and familiar with the distinctive way IB students work in science. These revised books provide a greater emphasis on the global contexts for learning in science, ranging from the challenge to provide better and more equal access to medicines worldwide, to considering global environmental challenges such as global warming. The books emphasise investigative and experimental work and expect you to work and think like a real scientist. As you will be well aware, the IB is also about encouraging you to develop effective learning skills that will stay with you for life, and you will see in these books many suggestions to help you with this challenge. We wish you all the success possible with MYP Science and beyond.

To the teacher

We have reviewed our original series, published in 2010–2011, to take account of the innovative developments and improvements in the MYP. In this new edition, we have deepened our coverage of MYP principles within each unit. The units are now much more contextual and more explicitly driven by the Statement of Inquiry. As you will be aware, the IB has attempted to give schools more flexibility in their delivery of the MYP and there certainly is no 'correct' model of how to put the MYP into practice. For that reason, we feel we should explain some of our approaches to constructing our units.

1. **Conceptual framework:** We have closely followed the suggested framework but have added a small number of extra related concepts that will be useful to teachers and will allow coverage of the US cross-cutting concepts. We have also used concepts from other subjects when we felt their use would enhance the unit. Importantly, we accept that the key to teaching conceptually lies in appropriate classroom practices. To help this practice, we have included activities and questions to help strengthen students' understanding of the conceptual framework as well as some further guidance in the teacher materials.
2. **Content:** We have included academically challenging content that will provide an effective transition from MYP 1 to 5, the new e-examinations, and to higher study in the Diploma Programme (DP) or in other national systems. This content should also help teachers meet the requirements of local curricula. We have covered all the expected content for MYP Sciences e-examination in Books 4/5. Some of this content is also covered in more detail in Books 1, 2 and 3. We have ensured that the scope and sequence of our MYP Books 1–5 is well thought out and offers a coherent framework for the development of deep understanding based on the big unifying concepts in science.
3. **Global Contexts:** The development of the Areas of interaction into the Global Contexts is very liberating and opens the door for much more creative uses of contexts in the planning of MYP units. To take advantage of this potential, we have associated the Global Context chosen for the unit with a more specific 'exploration into' statement. This 'exploration into' feeds clearly into the Statement of Inquiry for each unit. This has helped us to make the science content up to date, interesting and relevant to the real world.

4. **Statements of Inquiry:** We have written simple and clear Statements of Inquiry that are understandable to students and to teachers. We have been flexible in relation to trying to build all the chosen concepts into the Statements of Inquiry. Our priority has been to ensure that the Statement of Inquiry is easy to understand, has a conceptual feel, and, importantly, relates to the chosen Global Context.

5. **Assessment tasks:** Most science units will require more than one summative performance assessment task because it is artificial to try to bring together a number of the sciences criteria in one task. Therefore, most units include assessments relating to investigation work (criteria B and C), a performance-type task relating to the impacts of science (criterion D) and end-of-unit questions to assess criterion A. At the beginning of each unit, you will see a summative performance assessment task that relates closely to the Statement of Inquiry. We have given this task the most authentic performance nature possible. Other performance assessment tasks are included in each unit that can be used summatively or formatively. We expect that not all of the assessment suggestions will be used for summative purposes.

6. **Approaches to Learning:** We are very impressed by the revised Approaches to Learning framework based on the ten clusters of ATL skills. We understand that the effective implementation of ATL is a whole-school challenge but have made suggestions for when teachers can explicitly introduce these skills and dispositions, both as part of summative assessment tasks, and also more generally in their daily teaching. You will also see a simplified ATL framework in the appendices that we think will be of great help to teachers.

7. **Service learning:** We have also suggested a possible service learning activity (labelled 'TA' (Taking action)) for each unit.

The NelsonNet teacher website contains draft MYP unit plans, curriculum overviews, BLMs for experimental work and classroom activities, ideas for interdisciplinary tasks, further resources and advice for using the ATL framework, and answers to all questions.

We realise there may seem to be an inherent conflict between the idea of teachers working in a creative and collaborative way to produce MYP units of work and the use of a textbook. Schools will use this book in different ways. Some new schools might find it an invaluable stepping stone to getting a MYP Sciences programme up and running. Others may use it to enhance their existing courses. We encourage you not to use these books the way traditional textbooks have been used. Be creative, add to them, choose the bits you like, encourage the students to interact with them. They are there to help students in their deep learning of science, to encourage their interest and motivation. We hope the availability of materials of this kind will make your life as the teacher a little easier and give you more time to focus on the actual teaching and learning. Enjoy them.

Rick Armstrong (Series editor)

UNIT 1

BEING A SCIENTIST IN THE MYP

KEY CONCEPT
Relationships

RELATED CONCEPTS
Evidence

Patterns

Development

GLOBAL CONTEXT
Scientific and technical innovation: an exploration into how the world of science works

STATEMENT OF INQUIRY
Scientists develop our understanding of the world by looking for patterns and carrying out experiments to gain evidence to explain relationships.

INQUIRY QUESTIONS

FACTUAL
1. What are the steps involved in the scientific method?
2. What are the key features of MYP science?

CONCEPTUAL
3. Why is the control of variables (fair testing) important in science?
4. Why are concepts important to learning in science?
5. How does the use of global contexts help learning in science?

DEBATABLE
6. Does science provide the answers to all questions?
7. What factors may prevent science from solving problems or issues?

Introduction

Questioning is part of human nature. The need to understand, explain and measure inspires our need to create. Throughout time, humans have invented new ways of unlocking the mysteries of our world and the universe. Discoveries in health, medicine, technology, space and energy have influenced culture and society.

FIGURE 1.1 Scientific discoveries opened up the possibility of space travel.

FIGURE 1.2 The first magnetic compass was probably made in China during the Qin dynasty, 200 BCE and used for early navigation.

Without the discoveries of determined scientists, our lives would not be what they are today. Similarly, future discoveries will enrich our lives further. Here are just a few examples of how scientific discoveries and new technologies have changed our lives.

- Medicine – new technologies are helping people live longer, healthier lives. Years ago, cuts and scrapes that became infected could kill people, as could burns, disease and even childbirth. Vaccinations save thousands of lives from diseases that can be prevented.
- Communication – we can share our ideas in ways that were unimaginable in the past. We know almost instantly what is happening around the world, and can keep in close contact with family and friends.
- Agriculture – we can grow much more and better quality food.

- Arts – many more people are able to become artists, and more people can access high-quality art.
- Education – new technologies are improving access to education worldwide, and we understand much better how people learn.

Technology has also changed the way we play sport, use textiles and travel. But not everyone has benefitted equally from these developments. Bringing these technologies to everyone remains one of the most serious challenges facing the world.

Scientists are often portrayed as men and women in white coats studying an array of chemicals. In reality, they are people who are curious about the world or want to improve our lives. There are more types of scientists than there are letters in the alphabet! From archaeologists to zoologists, scientists carry out investigations to find answers to questions. Some become journalists, authors or politicians, and a special kind become teachers of the next generation of scientists.

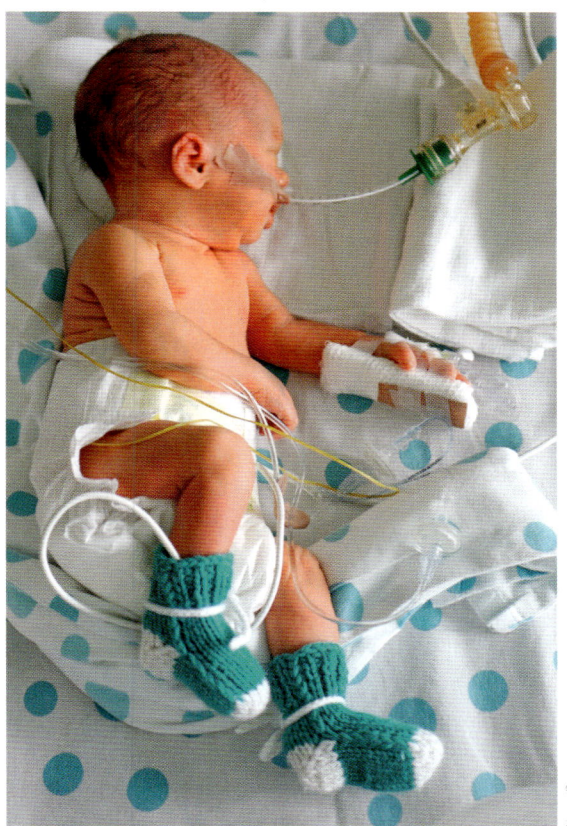

FIGURE 1.3 Modern medicine allows premature babies to be cared for and thrive, when once they may have died.

FIGURE 1.4 Technology such as computers, interactive whiteboards and projectors helps to improve education worldwide.

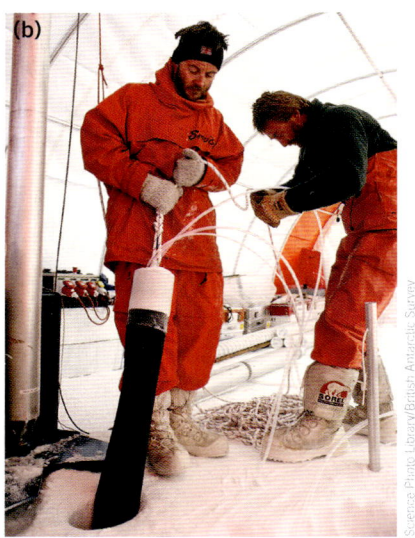

FIGURE 1.5 (a) Marine biologists and (b) climate scientists work in different environments to find answers to questions about the ocean and the climate.

FIGURE 1.6 Angela Merkel, Chancellor of Germany, was a scientist. She worked as a research chemist before becoming a politician.

Understanding how pendulums swing

INVESTIGATION 1.1

CRITERIA B AND C

 ATL

CRITICAL THINKING
Designing investigations. Designing, carrying out, and considering the results of any investigation in any subject requires a high level of careful and critical thinking.

Near the end of this unit, you will carry out a scientific investigation with little guidance from your teacher. You will use what you will learn from Investigation 1.2 into gummy bears, for which you will receive considerable guidance from your teacher.

YOUR CHALLENGE
To investigate how the length of a pendulum affects how fast it swings.

THIS MIGHT HELP
You can make a pendulum by attaching a weight to a piece of thin, flexible string. Tie the pendulum to the clamp on a clamp stand and check that it swings smoothly. It is difficult to measure the time for just one swing. It is best to measure the time for 10 swings and divide the result by 10.

Carry out and write up the investigation by following the guide in Appendix 3 on page 169, or as advised by your teacher.

> **ACTIVITY** Gallery walk of your ideas about science

On different coloured pieces of paper, answer the following questions.
1 Name four important scientists and describe their contributions.
2 Name four different sciences and describe each area of study, e.g. botany – the study of plants.
3 Suggest the four most important scientific discoveries of all time.
4 Suggest four qualities a good scientist should have.

Stick your answers on a wall and carry out a gallery walk of the answers.

How does science work?

Science is a way of explaining the natural world. Science is based on careful **investigation**, on collecting **evidence** and considering it critically. Scientific theories about the natural world can be changed, developed further or even rejected. You probably know that before the work of Copernicus in the 16th century, people thought the Sun moved around the Earth.

The idea of carrying out careful observations and experiments can be traced back to early times. For example, in Imperial China by around 300 BCE, people had studied how the symptoms of various diseases changed. In India around 600 BCE, people knew how to carry out operations for cataracts in eyes. Science flourished over the Islamic Golden Age from around 800 to 1300 and helped lay the foundation for the scientific revolution in Europe from around 1500 to 1700.

One of the first people to develop a more scientific way of working was the English physicist Sir Isaac Newton (1643–1727) (Figure 1.7). He carefully recorded his observations and repeated his investigations many times. Newton averaged his data, thought about his results, made conclusions and considered new ways to get better answers. His work led to a completely new theory about how objects move that we now call Newton's laws of motion.

FIGURE 1.7 Sir Isaac Newton used a scientific way of investigating motion.

Science is continually developing as theories are improved, and new theories sometimes replace older theories. Even Newton's ideas on motion have since been improved by Einstein's theories on relativity.

> **ACTIVITY** History of science

The origins of science go back a long time and involve many cultures. Carry out some research about the history of scientific developments that took place in one of the following cultures and share your results with the class in a 5-minute presentation:
- Ancient Babylon and Ancient Egypt
- Ancient Greece
- Ancient India
- Imperial China
- Islamic Golden Age
- Europe in the Middle Ages.

Care with scientific claims

We need to be careful about scientific claims, particularly in areas such as diet and medicine. Many of these claims are **pseudoscience** – they appear to be scientific but lack reliable evidence. Many people find it difficult to distinguish between reliable scientific claims and unreliable pseudoscience. For example, some people spend a lot of money on various minerals and vitamins, but in most cases there is no reliable scientific evidence for any health benefits from consuming these dietary supplements. This problem has increased with more widespread access to the internet.

A fully ripe banana with dark patches on yellow skin produces a substance call TNF (tumour necrosis factor), which has the ability to combat abnormal cells. The more darker patches it has, the higher will be its immunity enhancement quality. Hence, the riper the banana, the better the anti-cancer quality.

FIGURE 1.8 This seems like a pseudoscience claim about bananas.

Not all useful knowledge about the world is a result of scientific investigation. Personal experience can be a very valuable way of investigating something new. An example is an anthropologist looking to understand the customs of another culture. Many questions cannot be solved by a scientific approach, such as judgements about the quality of art or questions about religion. These are sometimes said to be examples of **non-science**. If you continue on in the IB until the Diploma Programme, then you will study these sorts of issues in Theory of Knowledge.

ACTIVITY

The science of superheroes

Some of the special powers of superheroes are inspired by science, even if in reality humans could only possess these powers with special technological support. It is interesting and educational to consider the scientific implications of these super powers. For example, how does Storm in X-Men produce lightning bolts?

Some superheroes are scientists. For example, Spider-Man (Peter Parker) is a science student, and the Incredible Hulk (Bruce Banner) is a nuclear physicist.

TASK 1 DISCUSS YOUR FAVOURITE SUPERHEROES

Choose one of your favourite superheroes and conduct some research into the scientific basis of their super power(s). Produce a poster explaining their super power(s) and discussing their scientific implications.

TASK 2 INVENT A NEW SUPERHERO

Invent a new superhero whose role is to protect the environment. Describe the super power(s) he or she has, discuss the science involved and create a short cartoon showing your superhero in action. You will see some examples from other students in the adjacent weblink.

Go to http://mypsci1.nelsonnet.com.au and click on **Superheroes**. Use the weblinks to help you carry out research into the science of superheroes.

Go to http://mypsci1.nelsonnet.com.au and click on **New superheroes** to see some examples of students inventing new superheroes.

FIGURE 1.9 The powers of superheroes can be inspired by science.

Being a brilliant MYP scientist

Science education in schools around the world has changed a lot in recent years. It used to mainly involve a lot of rote-learning scientific facts, a lot of study from books and a lot of talking from teachers. These days in most countries, the major aim of science education in schools is to help students develop the skills of real scientists. Therefore, students are taught to think in a scientific way, to carry out scientific investigations (Figure 1.10), to relate their science to real-world problems and to understand scientific ideas. This is particularly true in the MYP.

FIGURE 1.10 Students carry out scientific investigations as part of their science course.

The scientific method

Although different types of scientists work in different ways, there are a lot of similarities in their approach. This is sometimes referred to as the **scientific method**. Scientists often work collaboratively and discuss each step in their investigation (Figure 1.11). In the MYP, when we carry out scientific investigations, we can use the model in Figure 1.11 to help us. Each of the steps will be explained as you work through the unit.

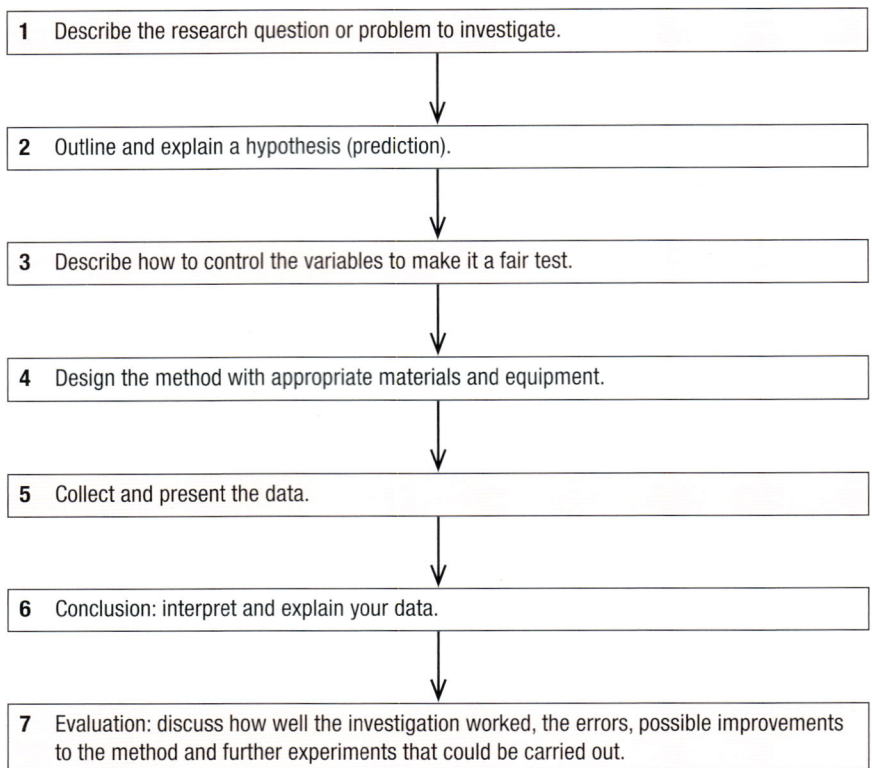

FIGURE 1.11 Steps in the scientific method

Investigation 1.2 is your first MYP scientific investigation to work on together as a class, step by step, with support from your teacher.

A practice investigation: the gummy bear challenge   INVESTIGATION 1.2

TRANSFER
Using skills in new situations. We are using a teaching idea called scaffolding during this investigation. This means we will give you the structure for how to carry out this scientific investigation so that next time you will be able to carry out the investigation with less guidance.

Gummy bears were first made in Germany in 1920. You can use any other gelatin-covered jelly sweet, such as jelly babies, for this investigation. Teachers may like to substitute this investigation with one on another topic if they prefer.

You will use the seven steps listed in Figure 1.11 to help you carry out your first MYP scientific investigation.

1 DESCRIBE THE RESEARCH QUESTION OR PROBLEM TO INVESTIGATE

First you need a question or a problem to investigate. This question or problem should be developed by you. Often, research questions come from

FIGURE 1.12 Gummy bears

observations we have made. Sometimes we carry out further research to find out more about the topic.

Put the gummy bear into a container with water, leave it overnight and observe what happens. This observation should give you some ideas for a good research question.

FIGURE 1.13 The growth of a gummy bear when left in water

What are you thinking? How fast did the gummy bear grow? How much did it grow? What happens if you add other substances to the water? What happens if you increase the temperature? Do gummy bears of all colours grow in the same way?

Here are some quite simple research questions.
- Do gummy bears of all colours grow at the same speed?
- How does the speed of growth change over time?
- Does the growth change if you add other substances such as sugar to the water?
- Does the temperature of the water affect how fast they grow?

A more sophisticated research question could be as follows.
- What factors control how much a gummy bear grows in water?

> Write your research question for your investigation. For this task, concentrate on the effect of adding sugar to the water.

2 OUTLINE AND EXPLAIN A HYPOTHESIS (PREDICTION)

Scientists usually have an idea or theory about the results they are likely to obtain. This idea or theory is called a **hypothesis**. A hypothesis is similar to a prediction. Try to suggest a reason for your hypothesis (this can be difficult in some situations). Here is an example.

'My hypothesis is that gummy bears of all colours will grow the same amount. I think this is because the colour is a very small part of the gummy bear and is unlikely to have any effect.'

> Write your hypothesis (prediction).

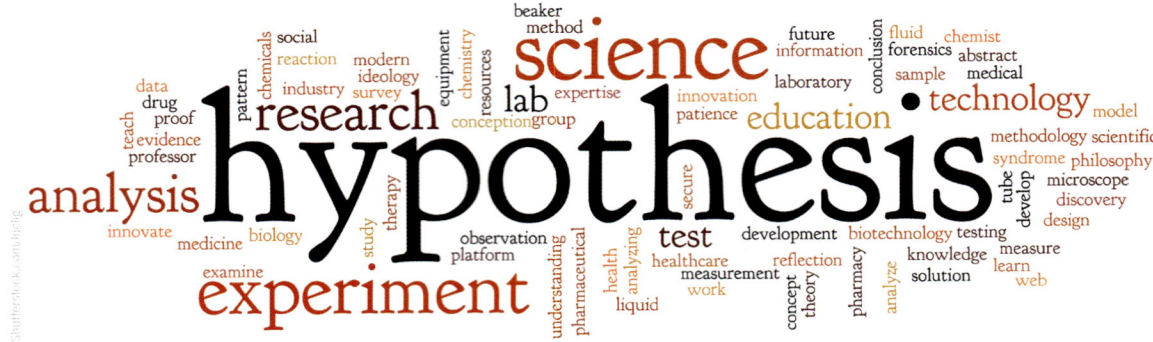

FIGURE 1.14 The hypothesis at the centre of scientific investigation

3 DESCRIBE HOW TO CONTROL THE VARIABLES TO MAKE IT A FAIR TEST

Your investigation needs to be a **fair test**. For example, if you were investigating the amount of sugar added to the water, and you used different-sized gummy bears in your experiment, it would not be a fair test. You could not compare the results from one gummy bear to another.

The word **variable** is very important in science. It means the property of something involved in the experiment that can change. Variables that you change are called **independent variables**. For an investigation to be a fair test, only one variable may be changed at a time – all other variables must be kept the same. For example, in this investigation you could decide to investigate the effect of changing the amount of sugar in the water. The amount of sugar would be the independent variable. The difference between the largest and the smallest values in the independent variable is called the **range**.

You need to keep the other variables the same. This would include keeping the type, size, and colour of gummy bear; the amount of water; the time; the temperature; and the size of the containers the same. These variables are called the **control variables**. If you control these variables, you can say that it was a fair test.

During an investigation, you will be measuring the outcome. In this investigation, this is the size of the gummy bear. This is called the **dependent variable** because it depends on the changes you are making to the independent variable. As you gain more experience with scientific investigations, you will state in your hypothesis the relationship between the independent and dependent variable.

Go to http://mypsci1.nelsonnet.com.au and click on **Variables** to see a video that explains the idea of variables.

> List one independent variable to investigate, the dependent variable to measure and the control variables that you will keep the same.

4 DESIGN THE METHOD WITH APPROPRIATE MATERIALS AND EQUIPMENT

You should have a detailed plan for your investigation. Before you start, think about the following types of questions.
- What equipment and materials do you need?
- How will you set them up?
- How will you make sure the method is safe?
- What steps will you follow to carry out your investigation?
- How will you change your independent variable?
- What data will you collect?
- How will you measure the change in size of the gummy bear?

Scientists need to share with other scientists exactly how they do their investigations, so a clear and logical plan is important. Your plan needs to be clear and easy to repeat so that other scientists can repeat your experiment. This is a very important aspect of how science works.

You should also state what data you will collect. In this case, you could simply say that you will carry out five different experiments: one with pure water and four with different numbers of teaspoons of sugar.

Where possible, scientists should repeat their results. Simply carrying out the experiments with one gummy bear each time would not be good science. Experiments can have errors and sometimes an unreliable result can be obtained. Repeating the experiment gives us more reliable results. In this case it is a good idea to use three or four gummy bears each time, or three or four different trials.

> Write your method for your experiments. A diagram is likely to help.

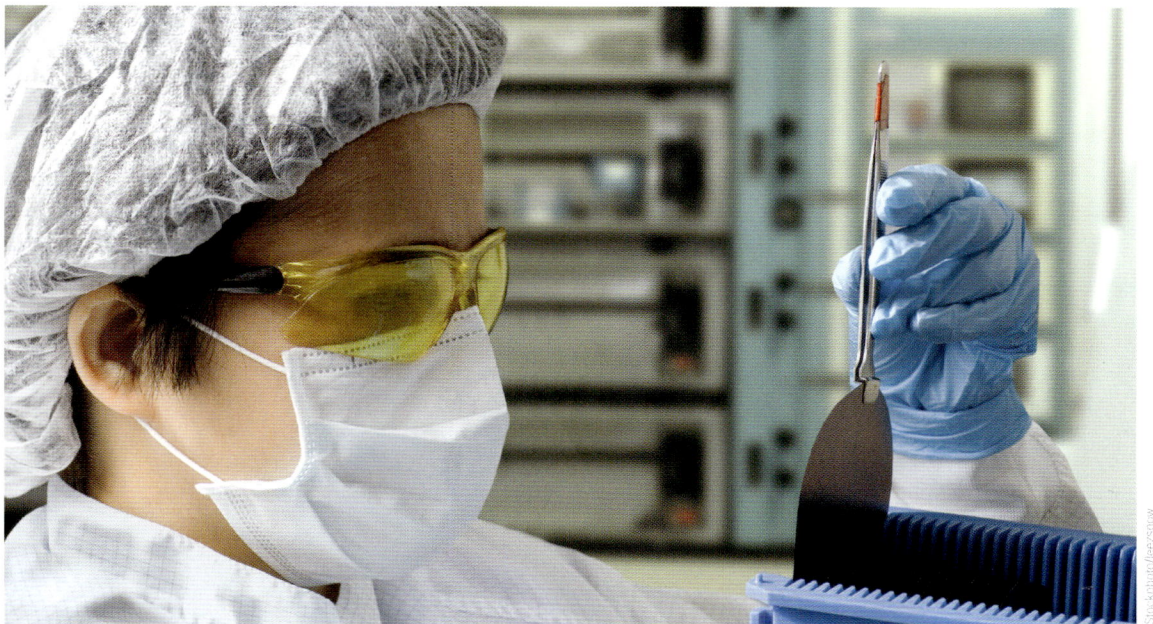

FIGURE 1.15 It is important that you design a method that is safe.

5 COLLECT AND PRESENT THE DATA

During your investigation, carefully watch any changes that occur and take any necessary measurements. This is called **experimental data**. Data can be collected in many ways, including measurements with suitable apparatus (for example, a ruler, photos or videos). The data is then recorded in a table. Sometimes it will be simply well-organised, written observations. If you have repeated your experiment and have more than one measurement, then you will often need to work out the **mean** (a type of average) of your results.

In your gummy bear investigation, you will need a table to record the original length of the gummy bear(s) and final length(s). Think about the headings your table will have. Don't forget to include the units of any measurements you have made. (Table 1.1 is given as an example.)

TABLE 1.1 Sample results table

Amount of sugar added (teaspoons)	Initial length of gummy bear (cm)	Final length of gummy bear (cm)	Difference in length (cm)

If your results include numbers, then a good way to show the results is by drawing a graph (Figure 1.16), such as a line graph, pie graph or column graph (bar chart). For this investigation, you could use a line graph. Talk with your teacher about how to draw and label the graph. You also need to draw a **line of best fit**, which is a straight line or curve that goes through as many points as possible, with an equal number of points above and below the line.

Design your results table, carry out your experiments to collect the data, and then present your results using a graph.

6 CONCLUSION: INTERPRET AND EXPLAIN YOUR DATA

When your investigation is finished, you need to communicate what you have learnt. Your explanation should be organised and well thought out and show good scientific thinking. Draw a graph to help see more clearly the relationship between the amount of sugar added to the water and the increase in length of the gummy bear. What pattern does the graph show? What shape is it? Are there any points that do not fit with the rest of your results? These points are called **anomalies** (or outliers) (Figure 1.17).

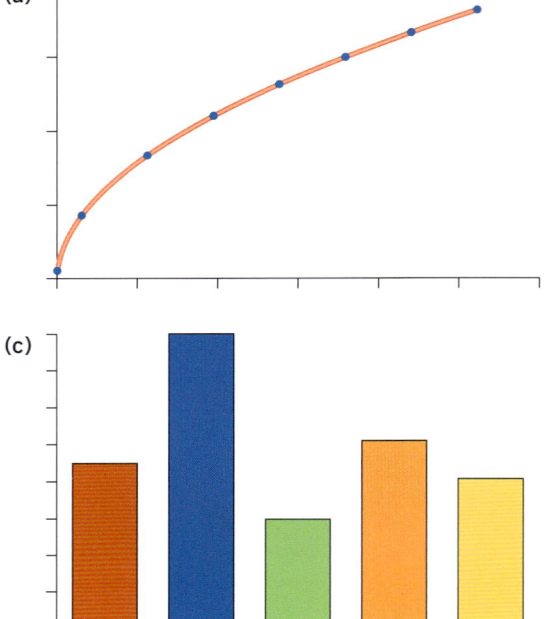
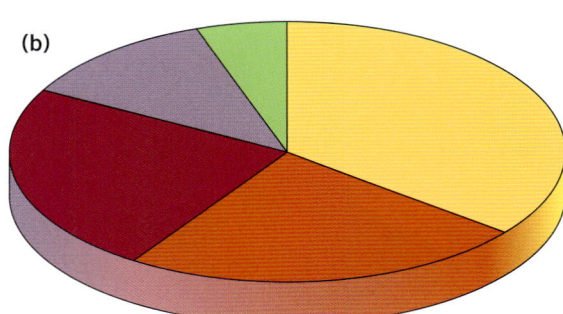

FIGURE 1.16 Experimental results can be displayed in a (a) line graph, (b) pie graph or (c) column graph.

The best science happens when you work collaboratively and you are prepared to argue about the interpretation of your results. It is important to be sceptical – question whether the method and the evidence were good enough to make these claims. Sometimes, results from experiments are not very clear, so you might need to say that there are no clear **trends**. In this case, it is likely more experiments need to be done.

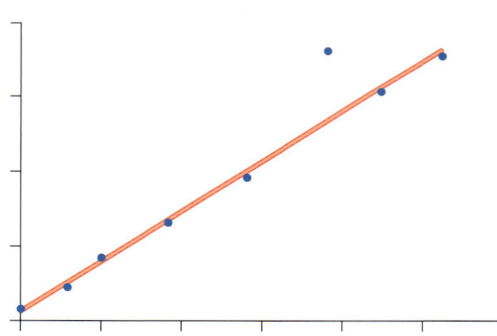

FIGURE 1.17 A line graph showing an anomalous result – an outlier does not fit with the rest of the line.

Write your conclusion to show how you have interpreted and explained your results.
Your teacher will probably guide you on this, particularly on the importance of being very careful about how you interpret the evidence and the need for very carefully written conclusions.

7 EVALUATION: DISCUSS HOW WELL THE INVESTIGATION WORKED, THE ERRORS, POSSIBLE IMPROVEMENTS TO THE METHOD, FURTHER EXPERIMENTS THAT COULD BE CARRIED OUT AND WHETHER YOUR RESULTS AGREED WITH THE HYPOTHESIS

This is the reflective part of an investigation. This can be challenging, but in science this is considered to be very important. Think about whether your investigation was successful – whether it actually tested the hypothesis. In a **valid** experiment, you can trust your data. All experimental measurements involve some errors. The important idea is that the results are sufficiently **accurate** and **precise** to make the experiment valid. A valid experiment also means that it really was a fair test. It means you really did control the variables sufficiently.

Try to suggest how to improve the experiment. How would you change the method? Also suggest other experiments you could do to find out more about this research question. For instance, in this investigation, you could change the independent variable to time, or to temperature.

Reflect on your hypothesis. What do the results tell you about your original theory? Perhaps you were trying to find out if adding sugar to water affected the amount the gummy bears expanded. Do your results support your original hypothesis?

> Complete your evaluation of the investigation.

That is your first MYP scientific investigation completed.
In the next section, you will learn about how this investigation could be assessed.

REVIEW

1. Outline what is meant by a scientific investigation.
2. State the seven steps in the model of scientific investigation described in this unit.
3. Outline what is meant by a fair test.
4. State what is meant by variables in a scientific investigation.
5. Outline the three types of variables that are involved in any scientific investigation.
6. Imagine that during an experiment, your partner looked at the results and quickly concluded what they showed, but you had doubts about the results and the validity of the experiment. Suggest what you might say to your partner.
7. When vinegar is added to baking powder, it fizzes and gives off a gas. An experiment was designed (see Figure 1.18) to measure the volume of this gas over 4 minutes.

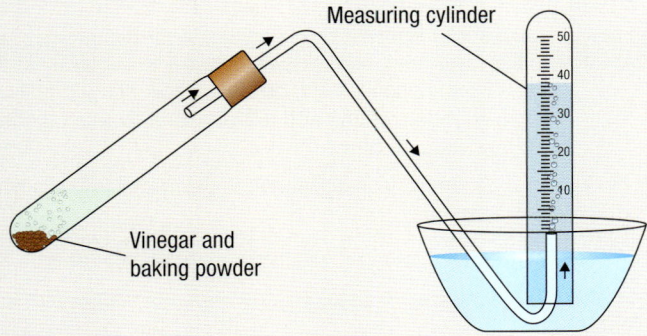

FIGURE 1.18 Apparatus used to measure the volume of gas given off

The results are displayed in the following table.

Time (min)	Volume of gas (litres)
0.5	0.30
1.0	0.50
1.5	0.55
2.0	0.59
2.5	0.60
3.0	0.60
3.5	0.60
4.0	0.60

    a Plot a graph of the results.
    b Are there any anomalous results?
    c Interpret these results; that is, describe what happens to the volume of gas over time.
    d State the independent variable in this experiment.
    e State the dependent variable in this experiment.
    f State what the control variables could have been in this experiment.
    g Suggest a different independent variable that could be investigated in this experiment.
8 Suggest a hypothesis for an investigation into how increasing the amount of fertiliser affects the growth of plants. Try to explain your hypothesis.
9 a Write two questions that can be answered by science.
    b Write two questions that cannot be answered by science.
10 Explain what is meant by pseudoscience.

What makes MYP Science special?

Assessment in MYP Science

A special feature of MYP Science is the way the assessment works. You will gain levels in relation to four different **assessment criteria**. Table 1.2 shows the criteria and ways they could be assessed.

TABLE 1.2 MYP Science assessment criteria

Assessment criteria	Tasks that could be used for assessment
A. Knowing and understanding	Examinations, tests, quizzes, challenging questions, extended writing and explanations, presentations, posters, debates
B. Inquiring and designing	Scientific investigations (as described in the previous section)
C. Processing and evaluating	Scientific investigations or other experiments
D. Reflecting on the impacts of science (considering how science can be used to solve problems, for example, climate change)	Essays, presentations, debates, role plays, films

These four assessment criteria, and how they are used to award grades, are more fully explained in Appendix 1 on page 165. Successful MYP students learn to understand these assessment criteria. The criteria tell you what you need to do to gain top grades. Being a successful MYP Science student is not just about doing well in examinations. It is just as important to develop your experimental skills and to be interested in how science can be used to improve the world.

> **ACTIVITY** **Learning to use the assessment criteria**
>
> Use assessment criteria B and C to award levels to a write-up of the gummy bears investigation. Your teacher will give you a write-up from another student (or group of students). Your teacher will also give you some guidance on how to give and receive feedback. One commonly used approach for giving feedback is called 'two stars and a wish'. This approach acknowledges two areas where the student did well (the stars) and one area where they could improve (the wish).
> 1. Read the level descriptors for each of criteria B and C carefully and then decide which level the work corresponds to. It would be best to work on this in groups and to try to come to a consensus with the others in the group.
> 2. Give feedback to the original student(s) about the strengths and weaknesses of the work, and the level you would award. Also include feedback about how the work could be improved.
> 3. Discuss how you felt during this experience of giving and receiving feedback. How easy was it? How useful was it?
> Remember, feedback should be kind, specific and helpful.

REFLECTION
Self-awareness of learning, giving and receiving feedback. One of the best ways for students to improve their learning is through the use of **formative assessment**. This means students understand the assessment criteria well and are using them to assess their own work, and to assess the work of other students.

TA HELPING OTHER STUDENTS CARRY OUT SCIENTIFIC INVESTIGATIONS

You could offer to help primary school students carry out scientific investigations, particularly on the idea of variables and fair testing. You could design an investigation for them to carry out, which could possibly be based on growing plants or dissolving sugar.

Emphasising big ideas – the use of concepts

Our scientific knowledge is increasing rapidly and is easily accessible via internet, so it makes no sense for schools to try to teach you everything worth knowing in science. Science education should emphasise the big ideas in science – the ideas that give structure to science, that help you work and think like a scientist. The use of big ideas or **concepts** should help you to understand ideas better, or more deeply. When you learn something, the neurons in your brain send electrical messages (Figure 1.19). Learning is about building connections between neurons in your brain so that concepts, such as about gravity or how plants grow, are clearly organised.

Some students think that teachers simply need to explain the scientific ideas for students to learn. This is not true.

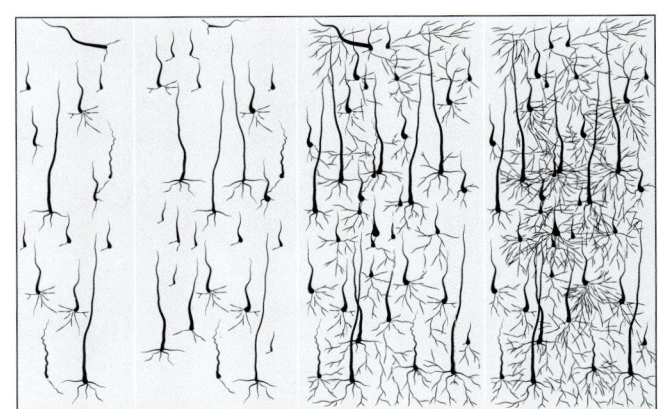

FIGURE 1.19 Neurons link up as concepts develop in the brain.

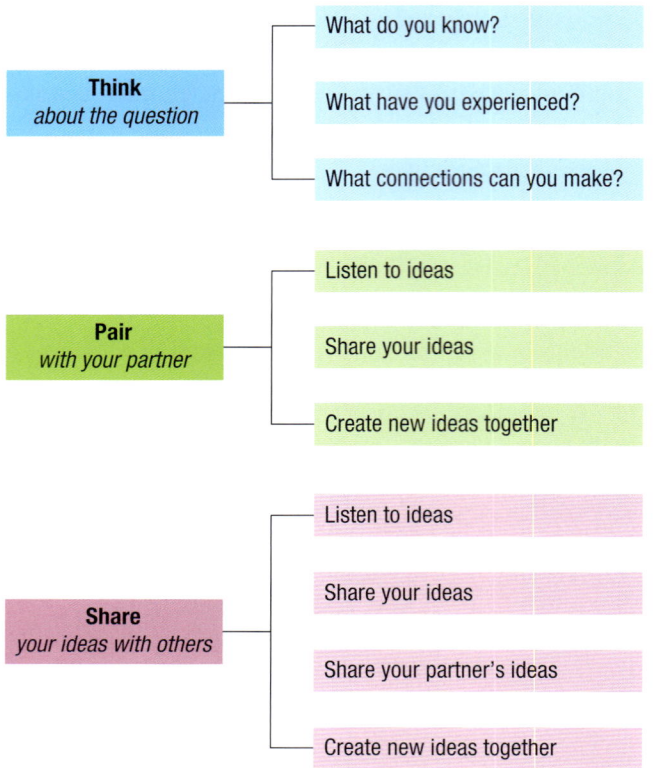

The learning is done by the student. The student is the one who needs to make an effort to ensure that their understanding has developed. This is why in science it very important that students ask questions and are prepared to discuss their ideas with other students. Teachers will often give you activities or questions to help you with these discussions. One such activity is called think, pair, share (Figure 1.20). Some students find mind maps very useful when organising their ideas (Figure 1.21).

FIGURE 1.20 A think, pair, share activity will help with your science learning.

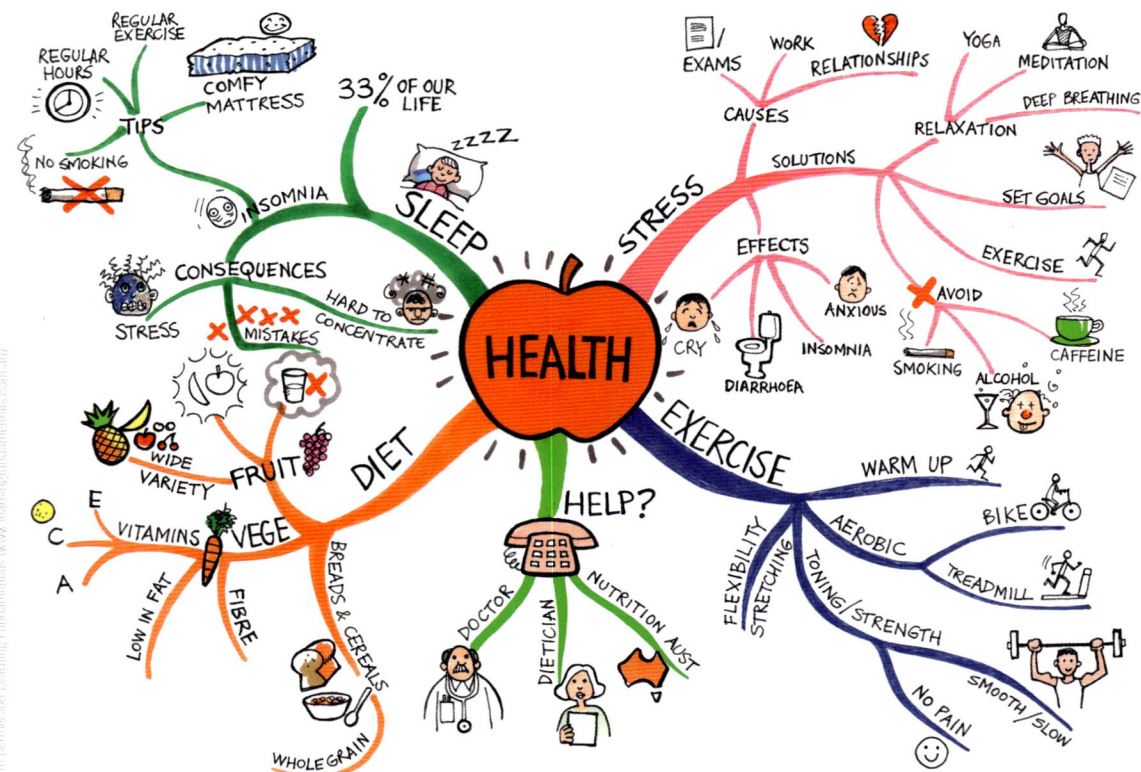

FIGURE 1.21 A mind map can help you learn about healthy living.

Misconceptions in science

In science, there is another difficulty about learning scientific concepts (theories). We all develop concepts about the world by simply being alive and being in the world. Sometimes these concepts are not scientifically correct and it is difficult to change these **misconceptions** to the correct scientific concepts. For example, some people think that electricity is used up in an electrical circuit, or that an object moving at a constant speed must have a force acting on it, or that plants get all their food from the soil. To overcome misconceptions, we need to have the opportunity to discuss our ideas with other people, and to answer special questions that challenge our thinking.

Key and related concepts in MYP Science

As you will be learning in other MYP subjects, each MYP unit of work is based on one key concept and usually two or three related concepts. These concepts are described in Appendix 4 on page 173. One key concept in science is systems, the idea of a group of related parts that move or work together. Examples include body systems such as the nervous system, and the solar system.

A related concept in science is patterns; for example, how scientists look for patterns in the weather, in the reactions of metals, and in results from experiments.

ACTIVITY   **Organising your ideas**

1. Use a think, pair, share activity to discuss the idea 'Looking for patterns is an important aspect of science'.
2. Discuss the following statements with another student or your teacher.
   - Energy is used up as a car moves.
   - A plant gets its food from the soil.
   - Gases do not weigh anything.
3. Use a mind map to show your understanding of an area of science you find interesting.

REFLECTIVE
Knowledgeable about aspects of learning such as the use of mind maps. Mind maps are very powerful tools to help you organise your ideas. They can help with organising a speech, writing an essay, or revising for examinations.

Relating MYP Science to the real-world use of global contexts

You will be learning in all subjects that every MYP unit of work is based on a **global context** (Table 1.3, page 18). This is to make sure learning has relevance for you. If you were a PYP student, you will recognise the global contexts as being very similar to the **PYP transdisciplinary themes**. In an MYP Science class, if someone asks you 'Why are you learning this?', you should be able to give a good answer. You might say 'I am learning about forces and motion because it will help me understand how to be safe in my life and hence support the development of my identity and relationships with others'.

TABLE 1.3 The use of MYP global contexts

Global context		
Identities and relationships	**Who am I? Who are we?**	
	In science, you could be involved in explorations relating to your health and/or your relationships with other people.	
Orientation in space and time	**What is the meaning of 'when' and 'where'?**	
	In science, you could explore key moments in science, and how new scientific discoveries have changed the world.	
Personal and cultural expression	**What is the nature and purpose of creative expression?**	
	You could explore the role of creativity in science and how culture affects science.	
Globalisation and sustainability	**How is everything connected?**	
	In science, you could consider issues relating to access to resources, including minerals and energy. Also, you could explore issues related to protecting the environment, recycling and the need for sustainable lifestyles.	
Fairness and development	**What are the consequences of our common humanity?**	
	In science, you could explore the rights of all people to an adequate diet, drinking water and health care.	
Scientific and technical innovation	**How do we understand the world in which we live?**	
	Science offers many possible explorations relating to this global context. You could explore how new scientific developments in materials and medicines are affecting our lives.	

UNIT 1 | BEING A SCIENTIST IN THE MYP | 9780170353403

ACTIVITY Use of global contexts

This activity will help you think about how the six different global contexts in the MYP can be used in science.

1 What are the global contexts and explorations chosen for the eight units in this book?
2 Imagine your teacher wants to teach the class about healthy diets. Explain how the use of each global context would change the way the unit is taught. For example, if the global context of fairness and development was chosen, then the teacher would emphasise considering the quality of diets of different people around the world.
3 Carry out some research into the Millennium Development Goals (Figure 1.22). Which global context could be used to study Goal 1 (Eradicate extreme poverty and hunger)?

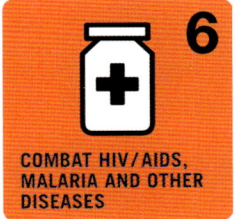

FIGURE 1.22 The eight Millennium Development Goals

4 Write a 400-word essay on the topic 'How science can help us to more fully meet Millennium Goal 1'.

Your teacher will discuss assessment criterion D with you – reflecting on the impacts of science. This will include a discussion of why other factors such as politics, economics and the environment are also part of the challenge to reduce poverty and hunger.

FIGURE 1.23 Doctors Without Borders (Médecins Sans Frontières) are helping meet the Millennium Goals.

Thinking about the profile of a successful scientist

If you were a PYP student, you will be very familiar with the IB Learner profile and its importance in the IB programs. Perhaps you could list all 10 attributes. The main idea is to remind us that the first purpose of education is to prepare students to become successful lifelong learners and internationally minded citizens. If you are new to the IB, then this is a good moment to learn more about the IB Learner profile.

Scientists showing the attributes of the IB Learner profile — ACTIVITY

Your teacher will provide you with a copy of the IB Learner profile. It includes the following 10 attributes: inquirer, knowledgeable, thinker, communicator, principled, open-minded, caring, risk-taker, balanced and reflective.

The following is a list of some attributes of a successful scientist.
- Can write up their investigations clearly
- Seeks and considers the points of view of others
- Has a natural curiosity and approaches problems with creativity and enthusiasm
- Is interested in relating their work to make a positive difference to the world
- Makes effective presentations at conferences
- Has a good life–work balance, and appreciates the importance of emotional and physical health
- Has high-quality research skills
- Shows a very reflective approach to experimentation and considers the evidence
- Reads scientific papers, attends conferences, and discusses with other scientists in other languages
- Is conscious of their strengths and weaknesses and the need for professional development
- Shows a careful, logical approach to the design of experiments
- Is honest in their work, and concerned about the social and environmental consequences of their work
- Enjoys a challenge and exploring new ideas, and copes well when things get tough
- Works effectively in research teams or other kinds of teams
- Has a deep understanding of their subject but also has interest in and good knowledge of other areas of science
- Analyses experimental results carefully and critically
- Shows a creative approach to their work

1. Read the IB Learner profile and think about how it would relate to being a successful scientist. Then work in small groups (or with the whole class) to associate each attribute, as described above, that scientists need to the corresponding learner profile attribute.
2. Compare your answers with those of other students.
3. Can you think of other attributes a successful scientist should have?
4. a What do you think are the three most important attributes for a scientist to have? Explain your answer.
   b Are these also the attributes that are needed in other professions? Explain your answer.

Becoming great learners

At their centre of all IB programmes is the idea of helping students to become successful learners (i.e. Approaches to Learning (ATL)). This is one reason why universities like IB students. The 10 MYP ATL skill clusters are:
- Communication
- Collaboration
- Organisation
- Affective
- Reflection
- Information literacy
- Media literacy
- Critical thinking
- Creative thinking
- Transfer of knowledge.

At times, your teacher will make a special effort to help you develop these skills.

FIGURE 1.24 Working collaboratively

ACTIVITY: Why ATL is important for science students

Read more about the 10 ATL learning clusters in Appendix 1 on page 165. Suggest one way each of the 10 ATL skill clusters could be developed though your work in science.

REVIEW

Use the appendices on pages 165–176 to answer the following questions.
1. List the four MYP Science criteria.
2. Name the three key concepts we use in science.
3. List six related concepts we use in science.
4. Give examples of how two global contexts could be used in science.
5. Which two ATL clusters would be most important in carrying out scientific investigations? Give your reasons.
6. What do you think are the two most important attributes for a scientist to possess from the IB Learner profile? Give your reasons.

UNIT QUESTIONS

CRITERION A

EXPLAINING SCIENTIFIC KNOWLEDGE

1. Write a hypothesis for each of the following testable questions. (Level 1–8)
   a. Do plants grow better in water or soil?
   b. Does Alka-Seltzer® fizz more as a whole tablet or as small pieces?
   c. Does salt water, sugar water or pure water boil fastest?
   d. Which has more germs: a telephone handset or a restroom tap handle?

2. In the investigations a–d in Question 1, identify the: (Level 1–8)
   i. variable you are measuring
   ii. variable you will change
   iii. variables you will control (keep the same).

3. Compare and contrast a question that science can test and a question that science cannot test. (Level 7–8)

4. a. Explain what is meant by a fair test.
   b. Explain how this is related to an investigation being valid. (Level 5–8)

APPLYING SCIENTIFIC KNOWLEDGE AND UNDERSTANDING TO SOLVE A PROBLEM

5. Design an investigation to determine the best growing conditions for a new variety of tomato. (Level 1–8)

INTERPRETING INFORMATION

6. The following table shows the results for an investigation into how the time for sugar to dissolve changes as temperature is increased. (Level 1–8)

Temperature (°C)	Time for dissolving (s)
20	40
40	30
60	20
80	10

   a. Draw a graph to show these results.
   b. Make a conclusion about what these results show you.
   c. Outline the errors you predict could be involved in this experiment and suggest how these errors could be reduced.
   d. Outline some further experiments relating to this topic that could be worth carrying out.

REFLECTION

1. You have now been an MYP student for a few weeks. What similarities and differences do you see between MYP Science and your other subjects?
2. What do we mean when we say that science students need to be very careful about how they use the evidence they obtain from their experiments?
3. Discuss the idea that science theories are in a continued state of development.
4. Explain why the search for patterns is very important in science.
5. What type of questions can science not answer?
6. Suggest some reasons why millions of people in the world are dying of diseases even though we have the scientific understanding to cure most diseases.

UNIT 2
CLASSIFYING THE NATURAL WORLD

KEY CONCEPT
Systems

RELATED CONCEPTS
Patterns
Development
Evidence

GLOBAL CONTEXT
Orientation in space and time: an exploration into how scientists have used evidence over time to develop their understanding of the living world

STATEMENT OF INQUIRY
Throughout history, humans have sought to understand the natural world; through gathering evidence and identifying patterns, scientists have developed methods of classifying the world around us.

INQUIRY QUESTIONS

FACTUAL
1 What is living and non-living?
2 What are the six kingdoms?

CONCEPTUAL
3 How and why do we create dichotomous keys?
4 How do we group different organisms?

DEBATABLE
5 To what extent has binomial nomenclature enabled scientists to communicate globally?
6 To what extent has the classification of different species become clearer over time?

Introduction

At zoos, you will probably not see monkeys in the same cage as tigers, or antelopes in the same cage as lions, but you might see zebras in the same enclosure as giraffes. Animals in zoos are sorted into groups on the basis of their needs, such as how much space they need, what they eat, who eats them and how they reproduce.

Humans have sorted and grouped animals, and all other living things, since the time of Aristotle (384–322 BCE), an important Greek philosopher. In this unit, you will study the scientific way that we gather evidence to help us sort and group living things, and how we create systems of naming living things so that we can talk about them easily and without confusion.

Giving a historical lecture

You are an important scientific historian who has been asked to give a lecture on the question 'Over time, how has scientific discovery enabled us to have a deeper understanding of how to classify living things?'. You can use a white board, slide show or video to present your lecture to your class. You should include:
- an introduction to the topic
- two different scientific discoveries
- information on how the discoveries have developed our knowledge of classification
- good scientific language
- at least two documented sources.

COMMUNICATION
Selecting your presentation technique so it is appropriate for your audience.

ORGANISATION
Planning your presentation and setting deadlines to ensure it is completed on time.

Sorting things

Who sorts things

You may not realise it, but you sort and group every day. Humans start grouping objects from a very young age. Even as babies, we use our sense of smell to recognise who is family and who is not. As we grow older, we sort our toys and our books, developing skills that we will use later in life. We do this by identifying different patterns that can be seen in the world around us. These patterns include the colour or shape of different items. Figure 2.1 shows a baby sorting blocks by shape. These classification skills are important in many school subjects; for example, in English, we classify types of words such as adjectives or nouns, and in Science, we classify different chemicals as corrosive or harmful.

FIGURE 2.1 A baby sorting blocks is classifying them according to colour or shape.

Why we sort things

'Hey, look at that four-legged grey thing with a tail!' yells your friend. You look, not knowing if you are going to see a tortoise, a rabbit, a cat, a squirrel or another type of animal. In fact, you see a horse. If your friend had instead said, 'Hey, look at that grey horse', you would have known what to expect. You know what a horse looks like because all horses have the same set of features and you have seen a horse before.

Humans have a natural tendency to want to sort large groups of objects into smaller groups. The groups are usually based on what the object looks like. Sorting helps us make sense of what is going on around us. It also makes us feel more secure because we can predict what might happen in the future in a particular situation. It makes talking about the objects a lot easier as well.

How we sort things

We usually sort things into groups on the basis of the features that they have in common. Identifying these patterns enables us to group the items.

ACTIVITY: Sorting old phones

This activity uses mobile phones, but you could use any object that comes in a number of different types, shapes and colours, such as buttons, shoes or wooden blocks of different shapes, sizes and colours.

WHAT YOU NEED
- old used mobile phones collected from the whole class or school
- digital camera

SAFETY
Make sure that the SIM cards are no longer in the phones and all personal details are deleted.

WHAT TO DO
1. Work in a group of three. Collect at least 10 mobile phones. Choose one feature (such as colour) to sort them into two approximately equal groups. Take a photo of your two groups.
2. Choose another feature that will sort each group into two more groups. You do not need to use the same feature for each group of phones. Keep note of what feature you used each time. Keep sorting into groups until each group only contains one mobile phone.
3. Insert the photos into a multimedia presentation or print them and glue them onto an A3 sheet of paper.
4. Present your sorting and grouping system to the class.

WHAT DO YOU THINK?
1. Can the class work out what features you used each time you sorted the phones into groups?
2. List the features that you used to sort the phones into groups. Show this as a diagram.
3. What features did the rest of the class use to sort their phones into groups?
4. Were some phones hard to sort into groups? Why was this?
5. What can you conclude?
6. Look at the list of features that you used to sort your mobile phones into groups. What do all these features have in common?
7. Were the mobile phones in each group more similar at the beginning of the activity (when they were in one big group) or at the end after you had developed your sorting system (when they were in smaller groups)? Explain your answer.

TA RECYCLING MOBILE PHONES

Mobile phones are made up of many useful materials: 1 kg aluminium, 30 kg steel, 4 kg copper, 2 kg manganese, 1 kg nickel, 1 kg cadmium (a heavy metal that should never end up in landfill), 3 kg plastics and 1.5 kg brass can be recovered from 1300 mobile phones. Find out how to recycle mobile phones in your country, so these materials do not go to waste. At the end of the previous activity, you can donate all the mobile phones to a recycling centre in your country.

Go to http://mypsci1.nelsonnet.com.au and click on **Recycle mobile phones** to get some ideas about where, how and why we recycle.

FIGURE 2.2 Old mobile phones for recycling

REVIEW

1. Why do Suggest a reason for why humans tend to want to sort things into groups.
2. Outline the principles of sorting and grouping.
3. As the groups get smaller, do the objects within a group become more or less similar?
4. Imagine there is no sorting and grouping of the natural world. People communicate only by describing things to one another. Rewrite the sentence 'My cat ate a mouse' without using the words 'cat' or 'mouse'. Make sure that someone else would understand what you are trying to say.

Sorting and grouping the natural world

The natural world is made up of a huge number of different things: from stars to rocks, water, grass, animals and trees, just to name a few. To sort and group, or **classify**, all the things that we find in the natural world, we first need to determine whether they are **living** or **non-living**. But what does that mean? How do we define 'life'?

Living or non-living?

In Figure 2.3 you can see eight items from the natural world. Some of these are living and some are non-living.

FIGURE 2.3 Which of these are living and which are non-living?

Scientists use a list of criteria to work out if an object is living or non-living. If the answer to each criterion is 'Yes', the object is living. The criteria are as follows.
- Is it made up of one or more cells?
- Is it able to move? (This can be movement within the cell known as **cytoplasmic streaming**. See the adjacent weblink.)
- Does it respond to **stimuli**?
- Does it produce waste?
- Does it exchange gas with the environment?
- Does it need water?
- Does it need food in some form?
- Is it able to reproduce to make more individuals like itself?

Go to http://mypsci1.nelsonnet.com.au and click on **Cytoplasmic streaming**. You will see cells from the freshwater plant *Elodea*. The moving objects are the chloroplasts inside the cell moving around in the cytoplasm. This is a sign that the cell is living.

Classifying the living world

In the second half of the 17th century, Antoni van Leeuwenhoek (1632–1723), a Dutch tradesman, began experimenting with lenses. He found that lenses could be used to **magnify** objects – make them look bigger. One of his discoveries was 'little animalcules' – or what we now know as **micro-organisms**. Up until this time, the existence of micro-organisms was unknown, so van Leeuwenhoek's discovery was met with a lot of doubt. It was not until 1680 that the Royal Society began to believe what he was saying. Van Leeuwenhoek continued observing and describing micro-organisms until his death.

Making the invisible visible

It is hard to believe, but a world-changing discovery was made because people didn't brush their teeth! On 17 September 1683, Antoni van Leeuwenhoek wrote a letter to the Royal Society in London describing 'a little white matter, which is as thick as if it were batter'. What he was describing was dental plaque – the white material that forms on your teeth if you don't brush them properly. Van Leeuwenhoek was studying plaque using a microscope he had made himself. He did not limit his investigations to his own teeth. He also looked at plaque from his wife, his daughter and 'two old men who had never cleaned their teeth in their life'.

Van Leeuwenhoek shared his observations with the Royal Society: 'I then most always saw, with great wonder, that in the said matter there were many very little living animalcules, very prettily a-moving. The biggest sort … had a very strong and swift motion, and shot through the water [most likely spit] like a fish does through water.'

What van Leeuwenhoek was describing were the **bacteria** that live in plaque and cause tooth decay. He was the first person to see these micro-organisms. This discovery opened up a new world of microscopic organisms to the scientists of the day.

Once they knew about this mini-world, inventors went to work, building more powerful microscopes to see these mysterious tiny organisms in more detail. Figure 2.4 shows an image of the bacteria that are present in plaque, taken with a more powerful microscope than the one that van Leeuwenhoek used.

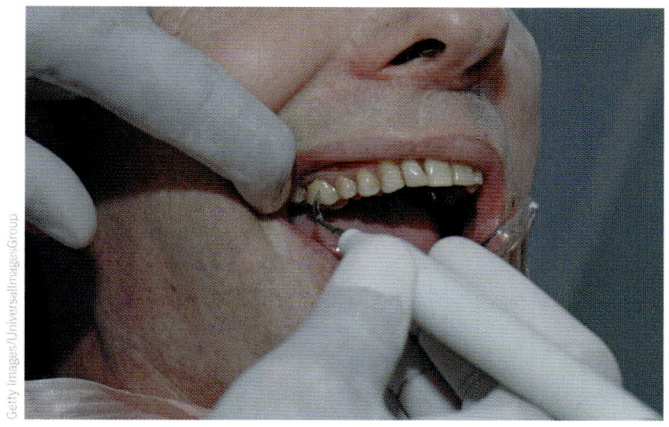 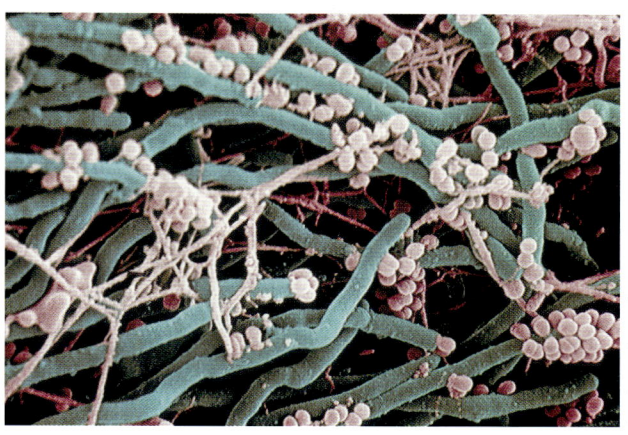

FIGURE 2.4 Dental plaque contains bacteria, which can be seen under a microscope.

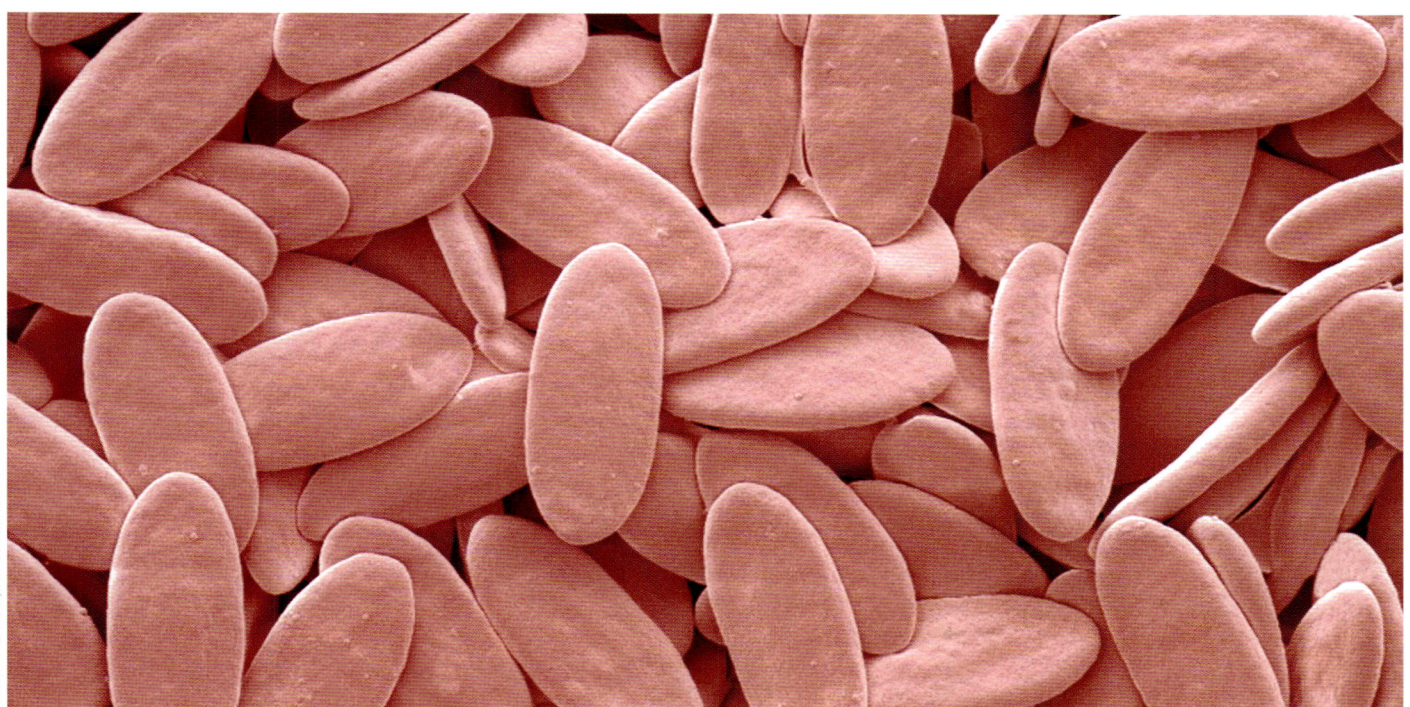

FIGURE 2.5 This is a highly magnified image of bird red blood cells, taken with a very powerful microscope.

REVIEW

1. State four different ways we know something is living.
2. **a** Make a list of the differences between a living thing and a non-living thing.
   b Is a dead tree living or non-living? Explain the arguments to support your choice.
3. Define the term 'magnify'.
4. What did van Leeuwenhoek call the living organisms that he saw under the microscope? What do we call them today?
5. Describe how the invention of the microscope changed the way that people viewed the living world.

Go to http://mypsci1.nelsonnet.com.au and click on **Royal Society**. Investigate the Royal Society and see some of the excellent work that they still do today.

Living kingdoms

Carl von Linné (1707–1778) was a young medical student in Sweden, who was working around the time that van Leeuwenhoek died. He later Latinised his name to Carolus Linnaeus. Von Linné was trying to sort and group all living things (see page 39). He proposed that all living things could be sorted into two large groupings (**kingdoms**): the plant kingdom and the animal kingdom. Von Linné did not consider van Leeuwenhoek's observations, so micro-organisms did not fit into his system. It was not until 1866 that a third kingdom, the protist kingdom, was proposed to account for micro-organisms.

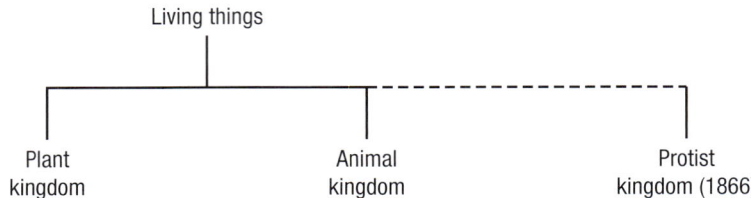

FIGURE 2.6 The initial kingdoms in von Linné's classification system. The protist kingdom was added in 1866.

FIGURE 2.7 Mushrooms are part of the fungi kingdom. They obtain their food by absorbing the decaying remains of other organisms.

Improved technology allows us to study living things in much more detail. This means that scientific knowledge is still expanding. In 2004, scientists agreed to classify living things into six kingdoms: **protist**, **archaebacteria**, **eubacteria**, **fungi**, plants and animals. As more evidence is collected and we develop our learning and technology, these classifications may need to be changed and refined.

The features used by scientists to divide all living things into these six kingdoms are:

1. how they obtain their food. Organisms can eat other living things, as animals do; make their own food, as plants and some bacteria do; or absorb the products of decay, as fungi do (Figure 2.7).
2. how complex their cell(s) are. The structure of a cell can be very simple, such as that of a bacterial cell, or very complex, such as that of a human cell (Figure 2.8).
3. how many cells make up the organism. An organism can be made up of one cell, such as a micro-organism, or up to billions of cells, such as a human (Figure 2.9).

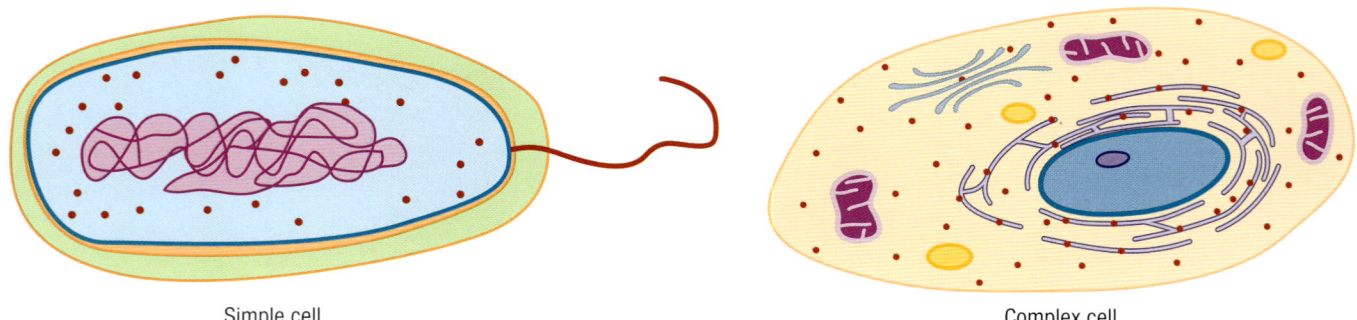

FIGURE 2.8 The complexity of an organism's cells can tell us which kingdom the organism belongs to.

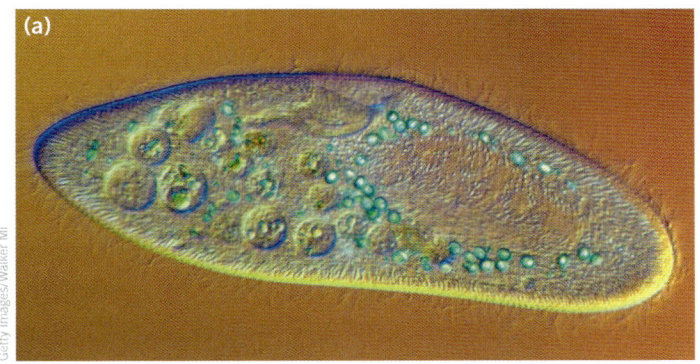

FIGURE 2.9 (a) A paramecium is a unicellular organism (made up of one cell). (b) Onion skin is multicellular (made up of many cells).

Dichotomous keys

Scientists use a visual organiser called a **dichotomous key** to help them classify things. A dichotomous key involves levels of questions, where each question has only two possible answers. (The term 'dichotomous' means 'two parts'.) For example, if you use a dichotomous key to classify your mobile phone, you could ask, 'Is the phone black?' The answer would be 'Yes' or 'No'. This would be a level 1 question (Figure 2.10).

You can then sort your mobile phone further by asking another question (a level 2 question), such as 'Is it a flip phone?' Again, the answer to this question would be 'Yes' or 'No' (Figure 2.11).

Asking more questions helps to further refine your groups. A dichotomous key for mobile phones with three levels is shown in Figure 2.12.

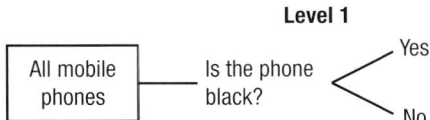

FIGURE 2.10 First level of a dichotomous key

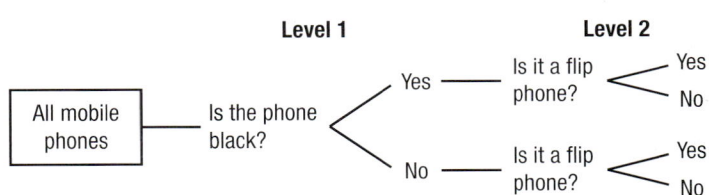

FIGURE 2.11 Second level of a dichotomous key

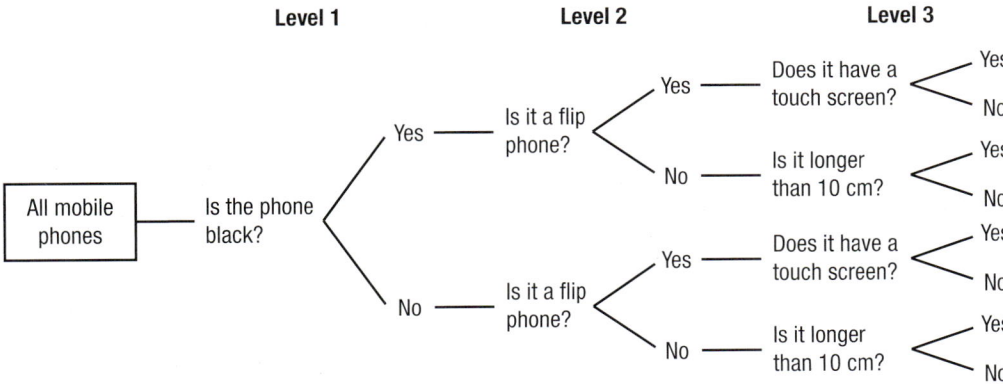

FIGURE 2.12 A dichotomous key for mobile phones

Go to http://mypsci1.nelsonnet.com.au and click on **Natural History Museum**. Learn how the Natural History Museum has collected data on trees in urban areas to gain evidence of the different trees found in the UK. You could do a similar project with your class.

A dichotomous key for leaves

ACTIVITY

You will need to go to an area near your school to collect leaves for constructing your dichotomous key. You will need at least 15 different leaves.

WHAT TO DO

As a class (or in smaller groups), create a dichotomous key to classify the leaves. Put in as many levels as you can so that each leaf ends up in its own group.

WHAT DID YOU FIND?

Copy the dichotomous key into your workbook. Then go to the adjacent weblink to learn more about why tree identification is important.

The six kingdoms

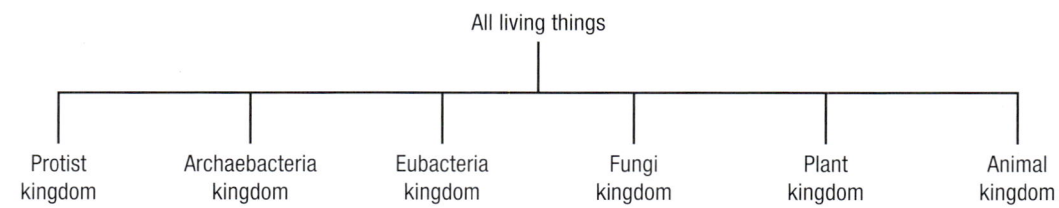

FIGURE 2.13 All living things are divided into six kingdoms.

Protists

The protist kingdom includes a wide range of organisms that don't fit into any of the other kingdoms. Protists vary from very simple microscopic organisms called protozoa, to very large organisms such as brown kelp in the ocean (Figure 2.14). Some species of protozoa cause diseases. One example is malaria, which kills more than a million people every year. The protist kingdom may be reclassified when more is known about its members.

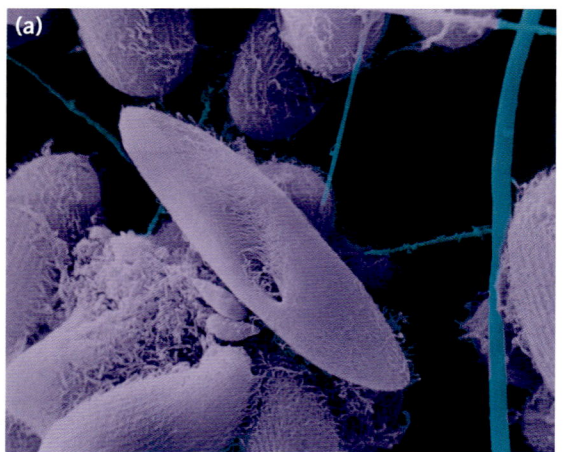

FIGURE 2.14 Members of the protist kingdom: (a) protozoa and (b) brown algae.

Archaebacteria

Members of the archaebacteria kingdom are among the oldest living things on Earth. They have a simple cell structure – they occur as single cells. They are distinguished by where they can live. Archaebacteria can be found in the most extreme **anaerobic** environments, such as in salt plains and swampy marshes, inside our intestines, and in highly acidic and very hot volcanic vents. They generally obtain their nutrition from chemical reactions, such as the mixing of hydrogen and carbon dioxide to make methane (Figure 2.15).

Eubacteria

All of the members of the eubacteria (also known as bacteria) kingdom are microscopic. They have a simple cell structure and occur singly or joined together to form a long chain, much like a string of pearls. Eubacteria are very simple organisms that generally look like tiny sticks or rods. They live in less extreme environments than the archaebacteria do – even on our skin. Most are harmless, and many are very useful. In fact, we could not live without them. However, some can cause diseases, such as Legionnaires' disease, tetanus, gangrene and whooping cough.

Go to http://mypsci1.nelsonnet.com.au and click on **Bacteria in outer space**. Find out how bacteria survive the extreme conditions of outer space.

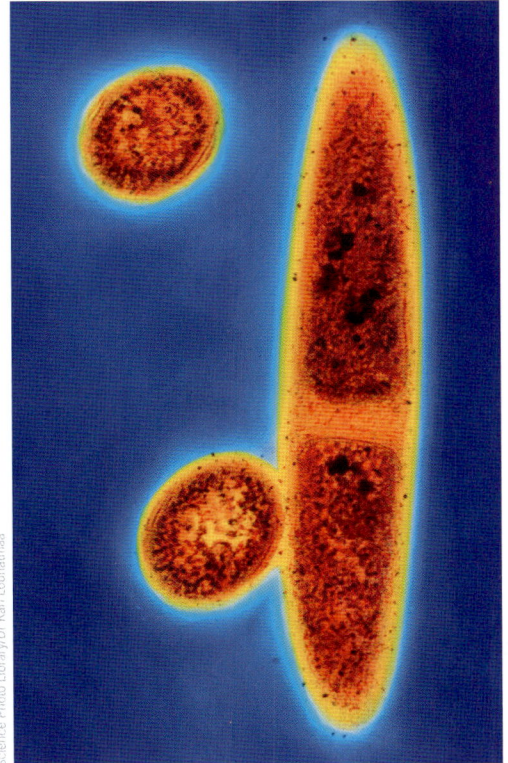

FIGURE 2.15 *Methanospirillum hungatii* is a member of the archaebacteria kingdom, which obtains its energy from the reaction of hydrogen and carbon dioxide to produce methane.

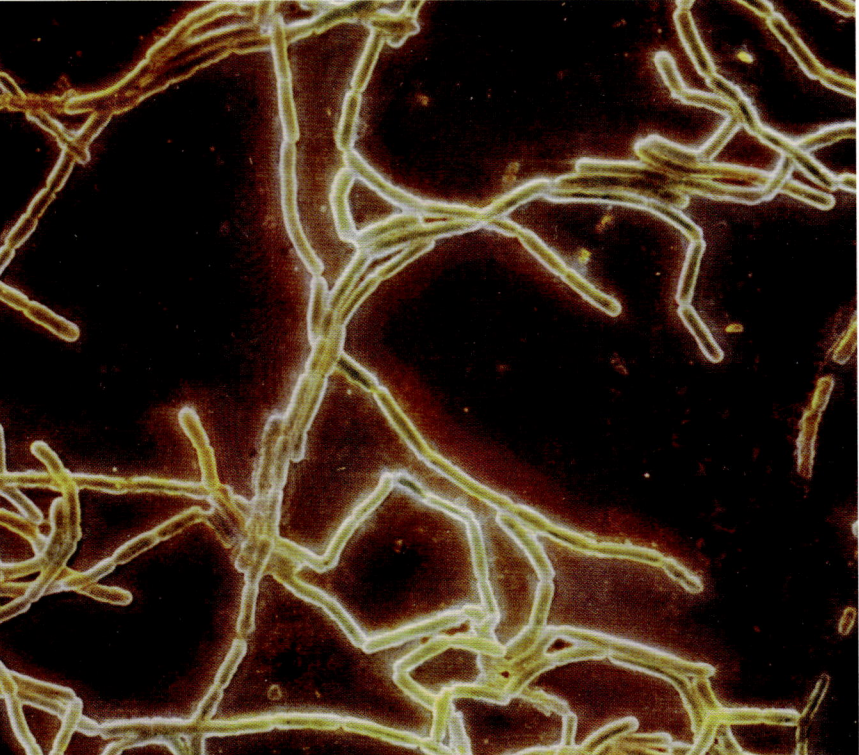

FIGURE 2.16 Bacteria, such as these rod-shaped *Bacillus magaterium*, are members of the eubacteria kingdom.

Fungi

You will most certainly have eaten bread or buns made with yeast. You may have tried mushrooms. If you have, you have eaten members of the fungi kingdom.

Fungi were originally thought to be plants, but we now know that they are more closely related to animals. Another member of the fungi kingdom is mould. The white, powdery coating on a camembert or brie cheese is a mould that is safe to eat. *Penicillium* was the mould used to make the drug penicillin, which was developed during World War II to fight bacterial infection.

FIGURE 2.17 Mushrooms are members of the fungi kingdom.

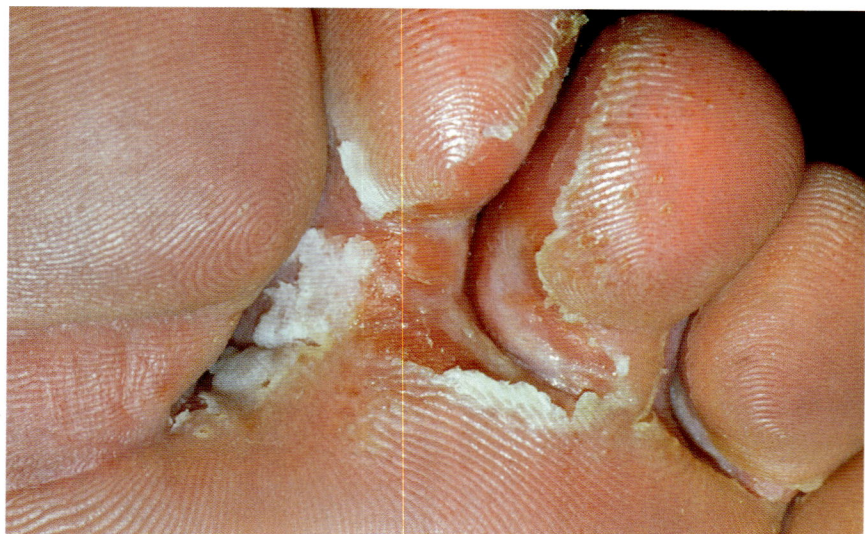

FIGURE 2.18 Tinea is a fungus that can grow on human skin.

Not all fungi are useful. Some can cause diseases. Tinea (also known as athlete's foot) (Figure 2.18) and ringworm are examples of fungal infections. Fungi live by eating organisms, such as wood, leaf litter or dead animals.

Plants

All members of the **plant** kingdom are complex, **multicellular** organisms. They can be as small as moss or as large as an oak tree or a redwood tree. All members of this kingdom make sugars by a process called **photosynthesis**.

FIGURE 2.19 (a) Moss and (b) oak trees are both members of the plant kingdom.

INVESTIGATION 2.1 — Living lunch

CRITICAL THINKING
Logically design your scientific investigation. Use the advice given in Unit 1.

YOUR CHALLENGE
Fungi are the main reason why you cannot leave your lunch in your schoolbag for a week, or store fruit and vegetables for too long. Work out what kind of bread, filling and sandwich wrapping can best withstand 'mould attack'.

THIS MIGHT HELP
Your teacher will provide you with a variety of breads, fillings and wrappers. Read the safety advice on this page before designing and starting your investigation. Also work out a way of recording what you do and all your observations before you start. This may include using a digital camera to photograph the progress of your moulds.

THINGS TO THINK ABOUT
- A stereomicroscope, or a good magnifying lens, will be very helpful when detecting any mould invasion and identifying any differences between the kinds of moulds that grow.
- Some questions you might like to investigate are:
  – What lunch wrappings are best at resisting mould growth?
  – Do some types of bread resist mould growth better than others?
  – What lunch fillings are best at resisting mould growth?

You may also think of other questions, or other factors affecting mould growth that you want to test.

Carry out and write up the investigation by following the guide in Appendix 3 on page 169, or as advised by your teacher.

SAFETY
1. Some moulds can make you very ill. Ensure that once you have sealed your food in the food wrap, you do not take it out again. Your teacher will help you make your observations safely if you try wraps that you cannot see through, such as paper or aluminium foil.
2. Always wash your hands thoroughly with soap and water after performing your experiments.

Animals

You are probably most familiar with the members of the **animal** kingdom. Animals are all complex, multicellular organisms that get their food by eating members of their own or other kingdoms. They can be as varied as jellyfish, earthworms, frogs, beetles, birds and humans.

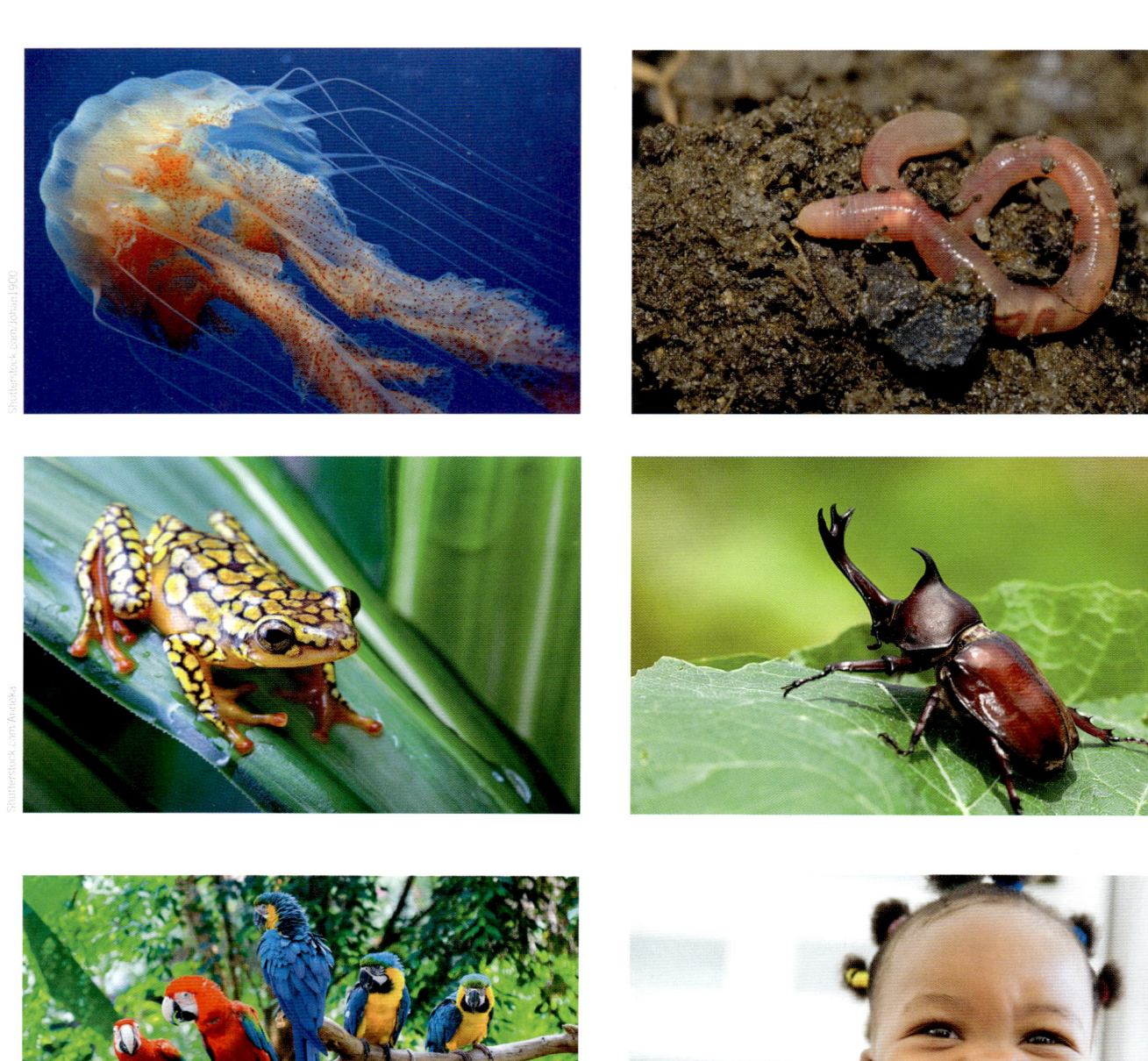

FIGURE 2.20 Members of the animal kingdom

A timeline of classification

Throughout the unit, you have learnt about a number of developments and new methods of acquiring evidence that have changed the system we use to classify organisms. Scientists from all over the world have collected this evidence over thousands of years. The timeline in Figure 2.21 shows some of the main scientists and developments involved in creating the system we have today, from Aristotle's

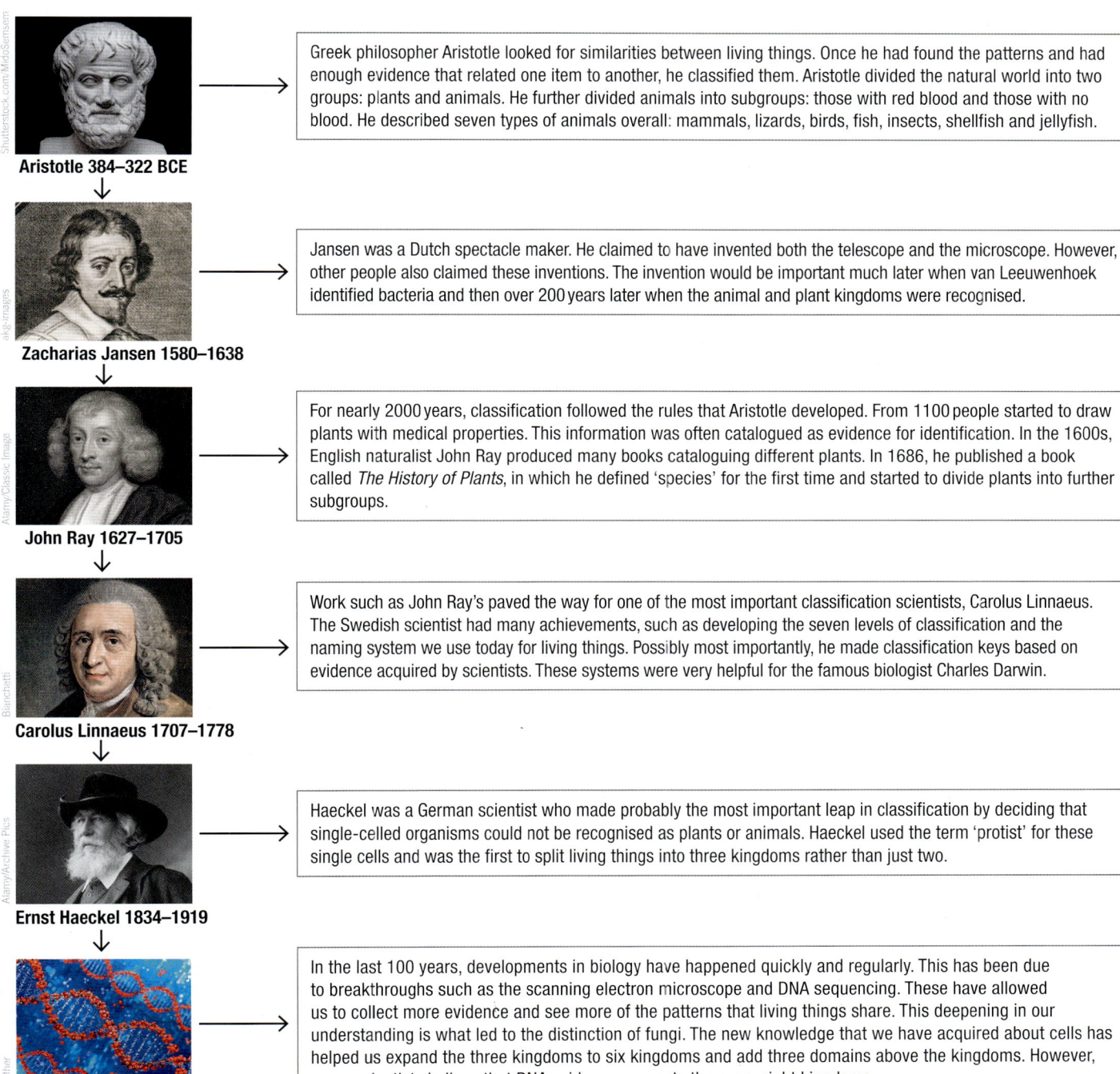

Aristotle 384–322 BCE

Greek philosopher Aristotle looked for similarities between living things. Once he had found the patterns and had enough evidence that related one item to another, he classified them. Aristotle divided the natural world into two groups: plants and animals. He further divided animals into subgroups: those with red blood and those with no blood. He described seven types of animals overall: mammals, lizards, birds, fish, insects, shellfish and jellyfish.

Zacharias Jansen 1580–1638

Jansen was a Dutch spectacle maker. He claimed to have invented both the telescope and the microscope. However, other people also claimed these inventions. The invention would be important much later when van Leeuwenhoek identified bacteria and then over 200 years later when the animal and plant kingdoms were recognised.

John Ray 1627–1705

For nearly 2000 years, classification followed the rules that Aristotle developed. From 1100 people started to draw plants with medical properties. This information was often catalogued as evidence for identification. In the 1600s, English naturalist John Ray produced many books cataloguing different plants. In 1686, he published a book called *The History of Plants*, in which he defined 'species' for the first time and started to divide plants into further subgroups.

Carolus Linnaeus 1707–1778

Work such as John Ray's paved the way for one of the most important classification scientists, Carolus Linnaeus. The Swedish scientist had many achievements, such as developing the seven levels of classification and the naming system we use today for living things. Possibly most importantly, he made classification keys based on evidence acquired by scientists. These systems were very helpful for the famous biologist Charles Darwin.

Ernst Haeckel 1834–1919

Haeckel was a German scientist who made probably the most important leap in classification by deciding that single-celled organisms could not be recognised as plants or animals. Haeckel used the term 'protist' for these single cells and was the first to split living things into three kingdoms rather than just two.

The last 100 years

In the last 100 years, developments in biology have happened quickly and regularly. This has been due to breakthroughs such as the scanning electron microscope and DNA sequencing. These have allowed us to collect more evidence and see more of the patterns that living things share. This deepening in our understanding is what led to the distinction of fungi. The new knowledge that we have acquired about cells has helped us expand the three kingdoms to six kingdoms and add three domains above the kingdoms. However, some scientists believe that DNA evidence suggests there are eight kingdoms.

FIGURE 2.21 A timeline of classification

patterns to the **scanning electron microscope** and **DNA** sequencing. In the future, we will use technological developments to identify more patterns and gain more evidence. This research will mean that the timeline will continue to develop and change.

REVIEW

1. **a** Explain the term 'classifying'.
   b Outline why humans classify the natural world.
2. What is a dichotomous key? Use an example to explain how it works.
3. **a** Outline the technological development that caused the change from the two-kingdom system to the three-kingdom system.
   b Outline why the system of classification of the natural world has changed from two kingdoms to three kingdoms to six kingdoms.
   c Discuss the possibility of there being more than six kingdoms in the future.
4. Copy and complete Table 2.1 in your workbook.

TABLE 2.1

Kingdom	How they obtain their food	How their cells are put together	How many cells make up the organism
Protist		Simple	
Archaebacteria			Single-celled
Eubacteria			
Fungi			
Plant		Complex	
Animal			Multicellular

5. If you found a living organism that was made up of more than one cell and made its own food, in which kingdom would you place it?
6. Explain why scientists need to be flexible in their thinking.

Seven levels of classification

All living things are sorted into six kingdoms on the basis of how they get their food, their cell structure and their number of cells. Each kingdom can be sorted into smaller groupings using different characteristics. These smaller groupings are called phyla (singular **phylum**). Phyla can also be sorted and grouped into smaller groupings. Each smaller grouping is called a **class**.

This sorting and grouping continues through **family** and **order** until we get to the **species** level. With each level of grouping, the number of organisms gets smaller and the organisms become more similar. Table 2.2 shows the classification of humans from kingdom to species level.

TABLE 2.2 Human classification

Level of classification	Example	Features of the group	Organisms found in this grouping
Kingdom	Animal	Complex, multicellular organisms that eat other living things	Earthworms, sponges, beetles, frogs, birds, whales, cows, dogs, horses, lemurs, baboons, monkeys, apes, humans
Phylum	Chordate	Possess a backbone	Frogs, birds, whales, cows, dogs, horses, lemurs, baboons, monkeys, apes, humans
Class	Mammal	Possess hair, feed their young on milk	Whales, cows, dogs, horses, lemurs, baboons, monkeys, apes, humans
Order	Primate	Eyes point forwards, reduced number of teeth, possess nails instead of claws at the end of their fingers and toes	Lemurs, baboons, monkeys, apes, humans
Family	Hominid	Able to walk on two legs, large brain	Monkeys, apes, humans
Genus	*Homo*	Small teeth and jaw, able to make and use tools, able to speak	Humans
Species	*sapiens*		Humans

TRANSFER

Improve your memory. A good way to remember the seven levels of classification (**K**ingdom, **P**hylum, **C**lass, **O**rder, **F**amily, **G**enus, **S**pecies) is to use an acrostic, such as King Paul Can Only Find Green Strawberries. Why do you think acrostics such as this help your memory? Can you make up some acrostics for other lists of information? Do you know any other 'tricks' to help you remember things?

Linnaeus' naming system

Have you ever smiled at a *Crocodylus johnstoni*, patted a *Canis familiaris*, eaten a *Malus pumila* or spoken to a *Homo sapiens*? Chances are that you have done the last three, probably many times. *Canis familiaris* is the scientific name for a dog, *Malus pumila* is an apple and *Homo sapiens* is a person.

These are odd names for organisms when everyone knows what a person or an apple is. They exist thanks to Carolus Linnaeus.

FIGURE 2.22 Carolus Linnaeus during one of his many collecting trips

Linnaeus invented a system of naming each species. Just as you have a first name and a surname (or family name), every species has a two-word name. These words are in Latin, one of the original languages of science. The first word of the name is the **genus** name, and the second word is the **descriptive name**. This two-word naming system is called a **binomial** system.

Carolus Linnaeus was born Carl von Linné, but he decided to Latinise his name to match his binomial system of naming living things. Some of the more bizarre scientific names that have been given to species include *Pieza kake* (a Brazilian fly), *Agra phobia* (a ground beetle), *Ytu brutus* (a water beetle), *Verae peculya* (a wasp), *Phthiria relativitae* (a fly), *Heerz tooya* and the closely related *Heerz lukenatcha* (two species of closely related wasps).

REVIEW

1. State the seven levels of classification.
2. Outline the features of mammals.
3. Suggest a reason for why Linnaeus is remembered more for his hobby than his profession.
4. Suggest a reason for Linnaeus first used his binomial naming system.
5. State the scientific name for a human.
6. Are you familiar with the scientific names of any other organisms?

Species

Species have common **features** that make them all belong to the one group. According to the seven levels of classification, there are usually several species within one genus. Members of the same species all look similar and can breed with one another to produce **fertile** offspring – offspring that in turn can produce offspring of their own. For example, humans belong to the genus *Homo* and the species *sapiens*. This means their scientific name is *Homo sapiens*. Domestic cats belong to the genus *Felis* and the species *catus*, so their scientific name is *Felis catus*. Different breeds of cat can mate and produce fertile kittens. This means that all breeds of cat belong to the same species.

Many living things have common names as well as scientific names. The scientific name for the species that is commonly called the white oak is *Quercus alba*. *Quercus* is its genus name and *alba* is its species name. The closely related *Quercus chapmanii* is the Chapman oak found in southeastern North America. Both trees have the same genus name, but they belong to different species. Organisms that have the same genus name are closely related, but they cannot breed to produce fertile offspring. A male donkey (*Equus africanus*) and a female horse (*Equus ferus*) are members of the same genus, but they belong to different species. They can breed to produce a mule, but the mule is **infertile**. A mule does not belong to any species as it does not fit the criteria for a species.

FIGURE 2.23 All domestic cats belong to the same species.

FIGURE 2.24 A male donkey and a female horse can produce an infertile offspring called a mule.

FIGURE 2.25 There are 400 000 species of beetle – that's a lot of relatives!

Finding new species

It is not known how many species live on Earth. We know that only a very small percentage (perhaps 2%) of them have been studied, described and named. Approximately 1.2 million species within the plant and animal kingdoms have been named; 57% of these are insects, including 400 000 species of beetle.

Scientists are constantly finding, studying and naming new species. In 2008, 1225 new species were studied, described and named. Each year, scientists compile a list of the top 10 new species. Go to the adjacent weblink to see the top 10 species for this year.

Many species are also under threat; over the decade 2001–2010, 10 species were declared extinct. With a growing human population and greater competition for resources and space, more species face extinction.

Go to http://mypsci1.nelsonnet.com.au and click on **Top 10.** Work out the criteria for judging the top 10 new species.

Endangered species ship

ACTIVITY

Visit a zoo, a safari park or an area with a number of different species to see.

Explore the area and find out about the endangered species that you can see. Make a fact sheet for one endangered species. This fact sheet will then be joined with the others in the class to make a small book to raise awareness of the plight of your species.

Your fact sheet must include:

- an endangered species
- at least one image
- the species' seven levels of classification
- information on why the species is endangered
- two ways that we are using science to protect the species
- a personal suggestion of a further way we could protect the species
- a record of at least two sources.

Your fact sheet should be no more than two pages long so that it can be printed back to back. Write about some other factors that need to be considered to ensure that your ideas for protection work in practice.

TA RAISING AWARENESS

Share your fact sheet with the school community. You can do this with hard copies but it would be better as an electronic document. This will help to raise awareness and supply evidence of the challenges your species faces.

REVIEW

1. What organisms are likely to have the most in common:
   a. Organisms in the same phylum or organisms in the same order?
   b. Organisms in the same family or organisms in the same genus?
2. State what is meant by the term 'species'.
3. A female red squirrel (*Sciurus vulgaris*) and a male grey squirrel (*Sciurus carolinensis*) are brought together in a zoo. Will they be able to produce fertile offspring?
4. a. Outline the binomial system of naming living things.
   b. Use resources to find out the scientific names for the common house mouse, African lion and Indian tiger.
5. Why is the binomial system of naming so useful for scientists?
6. Describe at least one similarity between the binomial system for naming living things and the way we name ourselves.

UNIT QUESTIONS

CRITERION A

EXPLAINING SCIENTIFIC KNOWLEDGE

1. State one way of observing very small organisms. (Level 1–2)
2. Give three reasons why we sort objects. (Level 3–4)
3. Describe two features of a mammal. (Level 5–6)
4. Are organisms within a phylum more or less similar than those within a family? Outline your answer. (Level 7–8)

APPLYING SCIENTIFIC KNOWLEDGE AND UNDERSTANDING TO SOLVE A PROBLEM

5. Identify the two non-living items in Figure 2.26. (Level 1–2)
6. Suggest a method of identifying whether something is living. (Level 3–4)
7. You are given 100 buttons of different shapes, colours and sizes. Give a detailed outline of the process you would use to sort them into eight smaller groups of similar buttons. (Level 5–8)

FIGURE 2.26 Living or non-living?

INTERPRETING INFORMATION

8 Identify two reasons we know that the organism in Figure 2.27 is a mammal. (Level 1–4)

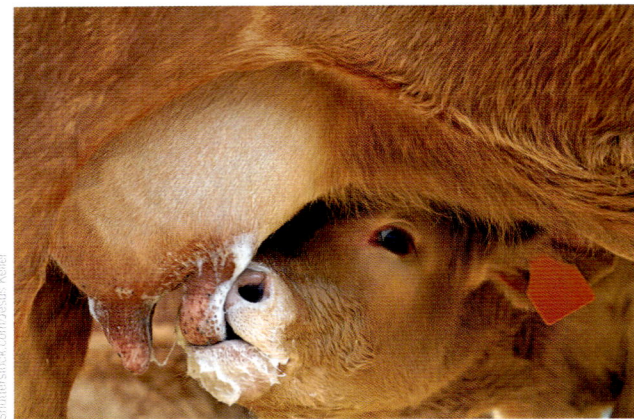

FIGURE 2.27 How do we know this is a mammal?

9 Fire can move, consume things, give off heat and carbon dioxide, and make more fires. Formulate an argument to classify fire as either living or non-living. (Level 5–6)

10 A Euglena is a single-celled organism that can absorb food from its environment. When food is scarce, it can make its own sugars by photosynthesis. Into which kingdom would you place Euglena? Explain why. (Level 7–8)

REFLECTION

1 Have technological developments allowed us to improve our methods of classification?
2 What are the benefits of identifying similar patterns between different species in different areas of the world?
3 Why is critically analysing evidence important in classification?
4 Why are organisational skills important in sorting and grouping objects?
5 To what extent has binomial nomenclature enabled scientists to communicate globally?
6 To what extent has the classification of different species developed and become clearer over time?

UNIT 3
LIVING IN A MANGROVE SWAMP

KEY CONCEPT
Systems

RELATED CONCEPTS
Environment

Interactions

GLOBAL CONTEXT
Globalisation and sustainability: an exploration into fragile ecosystems and the threats they are facing

STATEMENT OF INQUIRY
Organisms and the physical environment interact over generations to form successful and sustainable ecosystems; the increasing impact of humans is threatening many of these systems.

INQUIRY QUESTIONS

FACTUAL
1. What are adaptations?
2. What is a food chain?

CONCEPTUAL
3. How have organisms adapted to better suit their environments?
4. How does energy move through a system?

DEBATABLE
5. To what extent have human interactions with ecosystems damaged environments?
6. To what extent will a loss of biodiversity affect humans?

Introduction

When you think of the seashore, you might envision blue skies, sunshine and lots of sand. But if you live along the tropical and subtropical coasts of Africa, Australia, Asia or the Americas, you might describe a coastline that looked more like a forest. The trees of this forest are known as **mangroves**.

Mangrove forests are one of many different delicate ecosystems that can be found on our planet. Within these ecosystems, organisms live by interacting with the physical environment. As the human population has grown, many of these ecosystems have become threatened. In this unit, you will study the specific case of the mangroves and link this to environments near you.

INFORMATION LITERACY
Select information about mangrove planting programs from a range of sources. An example is in the weblink. You will then use this in your newspaper article to inform others.

Mangroves: protecting communities and diversity

The replanting of mangroves on the coast could help save many of the lives that would otherwise be lost in tsunamis, typhoons and hurricanes. Planting programs would also increase habitats for organisms living in mangroves. Investigate the pros and cons of this human interaction with the environment and what large-scale replanting projects can achieve. Write an informative newspaper article to share your findings with the wider community. Your article should:
1 explain the benefits and implications of replanting mangroves to protect communities and develop diversity
2 use scientific language that relates to environments and ecosystems
3 refer to sources of information to support your arguments.

Life on the coast

Mangroves

Go to http://mypsci1.nelsonnet.com.au and click on **Mangrove forests.** Read the informative article on Sri Lanka's protection of its mangrove forests.

Mangroves are woody plants that grow in the water where the land meets the sea. They experience the extreme conditions of high winds, salt water and high and low tides. Many other plants could not survive here. Mangrove swamps also act as a **buffer** between the land and the sea. They are home to many other **organisms**.

Protective mangroves

FIGURE 3.1 A mangrove swamp

On 26 December 2004, a tsunami hit Sri Lanka. According to the International Union for Conservation of Nature (IUCN), two people died in the settlement protected by dense mangrove and scrub forest, while up to 6000 people died in the village without similar vegetation.

Mangroves and humans

Mangroves are very valuable resources in traditional coastal cultures. They have been used in medicine, where the healing properties of their bark and leaves have been used to treat headaches, boils, ulcers and stings from marine animals.

The leaves of mangroves, crushed and placed in water, are used for fishing. The liquid stuns fish so that they float to the surface and can be caught easily.

Across the world, many mangrove swamps have been destroyed so that the valuable land could be used for other purposes, such as fisheries or tourist resorts. The largest surviving mangrove swamp is in the Sundarbans on the edge of the Bay of Bengal in eastern India and part of Bangladesh (see Figure 3.3).

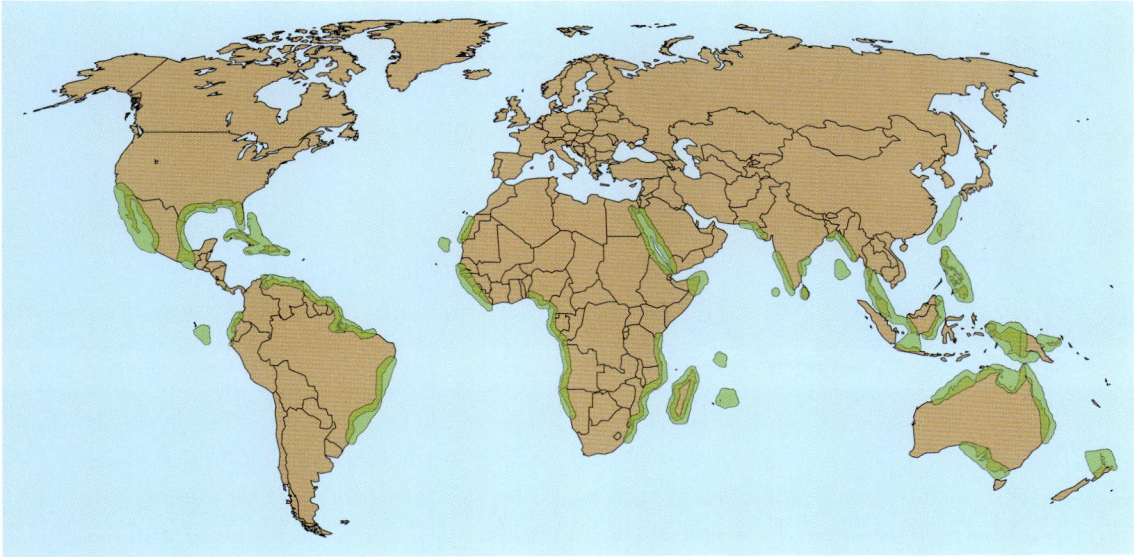

FIGURE 3.2 At one time, most of the world's tropical coastlines had a barrier of mangrove forests, but only about 70% of these remain.

FIGURE 3.3 This is a satellite image of the world's largest mangrove swamp (dark blue-green area) in the Sundarbans, India.

AFFECTIVE

Be resilient in coping with difficulties. One of the characteristics of scientists is honesty In real science, experiments often don't work and resilience is needed to overcome these difficulties.

FIGURE 3.4 Dealing with the salt – mangroves can expel excess salt through their leaves.

How mangroves survive

The environment of the mangrove is very hostile. During low tide it can be very hot and dry. During high tide, the temperature decreases and the mangroves can be almost covered by salt water. Under these conditions, the mangroves are beaten by waves and wind.

Most land-dwelling plants absorb oxygen through their roots from in between the soil particles, but mangroves cannot do this. The soil they live in is waterlogged and has little oxygen. Over millions of years, mangroves have developed ways to survive in their harsh, natural environment. These survival mechanisms are called **adaptations**.

Mangrove adaptations
Filtering salt

Mangroves are covered with salt water for half of their life. Most plants take in water through their roots, but if mangroves did this they would also absorb the dissolved salt. Many mangroves have an adaptation that enables them to cope with the excess salt entering the root cells. The grey mangrove can remove salt through its leaves. These leaves have special salt glands that expel the salt to the surface of the leaf.

How much salt is too much?

INVESTIGATION 3.1

YOUR CHALLENGE
Design an experiment to test how much salt a plant can tolerate.

THIS MIGHT HELP
Your teacher will provide you with one species of plant (bean or pumpkin seedlings would be good).

THINGS TO THINK ABOUT
1. Create a research question to guide you.
2. State a hypothesis.
3. What variables are you testing and how will you control variables to test your hypothesis fairly?
4. How are you going to test your hypothesis? Write your method before you begin the investigation.
5. How will you collect and represent your data?

Carry out and write up the investigation by following the guide in Appendix 3 on page 169, or as advised by your teacher.

Keeping upright

High winds and water movement due to high and low tides mean that mangroves are constantly being pushed and pulled. In Figure 3.5, the branch-like structures growing out of the stem and into the ground are called **prop roots**. They keep the mangrove upright and in one place.

FIGURE 3.5 Prop roots on a mangrove keep the mangrove in place.

FIGURE 3.6 Pneumatophores on a mangrove are roots above the ground that take in oxygen.

Storing oxygen

Most plants take in oxygen through their underground root system. Mangroves cannot do this because their roots are mainly sitting in water. Some mangroves have developed aboveground roots called **pneumatophores** (Figure 3.6). Oxygen is drawn in through the pneumatophores and stored in special cells within the roots for use while these roots are underwater during high tide. To avoid being covered by mud and silt, pneumatophores grow up instead of down.

REVIEW

1. Where would you be most likely to find a mangrove swamp?
2. Describe the environment in which mangroves live.
3. State two reasons why people cut down mangrove forests.
4. Suggest a consequence of cutting down mangrove forests.
5. Compare and contrast mangroves to land-dwelling plants.
6. Outline three adaptations that help mangroves survive in their natural environment. Explain what each adaptation is for.

A mangrove feast

When you walk through a mangrove swamp, your boots stick in the mud. If you are not careful, your boots could be pulled off by the suction from the mud.

Mangroves produce a lot of leaf litter. It has been estimated that up to 1 kilogram of mangrove leaf, bark, fruit and flower litter is produced each year for every square metre of mangrove swamp. In the leaf litter live bacteria and fungi. They break down the litter, causing it to **decay** into a muddy mixture. One teaspoon of this mixture contains as many as 10 billion bacteria.

Much of the muddy leaf mixture is carried out to sea by the action of tides and provides food for many sea-dwelling creatures. The litter that remains provides a perfect feast for the fish, shrimp, plankton and mud whelks that live among the mangroves. Where there are small sea creatures, there are birds. Birds such as ibis and heron make their home in the mangrove swamps because of the ready availability of food.

FIGURE 3.7 An ibis browses for food in a mangrove swamp.

Birds of the mangroves

A mangrove swamp is a perfect place for birds to live. There are many perches on the mangrove branches, not many predators, and ample food and fresh sea air. Birds of the mangroves have special adaptations to help them survive in this environment.

Beaks

The little marine organisms that live among the mangrove plants can be difficult to catch. It is important that birds have the right-shaped beak to help them catch their food.

EXPERIMENT 3.1 It's all in the beak

CRITICAL THINKING
Understand the importance of predictions/hypotheses in scientific investigation.

AIM
To work out which beak shape would be best suited for birds living in a mangrove swamp.

PREDICTION (HYPOTHESIS)
Write your prediction for which beak shape would be the most suitable for birds living in a mangrove swamp. Explain your reason for this prediction.

MATERIALS
- scissors
- tweezers
- tongs
- pegs or icy pole sticks
- marbles
- toothpicks
- string
- broad bean seeds
- foam

PROCEDURE
1. Work with a partner. Share the work evenly.
2. Your 'beaks' are the scissors, tweezers, tongs, pegs and icy pole sticks. Use each of these in turn to pick up your 'food'.
3. Your 'food' is marbles (water snails), toothpicks (insects), string (worms), broad beans (crabs) and foam (shrimp).

RESULTS
1. Draw up a table to record your results.
2. Explain why you chose each beak to pick up the food.
3. Which beak shape was best adapted to pick up the food?

CONCLUSION
1. What can you conclude from your results about the shape of the beaks of birds that live in mangrove swamps? Was your prediction valid?
2. Look at Figure 3.7 to see the shape of an ibis' beak. Do your results fit in with their beak shape? Explain.

EVALUATION
Discuss how well your method worked. Suggest ways the method could be improved.

EXTENSION
Which beak would be best adapted if the snails, crabs and shrimp were removed from the mangrove swamp? Plan an investigation to find out, and carry it out if you have time.

Feathers

Feathers are the most distinguishing characteristic of birds. Feathers provide **insulation** against heat and cold and enable birds to fly. Brightly coloured feathers also help birds to attract a mate.

Downy feathers, or **down**, look very fluffy. They keep birds warm. Flight feathers have a strong **shaft**, with many small thread-like filaments attached to either side of the shaft. Each filament has hundreds of tiny hooks that hold the filaments together to make a long, flat surface called a **vane**. The vane is the main reason why birds can fly: it provides a large, flat surface that can withstand the air resistance during flight. Sometimes the filaments can detach but can be reattached by the bird during **preening**.

Figure 3.8 shows the parts of a feather. Feathers are 90.8% protein, 1.3% fat and 7.9% water. (Your hair and fingernails are mostly made of proteins as well.) Some birds can have up to 25 000 feathers, which can account for up to 20% of their body weight. Birds periodically shed and renew their plumage by **moulting**, usually two or three times in the first year to rid them of their downy feathers, then once or twice a year after that. Moulting needs a large input of energy by the bird, so it is usually timed to occur just after breeding season while food is still abundant.

FIGURE 3.8 Parts of a bird's feather

Go to http://mypsci1.nelsonnet.com.au and click on **Bird brains**. Find two interesting facts about bird brains. Click on **Backyard bird watch**. It will help you recognise birds in your own backyard.

Why feathers are special

ACTIVITY

In this activity, you will look at a variety of feathers and to try to work out their function.

WHAT YOU NEED
- flight feathers
- downy feathers
- hand lenses or stereomicroscopes
- synthetic insulation from a coat, sleeping bag or ski parka

WHAT TO DO
1 Rule up a table with three columns: the first headed 'Object', the second 'Drawings' and the third 'Observations'.
2 Use a hand lens or stereomicroscope to examine the flight feather. Draw the feather in your table. Examine the shaft. Hold it by the thicker end and carefully bend the opposite end a little bit. What happens when you let go of the bent end? Record your observations.
3 Carefully separate the thread-like filaments near the middle of the feather. What do you notice? Record your observations.
4 Use a hand lens or stereomicroscope to examine the downy feather. Draw the feather in your table.
5 Compare the shafts and filaments of the downy feather with those of the flight feather. Why do you think they are different? How does each type support its function? Record your observations.
6 Birds are warm-blooded. This means that, like ours, a bird's body produces its own heat energy. People and birds retain this warmth with the help of protective coverings. Examine the synthetic material. Compare this material with the downy feathers. How are they alike? How are they different? Record your observations.

WHAT DID YOU DISCOVER?
1 What did you find out about the two types of feathers? How are they alike and how are they different?
2 How does the synthetic material compare with downy feathers?

WHAT DO YOU THINK?
1 Why do you think birds have downy feathers?
2 What features of flight feathers make them suitable for flying?
3 If you were getting a new duvet, would you prefer goose down or a synthetic filling? Why?

REVIEW
1 Outline why mangrove swamps are a great place for birds to live.
2 Outline three adaptations that birds have that make them suited to living in mangrove swamps.
3 Draw a feather and label the shaft, filaments and vane.
4 Research how birds moult. Draw a concept map to represent the process.
5 Draw, or take a photo of, one plant or animal that lives in your local community that is well suited to its environment. What are its adaptations that led you to choose it?

Interactions in a mangrove swamp

People interact with one another through family, school, work and friendships. Other living things also interact with one another in the natural world. They eat, or are eaten by, other organisms; they shelter under trees or leaves; they mate; and they fight with other organisms from their species. These interactions help form systems that enable successful populations of organisms to thrive in their environment. Mangrove swamps are no exception, with interactions between their living parts.

Producers and consumers

Plants make their own food during photosynthesis. Mangroves use energy from the Sun, water from the swamp and carbon dioxide from the air to produce the simple sugar **glucose**. For this reason, they and other plants are called **producers**. Producers are the ultimate source of energy for all the other living organisms on Earth. Many animals, such as fish, shrimp and crabs, feed on the mangroves or decayed parts of the mangroves. These animals are called **consumers** because they eat other living material.

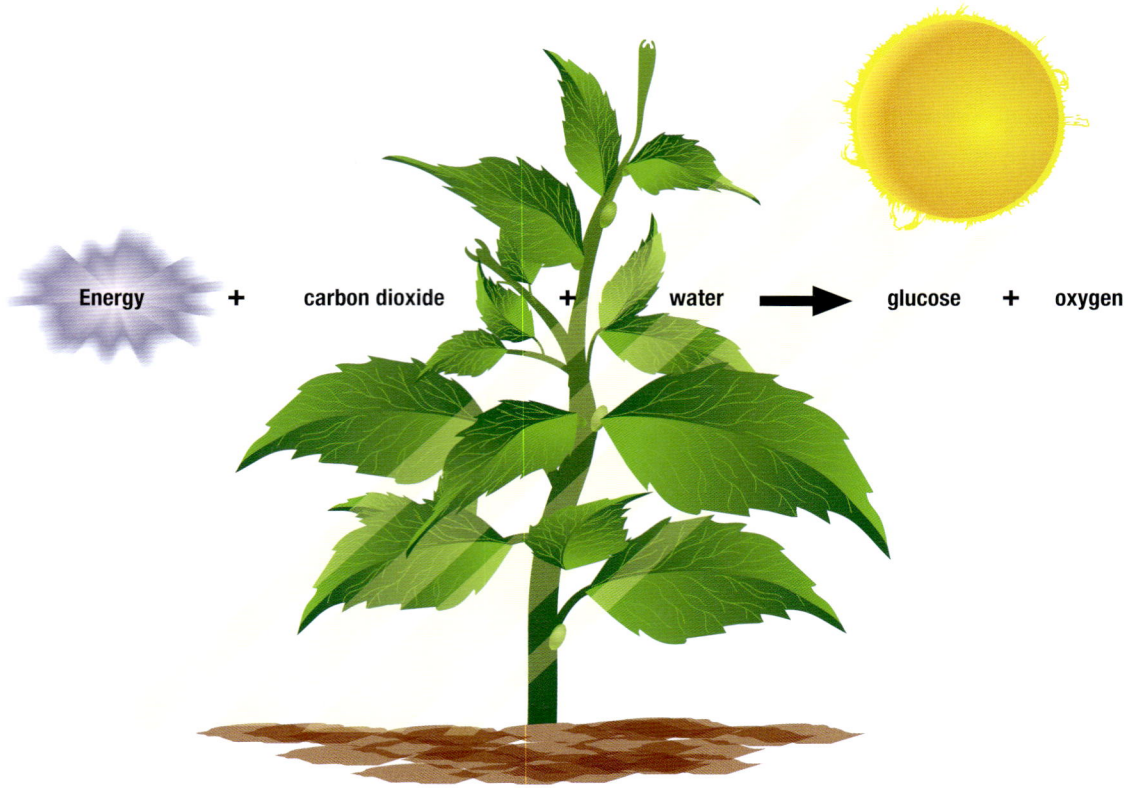

FIGURE 3.9 Plants are able to produce their own sugar in the process of photosynthesis.

Food chains

The **relationship** between the producer mangrove and the consumer animals can be shown as a **food chain** (Figure 3.10). A food chain is a diagram that shows who gets eaten by whom. Primary consumers eat the producers.

Birds such as ibis look for food among the water and mud surrounding the mangroves. Their long legs make them well adapted to this task. Their daily feast includes shrimp, insects, crabs and fish. The food chain in Figure 3.10 is extended in Figure 3.11 to show where the ibis fits in. The ibis is a secondary consumer because it eats a primary consumer.

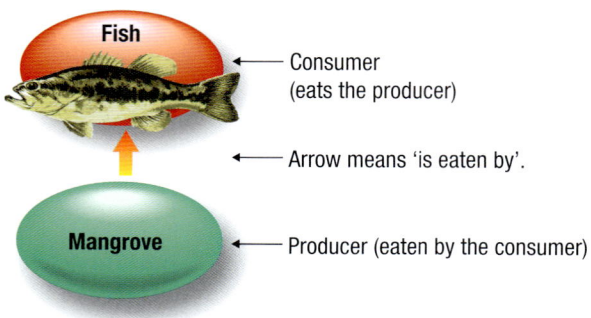

FIGURE 3.10 Food chains contain producers and consumers.

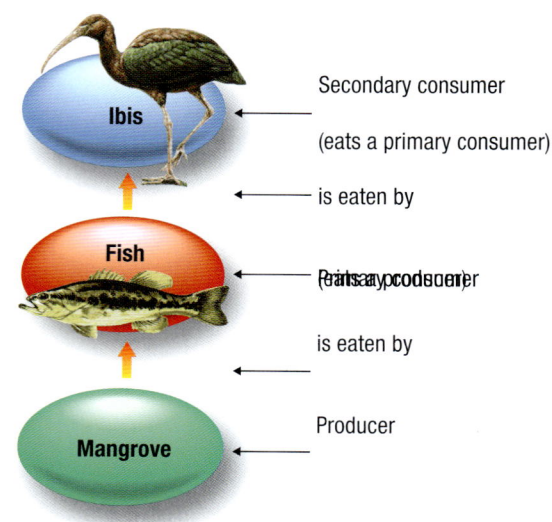

FIGURE 3.11 This food chain contains two levels of consumers.

Predators and their prey

Heron and ibis kill and eat other animals, such as fish, shrimp and crabs. The heron and ibis are described as **predators**, and the animal species they eat are their **prey**. This is known as a **predator–prey relationship**.

ACTIVITY: Using a simulation to study a predator–prey relationship

It is very difficult to study predator–prey relationships in nature when you are at school, especially over long periods of time. Fortunately, scientists have collected this type of information and made it available through computer simulations. A simulation reproduces the behaviour of a system. For example, simulations can be used to help us test the strength of buildings or learn how to fly an aeroplane. In this case, the simulation in the weblink will help you study the population relationship between wolves and moose.

1. Read the instructions and then run the simulation.
2. Describe the patterns in the graph.
3. Why do the populations of the animals change in this way?
4. Change one of the variables a number of times and re-run the simulation.
5. What did you learn about the effect of this variable on the predator–prey relationship?

Go to http://mypsci1.nelsonnet.com.au and click on **Predator prey simulation**. Use this site to carry out the wolves–moose simulation.

Parasites and their hosts

In between the feathers of a heron live very small animals called ticks. They feed by biting and sucking blood out of the heron. Species living on another species are called **parasites**. The heron is called the **host** because it supplies the tick's needs. The relationship between the heron and the tick is a **parasite–host relationship**. When a parasite invades its host, the host is usually weakened and sometimes dies.

Humans are host to many parasitic species, such as head lice, leeches and intestinal worms.

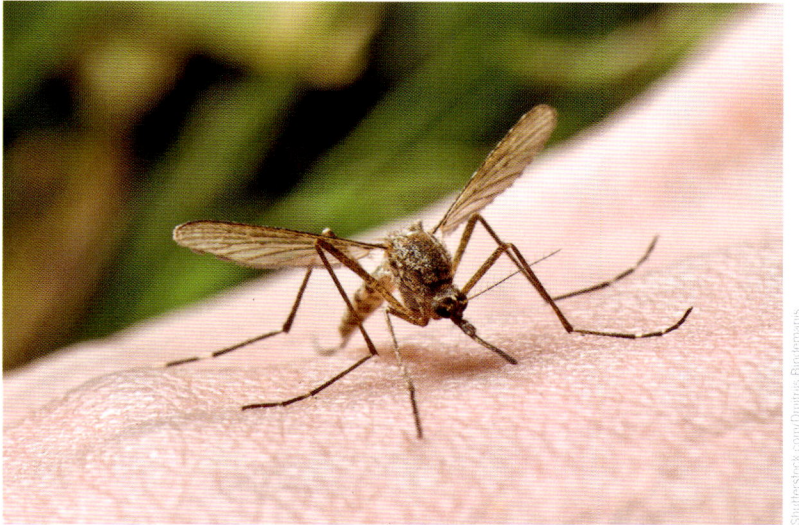

FIGURE 3.12 A mosquito (parasite) bites a human (host). The mosquito benefits from this relationship but the human can be harmed.

FIGURE 3.13 This moray eel is being cleaned by several wrasse. Cleaner wrasse can be found off the coast of Africa, the Maldives, French Polynesia and Australia.

Mutualism

Small birds perch on the back of the heron and eat the ticks off its skin. The heron benefits because it is getting rid of the irritable ticks. The small bird benefits because it is getting its food. This relationship is called **mutualism** because both organisms benefit.

An interesting example of mutualism

Fish living off the coast of Egypt have a free vacuum cleaner service. Fish requiring a vacuum visit fish called cleaner wrasse. The wrasse nibble the parasites living on the fish's body and inside its mouth and gills.

It appears that the wrasse remove just enough parasites to keep the fish coming back. Fish are less likely to visit cleaning stations where they had previously been poorly cleaned or had to wait in a queue!

REVIEW

1. In nature, outline what is meant by a relationship.
2. Outline what photosynthesis is. Why is it an important process?
3. Why are mangroves called producers?
4. Outline what a consumer is. Give an example of a consumer within the mangrove swamp.
5. Consumers gain their energy by consuming other organisms. Where do producers get their energy?
6. For each of the following relationships, state an example from your own community.
   a Predator–prey
   b Parasite–host
   c Mutualism
7. For each of the following relationships, state which is the predator, prey, parasite or host.
   a A mosquito biting a person
   b A cat eating a mouse
   c A person eating a steak
8. Lichens are a combination of fungus and green algae. What type of relationship is this, and what part does each organism play in this relationship?

Ecosystems

An estimated 75% of the fish caught for commercial reasons depend directly on mangrove swamps for their nutrients. Some of the saltwater fish, crabs and other species make their way in between the mangroves to eat the leaf litter and small fish. Some of the birds living in the mangrove swamp fly inland and become food for foxes and feral cats. The combination of all the living organisms that make up a particular environment and all the non-living parts – the water, soil, rocks, air and wind – is called an **ecosystem**. In an **open ecosystem**, organisms can move in or out. This is so they can move between one ecosystem (such as the mangrove swamp) and another ecosystem (such as the sea).

The diversity of living things within an ecosystem is known as **biodiversity**. Biodiversity is often used as a measure of an ecosystem's health. An unhealthy ecosystem has a small number of different organisms living in it, whereas a healthy ecosystem has a large number of diverse organisms living in it.

Biodiversity is also about the variety within a species. People look different and they react differently. This is important for the survival of the species.

In 2001, the United Nations developed the Millennium Developmental Goals. These set out what the world hoped to achieve by 2015. Goal 7 (Ensure environmental **sustainability**) was concerned with working more sustainably with our environmental resources and reducing the loss of biodiversity. Mangrove swamps are highly biodiverse. Removing mangrove swamps to make room for other developments will harm that biodiversity. Humans must learn to live sustainably with mangrove swamps to ensure the survival of all species involved.

FIGURE 3.14 Millennium Development Goal 7: Ensure environmental sustainability

Weaving a web

The food chain shown in Figure 3.11 (on page 54) is a very simple way of looking at the feeding relationships in a mangrove swamp. The fish, prawns and crabs actually have a number of food sources, as do the birds. Organisms die and are returned to the mud, their decayed remains and nutrients are used by other plants to grow, and so the cycle continues. Such complex feeding interactions are called **food webs**.

Removing just one species in an ecosystem can have a huge impact on the other species and all their interactions. In Figure 3.15, if the small fish were poisoned by boats leaking oil and removed from this food web, fewer animals would be eating the mangrove plants. This could be a good thing for the crabs, mud whelks and shrimp, but less food would be available for the larger fish and in turn the ibis, herons, brolgas and foxes. Their numbers might decrease or they might disappear from this ecosystem. If these species disappeared, fewer nutrients would be returned to the soil by decaying organisms, which would affect the growth of the mangroves.

Go to http://mypsci1.nelsonnet.com.au and click on **Millennium Development Goals**. Find out about some of the great environmental projects the United Nations Development Programme has worked on over the 15 years.

Go to http://mypsci1.nelsonnet.com.au and click on **Food webs**. Practise constructing your own food webs online.

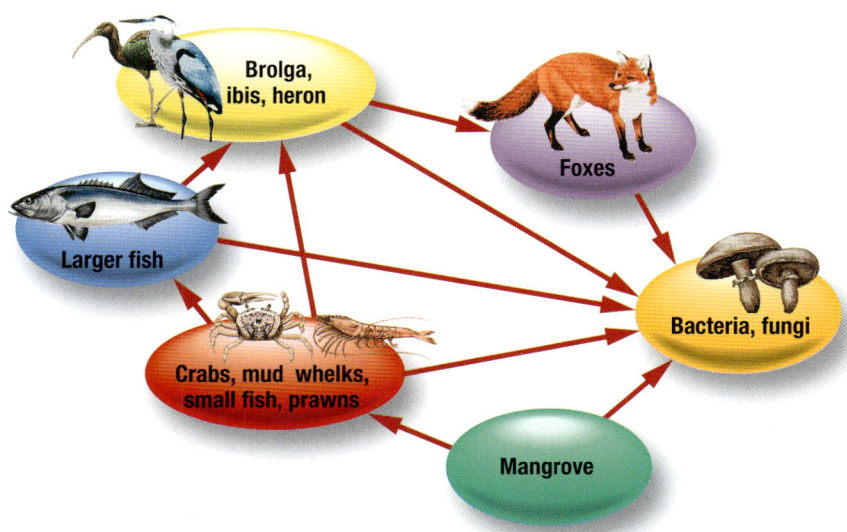

FIGURE 3.15 A simple food web from a mangrove swamp

TA PROTECTING BIODIVERSITY

Find out about environmental or community groups in your area that are working to protect the biodiversity of local ecosystems. What can you do to assist them?

Protecting your local environment ACTIVITY

There are plans to remove a wetland near your home in order to build a shopping mall. This wetland is home to many native species of birds, lizards, frogs and plants. Write a letter to the local politician in charge of planning in your area, stating your reasons why this wetland should not be removed, and the mall should be built elsewhere.

Protected environments ACTIVITY

Go to the UNESCO website. What natural areas in your country have been listed as World Heritage sites? What are five characteristics that are required for a site to be listed as a World Heritage site? Use these characteristics to determine whether mangrove swamps should be listed as World Heritage sites.

Go to http://mypsci1.nelsonnet.com.au and click on **UNESCO** to help you answer these questions.

Threats to the mangrove ecosystem

One of the greatest threats to mangrove ecosystems is **climate change**. Rising global temperatures are producing a warmer world. This means that sea levels are rising due to the melting of the glaciers and expansion of the oceans (as things get hotter, they also get bigger). It has been estimated that over the last 100 years, the sea levels have risen 10–25 centimetres. If climate change continues, mangrove pneumatophores will no longer be able to supply the mangrove with oxygen. This will lead to a loss of the mangrove plants.

Since the 1960s, the mangrove forests of South-East Asia have been slowly destroyed to make way for commercial shrimp farming. The South-East Asian **aquaculture** industry has been able to get around any laws intended to protect the mangrove swamps. Aquaculture has taken over most of the mangrove buffer zone, removing 70% of South-East Asia's mangrove forests.

FIGURE 3.16 A shrimp farm in Thailand. Aquaculture is threatening the survival of mangrove swamps.

As 75% of the South-East Asian commercial fish species spend part of their life in the mangrove forests, the loss of habitat has also brought about the loss of fish. This has in turn affected fishermen by decreasing the size and variety of their catch.

To add to their problems, the commercial feeds, **pesticides**, **antibiotics** and fertilisers used in shrimp farms have produced huge amounts of pollution. This has destroyed any remaining fish and harmed the coral reefs.

Left on its own, a mangrove ecosystem could survive for centuries. Unfortunately, humans have been moving in to clear mangrove swamps for commercial or private development. Such developments can be seen along many coastlines. Everybody loves a sea view!

> ### REVIEW
>
> 1. Outline what makes up the mangrove ecosystem.
> 2. Draw a food web that shows the eating relationship between a rabbit, insect, grass, frog, heron and a fox. Label the producer.
> 3. List the major threats to mangrove ecosystems.
> 4. Look at the food web in Figure 3.15 (page 57). The mangrove plant is a major producer for this ecosystem. What would happen to the food web if all the mangrove plants were removed?

A special ecosystem – tundra

Tundra comes from the Finnish word *tunturi*, meaning 'treeless plain'. Over one-fifth of the land on Earth is classified as tundra. Tundra is characterised by extreme cold. Temperatures in the Arctic tundra dip as low as −50°C in winter and only rise as high as 10°C in summer. Rainfall is below 25 centimetres annually. For almost all of the year, the soil and ground surface are frozen, with only brief periods of thaw in the summer.

Surprisingly, this ecosystem is home to many species of plants and animals. Plants are a very limited resource due to the cold conditions, lack of sunlight and frozen soil. Some grasses and caribou mosses do manage to survive.

FIGURE 3.17 The tundra ecosystem is very fragile.

These are eaten by lemmings, caribou, musk oxen and insects. Lemmings are the **keystone species** in the food web of the tundra, providing food for the small predators such as snowy owls and arctic foxes.

Polar bears and arctic wolves are the largest predators in the tundra food web. Their varied diet is made up of any of the smaller consumers.

All the living things eventually return to the soil of the tundra through the action of decomposing bacteria and fungi.

This ecosystem is extremely fragile due to the lack of producers. So if any of the smaller consumers are removed, the predators will not be able to find enough food to stay alive.

> ### REVIEW
>
> 1. Outline the characteristics of a tundra.
> 2. Would the requirements for photosynthesis be met on the tundra? Explain why or why not.
> 3. Suggest a reason why there are no trees on the tundra.
> 4. State what is meant by a keystone species.
> 5. Draw a food web for this ecosystem.
> 6. Outline why the role of the decomposers is important.
> 7. Suggest would happen to this ecosystem if all the producers died.
> 8. Suggest what would happen to this ecosystem if all the lemmings died.

UNIT QUESTIONS

CRITERION A

EXPLAINING SCIENTIFIC KNOWLEDGE

1 State whether the following relationships are predator–prey, parasite–host or mutualism. (Level 1–2)
   a Butterflies eat the nectar from a flower and spread the pollen to other flowers.
   b Insects eat the leaves of the snow gum.
   c A sheep is infested with tapeworm.
   d Venus fly traps (which are plants) suck the juices out of a mosquito.
   e A leech lands on your leg and sucks your blood.
   f Emus eat the fruit of a particular plant and deposit the seeds in a lump of faeces sometime later.
2 What adaptations do mangroves have to survive in their natural environment? (Level 3–4)
3 Describe using an annotated diagram how energy moves through the food chain. (Level 5–6)
4 Outline why producers are the most important part of a food web. (Level 7–8)

APPLYING SCIENTIFIC KNOWLEDGE AND UNDERSTANDING TO SOLVE A PROBLEM

5 Suggest one way that humans can have a positive impact on their environment. (Level 1–2)
6 List two ways that mutualism is important in ecosystems. (Level 3–4)
7 Explain two solutions that can enable us to achieve the seventh Millennium Development Goal of ensuring environmental sustainability. (Level 5–6)
8 You have just been appointed as Advisor to the Minister for the Environment. Outline how you will advise the minister about mangrove swamps and their importance. What will be your advice about actions that can be taken to protect mangrove swamps and inform the public? (Level 7–8)

INTERPRETING INFORMATION

Examine the food web shown in Figure 3.18 and answer the following questions.
9 Identify the primary consumers. (Level 1–2)
10 Draw the two food chains that involve sheep. (Level 3–4)
11 Suggest what might happen if the producer was removed. (Level 5–6)
12 Discuss what could happen if the number of rabbits was doubled. (Level 7–8)

REFLECTION

1 What impact do our lives have on coastlines?
2 What can we do to help support protected environments?
3 To what extent have human interactions with ecosystems damaged environments?
4 To what extent will a loss of biodiversity affect humans?

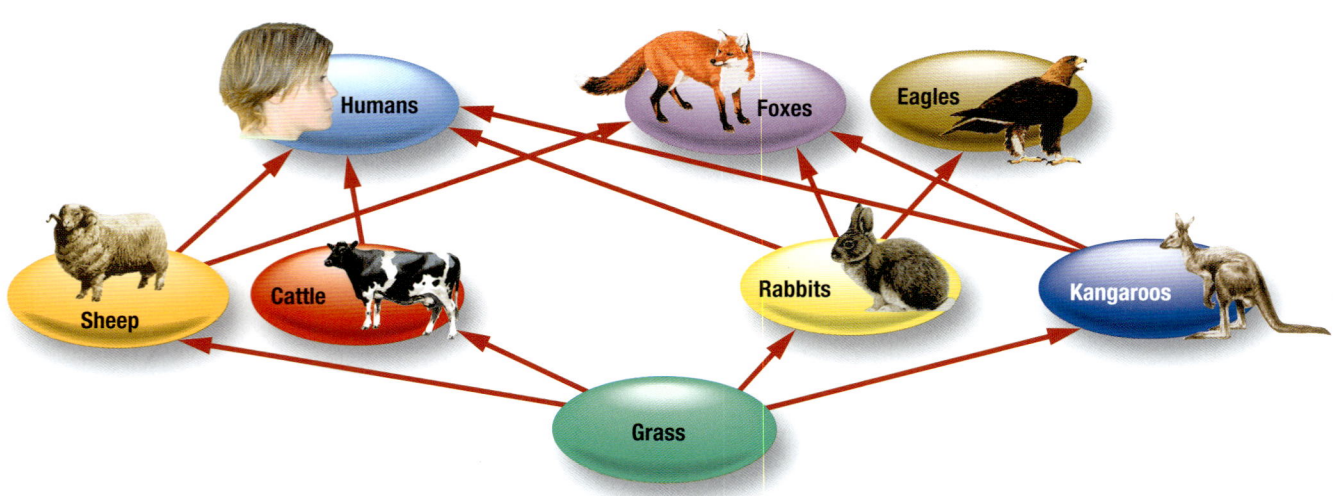

FIGURE 3.18 A food web

UNIT 4

EVERYDAY ACIDS AND BASES

KEY CONCEPT
Systems

RELATED CONCEPTS
Consequences

Evidence

GLOBAL CONTEXT
Globalisation and sustainability: an exploration into human impacts on the environment

STATEMENT OF INQUIRY
There is evidence that changes to pH in the environment caused by human activities are having serious consequences.

INQUIRY QUESTIONS

FACTUAL
1. What are the properties of acids and bases?
2. How do we use indicators to measure acidity?
3. What safety measures are needed when handling acids and bases?

CONCEPTUAL
4. What applications does neutralisation have in our lives?
5. How does the pH scale work?
6. How are the ideas of concentration and strength different in relation to acidity?

DEBATABLE
7. Are natural sources of acidity just as important as those from human activity?
8. Is the international community capable of solving issues such as acid rain?

Introduction

When you drink a fizzy drink, you experience a tingling sensation on your tongue. This is caused by the acids in the drink. One of these acids is **carbonic acid**. Carbonic acid is formed when carbon dioxide gas dissolves in water. You may have heard soft drinks being referred to as carbonated water. Other acids found in soft drinks are citric acid and phosphoric acid. Acids are everywhere in our lives – in our bodies, food, medicines, gardens and cleaning liquids. Acids are often part of pollution caused by cars and industries – this can be in the form of **acid rain**.

ATL

COLLABORATION
Show flexibility and willingness to make necessary compromises to accomplish a common goal when working in teams.

Taking action to tackle acid rain problems

Acid rain has a detrimental effect on the pH of lakes, other waterways, forests and buildings. Figure 4.1 shows the areas of the world that experience the greatest problems with acid rain.

Imagine you are a member of an environmental group in a country affected by acid rain. Work in groups to create an awareness campaign to convince people in your country that acid rain is a serious issue. Your campaign should be well coordinated and could contain items such as fact sheets, posters, badges, newspaper articles, videos for TV or to put on social networks, and petitions for people to sign. You will need to do some research into the acid rain problem in the country you have chosen.

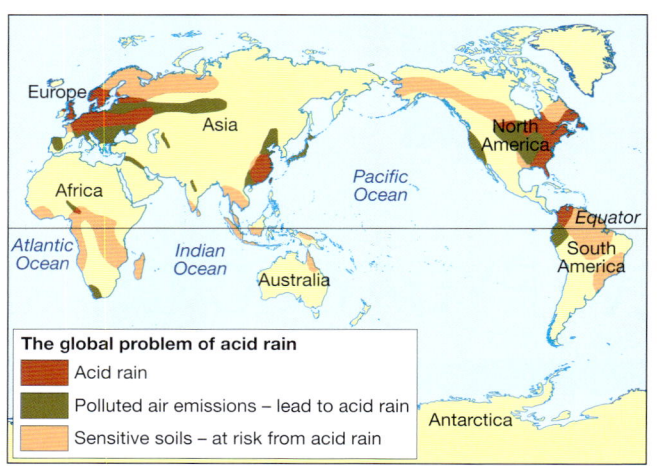

FIGURE 4.1 Acid rain is a global problem.

Acids and bases KWL chart

ACTIVITY

What do you already know about acids and bases? What do you want to know? In groups, divide a sheet of paper into three columns under the headings K, W, L.
- **K** stands for knowing. What do you already know about acids and bases?
- **W** stands for what you want to know or learn.
- **L** stands for the learning in class.

Leave the L blank for now, but remember to return to your KWL chart throughout the unit and keep adding to it.

Acids

Acid comes from the Latin word *acidus*, meaning 'sour'. If you have ever eaten a lemon, you will know what a sour taste is like. When you vomit, you can taste the sour hydrochloric acid that comes from the stomach.

Acids are also in common foods. Citrus fruits such as oranges contain citric acid and ascorbic acid. Acetic acid (the scientific name is ethanoic acid) is found in vinegar. These acids are fairly safe, but will sting if they get into a cut on your skin. Some acids, such as those used in cleaning, can harm your skin or eyes. Always treat all acids with great care. If you are using them in class, carefully follow all safety warnings. Some common acids in the home and laboratory are listed in Table 4.1.

FIGURE 4.2 Sour foods contain acids and are not always pleasant to eat.

TABLE 4.1 Some common acids

Common acids in the laboratory	Common acids in the home
Hydrochloric acid	Citric acid (oranges)
Sulfuric acid	Ethanoic acid (vinegar)
Nitric acid	Ascorbic acid (vitamin C)
	Lactic acid (milk)

Acid rain

Many cities have increased amounts of sulfur dioxide and nitrogen oxide in the air. These gases are released as by-products from the engines of vehicles and the burning of fossil fuels generally. Coal-fuelled power stations are a major source of sulfur dioxide.

When sulfur dioxide and nitrogen oxide dissolve in the moisture in the air, they form sulfuric and nitric acids. This is known as acid rain. If this rain falls on forests, it can kill the trees over time. It also can cause lakes to become acid, which affects the fish and plant life in the lakes. There are lakes where fish such as trout no longer can live. When acid rain falls on cities, anything made of marble will be slowly eaten away. Figure 4.3 shows a very old marble statue that has lost its detail because of acid rain.

FIGURE 4.3 This marble statue has been affected by acid rain.

Areas most affected by acid rain include large parts of Europe, particularly central Europe and Scandinavia (Figure 4.4), many parts of the United States and Canada, and the southwestern coast of China. The problem is complicated because much of the acid rain that falls in most countries comes from neighbouring countries.

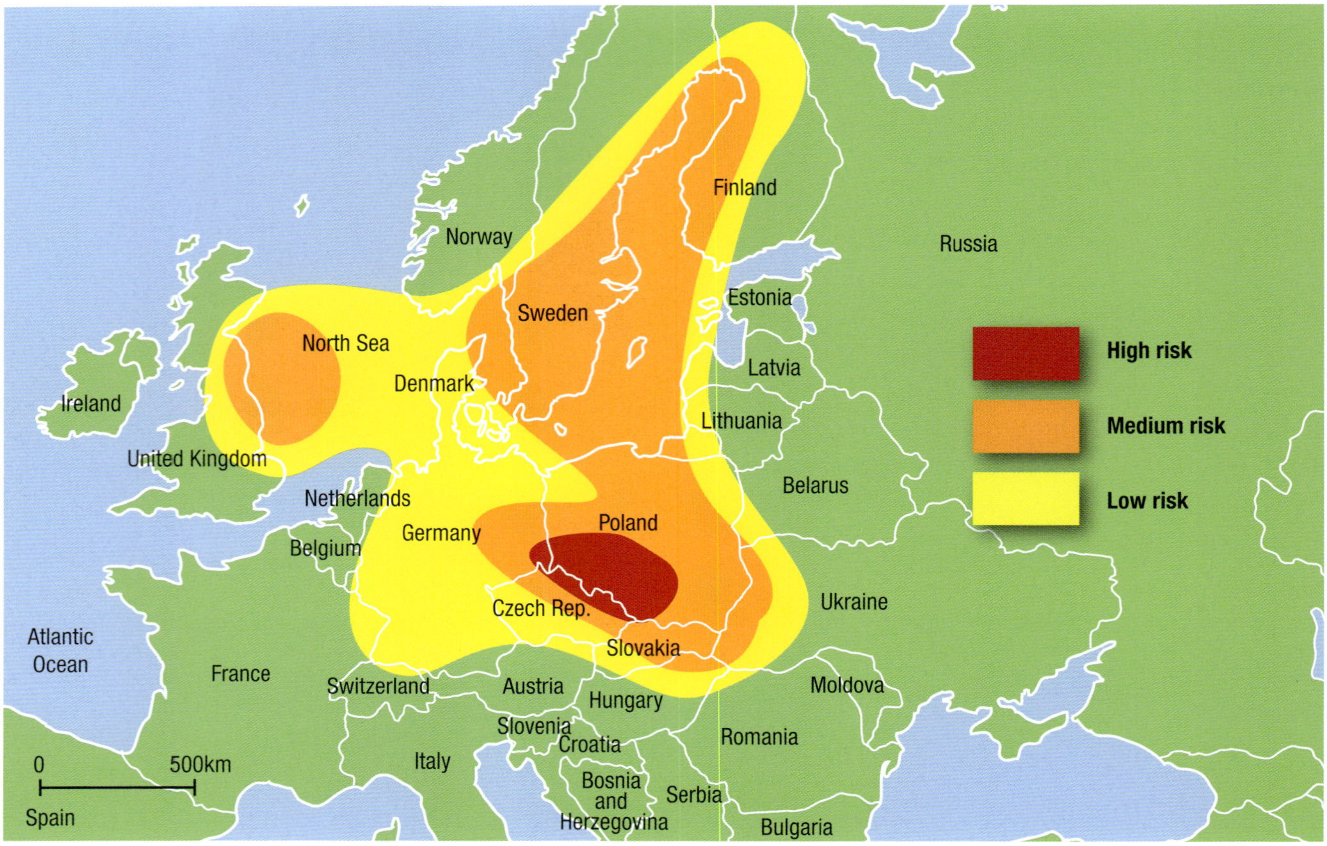

FIGURE 4.4 In Europe, central Europe and Scandanavia are particularly affected by acid rain.

Go to http://mypsci1.nelsonnet.com.au and click on **Acid rain**. Read 'The Tale of Lucy Lake' to learn about the effect that acid rain has on a lake and the surrounding plants and animals.

FIGURE 4.5 Lakes that are seriously affected by acid rain can no longer support life such as fish, tadpoles and frogs.

Bases

Bases are the chemical opposite of acids. They are substances that will react with acids, making them less acidic. While acids taste sour, bases tend to taste bitter. Some bases feel a little slimy, like wet soap. We use bases such as baking soda in cooking. Bleach and caustic soda are bases that are used as household cleaners (Figure 4.6). Some bases dissolve in water. This produces an **alkali** or an **alkaline solution**. A substance that dissolves in water is said to be **soluble** in water.

FIGURE 4.6 Toothpaste contains bases – it is slightly alkaline.

Alkalis are corrosive and can damage your skin and eyes. However, slightly alkali substances can be useful. For example, toothpaste reduces the acidity in your mouth that causes tooth decay (Figure 4.7). Antacids are bases or weak alkalis that are taken to reduce stomach acidity. The relationship between the terms base and alkali can be shown as a Venn diagram (Figure 4.8).

Some common bases are listed in Table 4.2 (page 66).

FIGURE 4.7 Household cleaners such as bleach and caustic soda are strong bases.

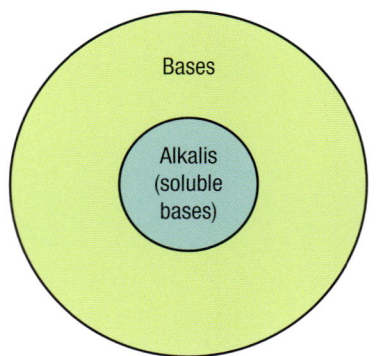

TABLE 4.2 Some common bases

Common bases and alkalis in the laboratory	Common bases and alkalis in the home
Sodium hydroxide	Sodium hydroxide (caustic soda)
Potassium hydroxide	Sodium carbonate (washing soda)
Ammonia solution	Calcium oxide (garden lime)
	Magnesium hydroxide (indigestion tablets)
	Sodium bicarbonate (baking powder)
	Ammonia solution (cleaning)

FIGURE 4.8 This Venn diagram shows the relationship between bases and alkalis.

REVIEW

The answers to these questions could be added to your KWL chart.
1. State what an acid is. Give an example of an acid you would find at home.
2. State the names of some acids you would find in soft drink.
3. State what a base is. Give an example of a base you would find at home.
4. Write a sentence that links acids and bases.
5. State what an alkali is. Name two alkaline substances found in your home.

Measuring acids and bases

FIGURE 4.9 A universal indicator colour chart, solution and paper strips – universal indicator turns a range of colours at different pH values.

One of the first characteristics that scientists used to identify acids was their sour taste. The more sour the substance, the more acidic it is. Now scientists measure acidity by using the **pH scale**. Most substances have a pH between 1 and 14. Acids have a pH below 7. The lower the pH, the more acidic it is. Bases that are soluble (alkalis) have a pH greater than 7. The higher the pH, the more alkaline it is. A pH of 7 is **neutral** – that is, it is neither acidic nor basic. Water usually has a pH of 7 – it tastes neither sour nor bitter. Scientists use instruments such as pH meters and pH probes to give a digital read-out of the pH of a solution. Alternatively, you can use an **indicator**. This is a substance that contains a dye that changes colour when you change the pH of the solution, showing what change has taken place.

The best indicator for quickly measuring the pH of a solution is **universal indicator**. It can turn a range of colours, depending on the pH of the solution (Figure 4.9). This makes it very useful. Universal indicator can be in the form of a solution or coloured paper strips. You just add one or two drops of the universal indicator solution – or a tiny piece of the universal indicator paper strip – to the solution you are testing. A colour chart helps you to decide the approximate pH of the solution.

Litmus paper is another indicator (Figure 4.11, page 68). It changes colour from red for acids to blue for bases (alkalis). Litmus paper is not as accurate as universal indicator but still can be very useful in some situations and is often used in the school laboratory.

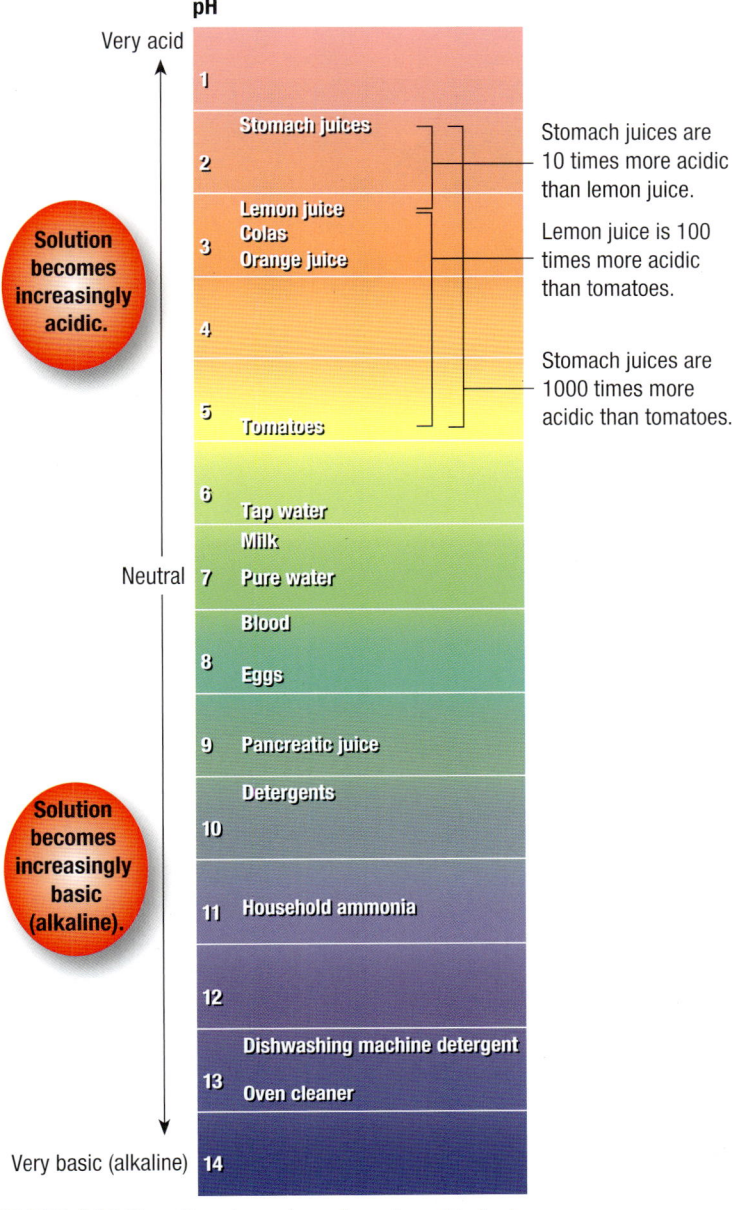

FIGURE 4.10 The pH scale as shown by universal indicator

The term 'pH' stands for the words 'hydrogen power' in Danish. This name came about because scientists discovered that all acids give away positively charged hydrogen atoms (called hydrogen ions) when they react with bases. Danish biochemist Søren Sørensen (1879–1963) devised the scale to show the amount of hydrogen ions. You will study more about pH in MYP 4 Chemistry.

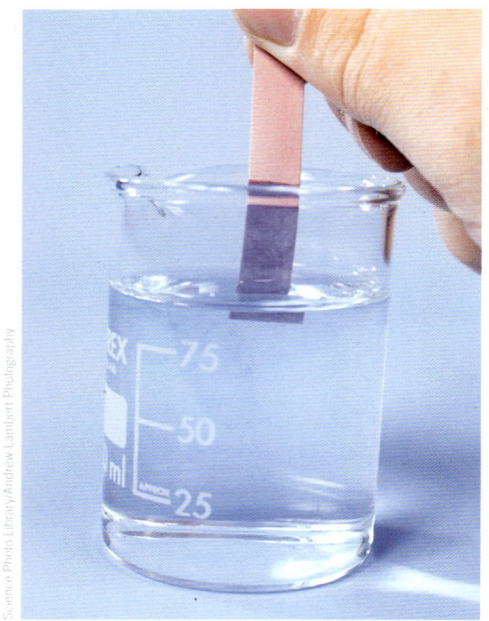

FIGURE 4.11 The use of litmus paper

FIGURE 4.12 A pH meter gives an accurate value for the pH of a solution.

Making an indicator

EXPERIMENT 4.1

COMMUNICATION
Read for meaning and understand the importance of following experimental instructions.

AIM
To make and test an indicator solution by using red cabbage leaves.

Note: this might be the first time you use Bunsen burners. Refer to pages 76–77 for instructions on how to use a Bunsen burner and guidance on safety.

MATERIALS

- large beaker
- Bunsen burner or hot plate
- tripod and gauze mat
- red cabbage leaves, cut into shreds
- filter paper and funnel
- storage jar with lid
- several small test tubes
- solutions to test (such as water, lemon juice, detergent, tomato, cola, orange juice, egg white, milk, a weak ammonia solution)
- teaspoon
- measuring cylinder or 1 cup measure (250 cm^3)
- universal indicator or pH meter

PROCEDURE

1. Put a handful of shredded red cabbage leaves into the beaker and add 1 cup of water.
2. Place the beaker onto the gauze mat on top of the tripod. Turn on the Bunsen burner and boil the leaves for 5 minutes.
3. When the water is very red, turn off the Bunsen burner and let the cabbage water cool.

4. Filter the liquid through the filter paper and funnel (see Figure 4.13), collecting the liquid (filtrate) in the storage jar. This is your indicator solution.
5. Use your indicator solution straight away, or refrigerate it for future use.
6. To use your indicator solution, put 2 teaspoons of the indicator solution into a test tube.
7. Add 1 teaspoon of the solution that you want to test. (Use a clean test tube for each solution you want to test.)
8. In a results table, record the colour that the indicator solution turns.
9. Test the pH of each solution with universal indicator or a pH meter.

Go to http://mypsci1.nelsonnet.com.au and click on **Alien juice bar** to learn more about using cabbage indicator to test acids and bases. Then use your knowledge to serve drinks to the aliens!

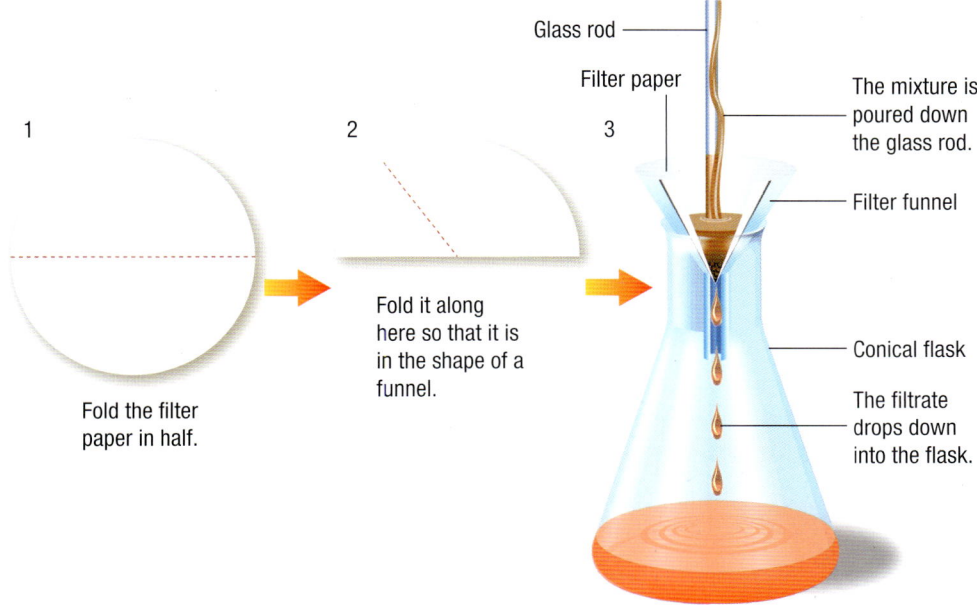

FIGURE 4.13 Steps for filtering the cabbage water.

RESULTS

1. Copy the results table into your workbook and complete it. Add as many rows as required.

Substance being tested	Colour the red cabbage indicator goes	pH as shown with universal indicator or pH meter	Acid, base or neutral?

CONCLUSION

Write a general conclusion explaining how red cabbage can be used as an indicator.

EXTENSION

Try to create a series of test tubes showing all the possible colours by carefully mixing two of these solutions.

Find information on other plant or animal extracts that can be used as indicators for acids and bases and carry out similar experiments using these.

Who needs to know about pH?

Nearly everybody needs to know about pH. For example, gardeners, cooks, food manufacturers and water authorities all need to consider pH in their professions.

FIGURE 4.14 A simple pH tester for soils. The gardener shakes up a sample of soil in water and then determines the pH by using an indicator.

Gardening

The pH of uncontaminated soils can range from less than 4.5 to nearly 8. Gardeners can test the acidity of soils with a simple kit (Figure 4.14). Most plants grow best in a slightly acidic or neutral soil, although plants such as azaleas and many indigenous Australian plants grow better in more acidic soils. Wholesale plant suppliers adjust the pH of the soils they use by adding chemicals. They also adjust the pH of the water they use on them.

FIGURE 4.15 Strawberry jam needs a specific pH for it to set.

Jam-making

Manufacturers of all foodstuffs need to closely check the pH during manufacturing. For example, pH is important in jam-making. If the pH is not just above 3, then the jam won't set, and instead remains a runny syrup. Strawberry jam must have a pH of 3.1 or 3.2 if it is to set properly.

Swimming pools

The pH of a chlorinated swimming pool must be carefully controlled. The pH of the water must be kept at about 7.5. If the water is too acidic, then it can sting a swimmer's eyes and irritate the skin. If the pH is too high (that is, too alkaline), then bacteria and algae will grow.

Water authorities

People who manage our water supply and the sewerage system must monitor the pH all the time. Most water authorities aim to keep the pH of drinking water between 6.5 and 8.5.

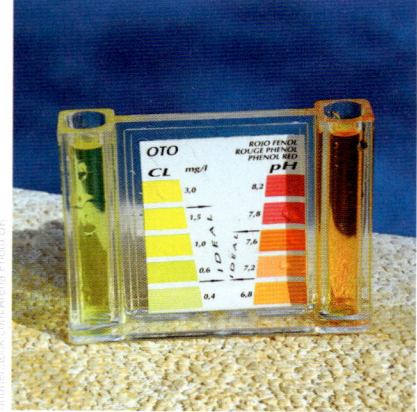

FIGURE 4.16 It is important to test swimming pools regularly to maintain the water at about pH 7.5.

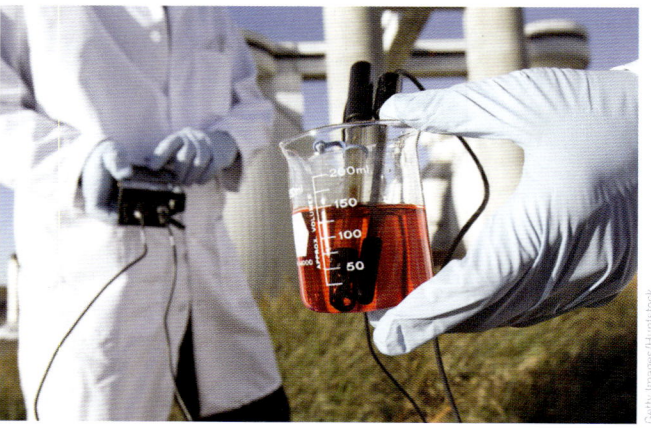

FIGURE 4.17 The pH of drinking water is kept between 6.5 and 8.5.

If the pH is lower than 6.5, then the water will taste sour and the acid will start 'eating away' the metal pipes – not to mention our teeth! If the pH is too high, then the water will taste bitter. Drinking water is also treated with chlorine to kill harmful micro-organisms.

At sewage-treatment plants and farms, the pH must remain between 6 and 10 so that bacteria can survive and break down the sludge.

Acid rain and soil

Acid rain increases the acidity (lowers the pH) of soils. This directly affects the growth of trees and plants. This change in pH can also increase the likelihood of attack by fungi, bacteria and other pests. A more serious problem is that increasing acidity can cause soils to lose nutrients needed for plant growth. This is a common problem around the world. In the Green Mountains of Vermont in the United States, 50% of the red spruce trees have died in the last 30 years.

Over cropping and soil acidity

If we grow too many crops, then the soil will lose nutrients and eventually become more acid. This affects soil quality and can lead to increased soil erosion. One solution which has been carried out for hundreds of years is to add lime to the soil to neutralise the acidity. Farming less intensively, using less artificial fertilisers and rotating crops can also help.

ACTIVITY Soil acidity

Use Table 4.3 to answer Questions 1–5.
1 Name a fruit that would grow well in a soil of pH 5.0.
2 Name a vegetable that would grow well in a soil of pH 7.2.
3 Name an alkaline-loving vegetable.
4 Describe what you would need to do to a soil of pH 6.8 to make it suitable to grow radishes.
5 Describe what you would need to do to a soil of pH 6.0 to make it suitable to grow cherries.

TABLE 4.3 Optimal pH of some common types of fruits and vegetables

Relationship to acid/ alkaline soil	Fruits	Vegetables	pH
Acid-loving	Blueberries, cranberries	Radishes, sweet potatoes	4.0–5.5
Acid-tolerating	Apples, raspberries, strawberries	Beans, broccoli, cabbages, carrots,	5.5–7.0
Alkaline-tolerating	Cherries, plums, pomegranates	Sunflowers	7.0–7.5
Alkaline-loving		Asparagus, garlic	7.0–8.0

6 Outline how human activity can reduce the pH of soils.
7 A farmer measured the pH of their soil every year for 10 years and obtained the following results.

2000	2001	2002	2003	2004	2005	2006	2007	2008	2009
6.8	6.7	6.6	6.5	6.5	6.5	6.6	6.7	6.7	6.7

a Plot these results as a graph.
b Describe the pattern in these results.
c Suggest a reason for these results.

> **REVIEW**
>
> 1 Draw a pH scale with pH 1–14 and label on it:
>   a a weak acid
>   b a strong base
>   c water
>   d toothpaste
>   e vinegar.
> 2 Compare the colour changes of universal indicator and litmus indicator.
> 3 Outline the importance of pH to gardeners and farmers.
> 4 Outline the consequence of the pH of a swimming pool being too high.
> 5 Explain why the colour of red cabbage can change during cooking.

Concentrated or dilute?

We can use the words **concentrated** and **dilute** to describe acids and bases. A concentrated acid solution has a lot of acid dissolved in a small volume of water. A dilute acid solution has a little bit of acid dissolved in a large volume of water. Can you think of other times when you use the words 'concentrated' or 'dilute'? You might have mixed yourself a drink using squash (or cordial) syrup and made it too dilute, so you added some more squash to make it taste better.

Concentrated acid and water react to produce a large amount of heat. You should always add acid slowly to water and not the other way around, because the water is much more efficient at absorbing the heat produced than the acid would be.

Concentrated acids and bases are **corrosive**. They can eat away at skin, metal and rock, so they must only be handled with suitable protective clothing and extreme care. Concentrated hydrochloric acid is used by bricklayers to clean cement from brick walls. Concentrated sulfuric acid is sometimes used by plumbers to unblock drains.

Concentrated sodium hydroxide (a base) is a common ingredient in many oven cleaners as it can dissolve baked-on fat and grease. Always wear thick rubber gloves when using oven cleaner to prevent the oven cleaner from touching your skin.

If a concentrated acid or base is diluted, the pH of the substance will change. Orange juice normally has a pH of 3.5. If the juice is diluted with water, the pH will become higher, moving more towards neutral (pH 7). This is because when the water is added, it makes the solution less acidic.

Safety considerations

Strongly acidic and alkaline solutions are hazardous. They can cause serious burns to skin and eyes. Some can blind you. This means they should never be handled without special rubber gloves, protective clothing, and safety glasses or a face shield. Figure 4.18 shows a warning symbol for corrosive chemicals.

You should never sniff strong acids and bases. Some will give off toxic, corrosive vapours. They must only be kept and handled in rooms that are very well ventilated. Examples of strong acids and bases that might be found in your home are:
- Strong acids: brick cleaner, concrete cleaner (see Figure 4.19)
- Strong bases: drain cleaner, oven cleaner, engine degreaser (see Figure 4.20).

Each of these products should have safety instructions on the label. **If there is a spill, inform an adult immediately. Do not try to clean it up yourself.**

FIGURE 4.18 European Union standard symbol for corrosives

The best thing to put on a spill is sodium bicarbonate (also known as bicarbonate of soda). This will help neutralise both strong acids and strong bases and absorb some of the liquid. The mixture can then be flushed away with a lot of water. Never try to neutralise a strong acid with a strong base, or vice versa, because this will produce a lot of heat and an even greater hazard. It is always wise to have bicarbonate of soda in a place that can be easily reached in case a spill happens.

FIGURE 4.19 Full protective gear must be worn when using acidic chemicals to remove graffiti from walls.

FIGURE 4.20 When cleaning the oven, wear gloves to protect the skin.

TA THE SAFE USE OF ACIDS AND ALKALIS IN YOUR HOUSE

With the permission of your parents, carry out a survey to find out which acids and alkalis are used in your house. Read the safety advice given for the use of each substance. Consider whether you think each substance is correctly stored in your house. You could have a conversation with your parents about whether they feel these substances are being used safely and stored well.

> **REVIEW**
>
> 1. Explain the difference between dilute acid and concentrated acid.
> 2. How do we dilute an acid?
> 3. What is meant when we say an acid is corrosive?
> 4. What happens to the pH of a strong alkali as it is diluted?
> 5. Make a list of five key safety recommendations for using acids and alkalis in the home.

Neutralisation

Reactions between acids and bases are described as **acid–base reactions**. During these reactions, the pH can change. When a base is added to an acid in just the right amount to make the pH about 7, we say it has **neutralised** the acid.

Uses of neutralisation

- A common treatment for a bee sting is to soothe it with calamine lotion. This is because a bee sting is acidic (formic acid) and the calamine lotion is basic and neutralises the sting.
- An indigestion (antacid) tablet works by reacting with stomach acid in a neutralisation reaction.
- Farmers add lime to soil to increase the pH of the soil, or sphagnum peat to reduce the pH.
- The reaction of baking soda with acids during cooking releases gases that help the cake or bread rise.
- Hair conditioner is acid and neutralises the alkalinity left in the hair by most shampoos.
- Lakes that have been affected by acid rain can be restored to health by the addition of limestone.

Baking soda and vinegar reaction

EXPERIMENT 4.2

AIM
To learn about the neutralisation reaction between baking soda and vinegar.

MATERIALS
- baking soda
- vinegar
- big container (to avoid a mess)
- paper towels
- tablespoon
- measuring cylinder
- safety goggles

PROCEDURE
1. Place 4 tablespoons of baking soda in the container.
2. Add 20 cm^3 of vinegar.
3. Watch the reaction.
4. Repeat steps 1–3 with different proportions of baking soda and vinegar.
5. Your teacher might allow you to make a volcano and do the reaction inside the volcano.

CONCLUSION
Describe the reaction in scientific language. What did you learn about the best mixture to use? Do you think a real volcanic eruption is caused by a reaction of this kind?

INVESTIGATION 4.1 Treatment of acid lakes

YOUR CHALLENGE
Investigate how effective adding lime to an acid lake is as a method of reducing the level of acidity.

THIS MIGHT HELP
Your teacher will provide you with vinegar solutions to use as a substitute for lake water. Usually garden lime (powdered calcium carbonate) is used. You could also use slaked lime (calcium hydroxide).

The basic method is to measure the pH of the vinegar, add the lime, and then re-measure the pH. You will need to experiment with the amounts needed and consider how many different amounts of lime are needed. Your teacher will advise you on the equipment to use.

Carry out and write up the investigation by following the guide in Appendix 3 on page 169, or as advised by your teacher.

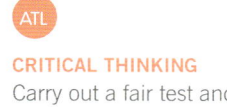

CRITICAL THINKING
Carry out a fair test and control variables.

FIGURE 4.21 Adding lime to an acid lake in Sweden can help restore it to health.

ACTIVITY Reducing the acid rain problem

One of the main sources of acid gases in the air has been coal-fired power stations. Coal usually contains some sulfur. When coal is burned, the sulfur is converted into acidic sulfur dioxide gas. This gas in then released through the chimney of the power station.

YOUR CHALLENGE
1. Use your knowledge from this unit to design some apparatus that could help reduce the amount of acid gas released to the air.
2. Discuss the reasons why good scientific ideas like your invention are not always put into practice. How could we solve this problem?

FIGURE 4.22 Emissions from a coal-fired power station contribute to acid rain.

How to use a Bunsen burner

Before you complete Experiment 4.1, you need to learn how to use a Bunsen burner. A Bunsen burner is a single gas jet often used in science laboratories for heating or burning things. Before you start, read the safety information about using Bunsen burners.

1. Place the burner on a heatproof mat next to a gas tap. Check that there is nothing nearby that could catch on fire.
2. Make sure that the gas is off. Your teacher will show you how to tell if it is off. Push the end of the rubber tube well onto the gas tap so that no gas can leak out.
3. Place anything else you need over the burner before you light it. (This might be a tripod, a gauze mat and a beaker containing water, as shown in Figure 4.23, but it will depend on the activity.)
4. Close the air hole by rotating the collar (see Figure 4.23). One person should light a match, while another should be ready to turn on the gas. Put the lit match next to the top of the burner and turn on the gas slowly. The more you turn the tap, the more gas you allow out and the bigger the flame. You should now see a bright yellow flame. This is a cool flame and is often called the **safety flame** or visible flame.
5. Slowly open the air hole. The more you open it, the more oxygen you allow in. This makes the flame look bluer and burn hotter. The blue flame is used for heating. A yellow flame puts black soot on objects and takes too long to heat things up.
6. If you have finished using the blue flame, but will use it again shortly, close the air hole to turn the flame back to yellow so that you can see it. If you have finished altogether, turn the burner off.

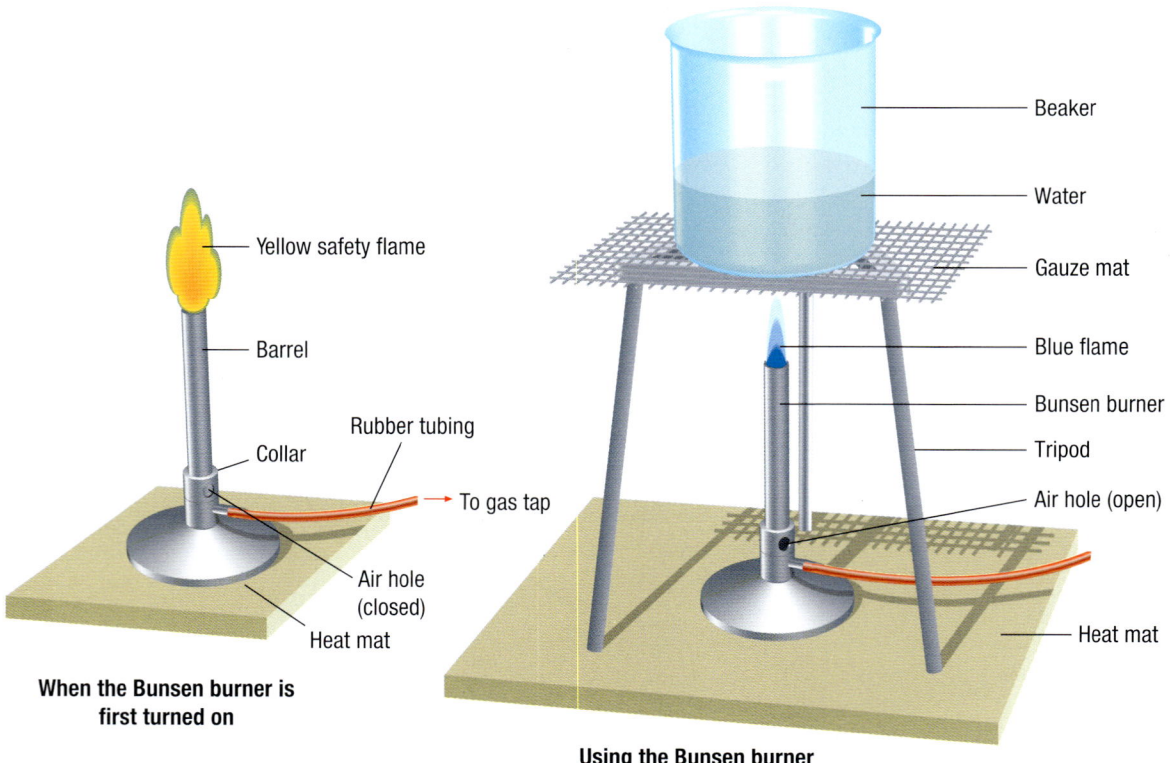

When the Bunsen burner is first turned on

Using the Bunsen burner

FIGURE 4.23 How to set up and use a Bunsen burner

Safety

When you use a Bunsen burner, follow these important safety instructions.
- Never light a Bunsen burner without a heatproof mat underneath it.
- Never light a Bunsen burner if a flammable substance is nearby.
- Tie back any long hair so that it cannot catch fire.
- Never play with matches or leave a matchbox open near the burner.
- If the burner does not light, turn the gas off immediately and start again. If it still does not work, ask your teacher for assistance. Your burner may have a blockage.
- Never put an empty glass container directly over or in a burner flame. The glass will shatter.
- Never stand over or near boiling liquids. They could spray onto your eyes and skin. Wear safety glasses just in case.
- Always have metal tongs or an oven cloth ready nearby in case you need to quickly move objects into or away from the flame.
- Never touch the burner or anything that has been over or in it until they are cold. Never put hot equipment in cupboards.
- Never try to speed up the cooling of hot objects by putting cold water on them. This can cause serious steam burns. It can also cause containers to crack and spill their hot contents.
- Ask your teacher to help as you take the hot container off the gauze mat so that you do not get burned.
- Do not touch hot equipment.

REVIEW

1. Define the term 'neutralisation'.
2. Give three examples of useful neutralisation reactions in the house.
3. Suggest how to reduce the pH of an acid lake.
4. If I add some strong alkali to a strong acid drop by drop, what do you think will happen to the pH?

UNIT QUESTIONS

CRITERION A

EXPLAINING SCIENTIFIC KNOWLEDGE

1. State whether the following statements are true or false. (Level 1–2)
   a. Lemons are alkaline.
   b. Bases feel soapy.
   c. Acids taste sour.
   d. Alkalis are sometimes called bases.

2. What am I? Select each answer from the following: citric acid, acid rain, sodium bicarbonate, universal indicator, magnesium hydroxide. (Level 1–2)
   a. I am the best thing to put on some spilt acid to make it less dangerous.
   b. I make lemons taste sour.
   c. I am the indicator that gives a range of colours when put in solutions of different pH.
   d. I form when sulfur dioxide in the air is dissolved in moisture in the air.
   e. I help ease the effects of indigestion.

3. Four soils have the following pH values: 9, 8, 7 and 5. Which soil most likely needs lime to make it neutral for healthy plant growth? (Level 1–2)

4. State the meaning of each of these terms. (Level 3–4)
   a. pH scale
   b. Acid
   c. Base
   d. Alkali

5. State three uses of acids and three uses of bases in everyday life. (Level 5–6)

6. Use your ideas about neutralisation and the pH scale to describe what happens when a strong acid is gradually added to a strong alkali. (Level 7–8)

APPLYING SCIENTIFIC KNOWLEDGE AND UNDERSTANDING TO SOLVE A PROBLEM

7. What can you tell about a solution if its pH is 4.5? (Level 1–2)

8. How would you recommend someone treat a bee sting? (Level 3–4)

9. Describe two safety precautions you should use when cleaning an oven with oven cleaner. (Level 5–6)

10. The owner of a swimming pool is complaining that their eyes are stinging after swimming. What advice would you give them about treating the water? (Level 5–6)

11. A lake is too acid to allow fish to live. Describe a possible reason for this and suggest two ways we could reduce this problem. (Level 7–8)

INTERPRETING INFORMATION

12. An advertisement claimed that a new shampoo had a pH of 7. Comment on this claim.

13. A gardener was surprised that her tomatoes had not grown very well over the last two years. Suggest some advice to give the gardener based on the work studied in this unit. (Level 3–6)

14. A student was carrying out a neutralisation experiment and obtained the results shown in Figure 4.24.

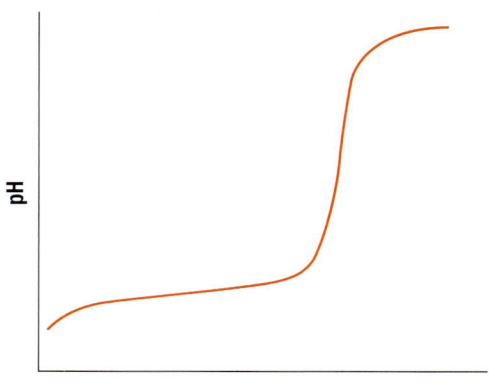

FIGURE 4.24 Results of a neutralisation experiment

   a. Interpret what the graph tells us.
   b. Suggest a reason for these results.
   c. Redraw the graph to show the results when an acid is added to an alkali. (Level 5–8)

REFLECTION

1. Describe the evidence that shows that acid rain is damaging the environment. Why do scientists need to be very careful how they use evidence to make conclusions?

2. Suggest some other consequences of humans' activities to our planet.

3. Discuss whether all acid soils are caused by humans' activities.

UNIT 5
SOLIDS, LIQUIDS AND GASES

KEY CONCEPT
Change

RELATED CONCEPTS
Models
Scales
Creativity

GLOBAL CONTEXT
Scientific and technical innovation: an exploration into the fundamental importance of the moving particle theory in science

STATEMENT OF INQUIRY
The creative use of the moving particle theory allows us to predict and understand the behaviour of solids, liquids and gases.

INQUIRY QUESTIONS

FACTUAL
1 What are the characteristics of solids, liquids and gases?
2 What causes air pressure?
3 What are condensation, evaporation and sublimation?

CONCEPTUAL
4 How do we distinguish the difference in phases at a particle level?
5 How do we explain the idea of expansion?
6 How does studying particle theory help us interpret weather patterns?

DEBATABLE
7 What role does creativity play in science?
8 How would the situations described in this unit be different on Mars?

Introduction

Consider the following phenomena. We put salt on the roads in cold weather. Cooking with natural gas can result in condensation on the windows of the house. We can smell someone's perfume a long way from them. If air enters a car's braking system, an accident can happen. We can travel in hot-air balloons. Ice can make a good building material. How do we explain all these different phenomena?

All matter is made of incredibly small particles, of a small scale beyond our normal experience. Even with most modern microscopes, we cannot see these particles. To help make sense of the behaviour of solids, liquids and gases, scientists use a **model** called the **moving particle theory**. Scientists use models in many situations. This is similar to engineers testing out models of new aeroplanes to better understand how to build the final aircraft. Economists use models of a country's economy to help them predict future economic trends. A good model allows people to be very creative in their thinking.

CRITERION A (I AND II) — SUMMATIVE PERFORMANCE ASSESSMENT TASK

 ATL

CREATIVE THINKING
Use your imagination. Do you enjoy being creative, playing with new ideas, taking risks?

Models: Using the moving particle theory to show understanding of air pressure

Your challenge

Design a poster to use the moving particle theory to explain one of the following situations.
- You blow into a balloon and it expands.
- Your balloon is left in the sun. The temperature of the air inside the balloon increases (more than the surroundings) and the balloon expands.
- You can use a straw to suck up and drink a liquid.

You could make your poster like a cartoon, giving the moving particles faces and words. Use your creativity! Display your posters on a wall and carry out a gallery walk of all posters.

The four states of matter

Everything is made from **matter**. The three most common states (or phases) of matter are solid, liquid and gas. There is also a fourth state of matter called **plasma**, but it is only found under special conditions, such as at the centre of stars.

Solids

A solid has a definite shape and usually cannot be **compressed**. Solids tend to maintain a constant shape and do not flow like liquids or gases. Their properties can vary. Some solids are hard and strong; others are quite flexible. Some, such as metals, conduct electricity; others are non-conductors. Some are very heavy for their volume (they are **dense**); others are quite light. Common solids include gold, ice and plastics.

FIGURE 5.1 A solid house being transported.

Liquids

Liquids do not have definite shapes. They are **fluids** – that is, they can be poured into different sizes and shapes of container. We say they can flow. Like solids, liquids cannot be compressed. They are quite dense, but usually less dense than solids.

Gases

Gases are very easy to compress. They fill up the entire volume of the space they are in. Like liquids, they also flow easily. They have very low **density**, much lower than the density of liquids.

Plasma

Plasma is a very complex state of matter. More than 99% of the known universe is plasma. As material is heated, it changes from solid to liquid to gas. If it is heated further, properties within the particles begin to change. When these properties change, we have the fourth state – plasma.

We use plasma in everyday life. For example, plasma is produced inside the glass tubing of neon advertising signs and plasma televisions.

Plasma is produced on the Sun and flung out from the surface as huge plumes of charged particles. These plumes are called solar prominences. They can contain 100 billion kilograms of matter and be as long as 350 000 kilometres. That's about 10 times the circumference of the Earth. A coronal mass ejection is a prominence gone wild. It is a huge body of plasma that erupts at speeds of up to 900 km/h. It's also very hot – tens of millions of degrees!

FIGURE 5.2 A liquid fuel being transported in a container

FIGURE 5.3 Natural gas is transported in pipes as it flows easily through the pipe.

Go to http://mypsci1.nelsonnet.com.au and click on **Solids, liquids and gases**. Watch some animations to help you understand the differences between the three states of matter.

FIGURE 5.4 A plasma TV

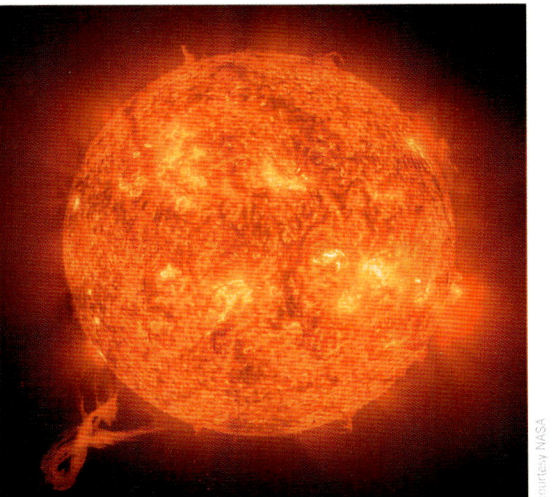
FIGURE 5.5 Plasma prominences often erupt from the Sun.

> **REVIEW**
>
> 1. Make a table to show the differences in properties between solids, liquids and gases.
> 2. Compare the ways you might transport solids, liquids and gases from one side of your classroom to the other.
> 3. Outline some of the uses for solids, liquids and gases.
> 4. Is jelly a solid or a liquid? Discuss.
> 5. Sand can flow. Is sand a solid or a liquid?

Moving particle theory

COMMUNICATION
Express scientific ideas clearly. Your ideas about concepts such as particles are likely to evolve slowly over time. For instance, students often understand that matter is made of particles. However, they can have incorrect ideas such as that particles have the same properties as the substance – that particles are coloured or that particles themselves become 'hot' when we heat up a substance. To improve your understanding of new concepts such as particles, it is important to use your ideas, to discuss them with other people, and to have patience that your understanding will gradually improve.

In order to explain the different properties of solids, liquids and gases; for example, why gases compress but liquids don't, we need to know what matter is made of.

In the mid-18th century, scientists such as Robert Boyle, Daniel Bernoulli and Joseph Louis Gay-Lussac developed theories about gases being made of moving particles. We often refer to the moving particle theory as the **kinetic** theory. The word 'kinetic' relates to the idea of movement.

Kinetic theory can be used to explain the properties of solids, liquids and gases. The moving particle theory suggests that all material is made of extremely small moving particles. In general, particles move fastest in gases. When you heat up a substance, what you are really doing is making the particles move faster.

There are spaces between the particles. These spaces are much larger for gases than for solids or liquids. Particles are attracted to each other. These attractions are very important in solids, a little less important in liquids, and less important again in gases.

Particles in a solid

The particles in a solid are all close together. They are also more or less fixed in their positions. They do not move too far from their position because they are strongly attracted to nearby particles. This is why solids have a fixed shape.

All of the particles vibrate about an average central position in all directions. They move up and down, back and forth, and side to side in a three-dimensional dance.

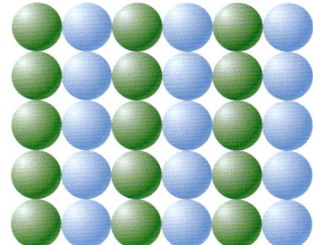
FIGURE 5.6 Particles in a solid are arranged close together.

Particles in a liquid

When energy is given to a solid, the particles vibrate more. They move farther away from the average central position and from one another. The particles become less attracted to each other, so they can move around more. The solid becomes a liquid.

There are still enough attractions to stop the particles separating completely from the other particles, but they are able to move more freely. This is why the liquid can flow and occupy the shape of a container.

FIGURE 5.7 Particles in a liquid are less attracted to each other than particles in a solid.

Particles in a gas

When energy is given to a liquid, again the particles move around faster until the attractions between them are no longer strong enough to hold them together. They escape the liquid to become a gas. They can now move very far apart from one another. The particles can move quickly to any part of the container.

This is how the smell of perfume can move through a room to your nose. The particles of perfume are far apart, as are the air particles. The perfume particles can get between the air particles to your nose. The spaces between the particles in a gas also make it easy to compress.

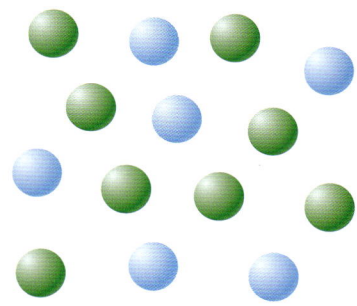

FIGURE 5.8 Particles in a gas are far apart from each other.

EXPERIMENT 5.1 Free space in solids, liquids and gases

AIM
To compare the amount of free space in solids, liquids and gases.

MATERIALS
- syringes (ideally one per student, working in groups of three)
- seals for the syringes
- water
- sand

PROCEDURE
1. Give each person in your group of three a syringe.
2. Take one syringe and fill it three-quarters with water. Make sure there is no air inside the syringe, only water.
3. Take another syringe and draw some air into it.
4. Place the sand in the other syringe.
5. Close the outlet of each syringe with a seal. You can use your fingers, but it might be messy!
6. Compress each syringe as hard as possible, and make sure you keep the end sealed.

CONCLUSION
1. What happened in each syringe? What were the differences?
2. Explain the results, using ideas about the arrangement of particles in solids, liquids and gases.

Go to http://mypsci1.nelsonnet.com.au and click on **Gas properties**. This is a simulation that allows you to test the compression of gases.

REVIEW

1. Outline the moving particle theory.
2. Compare the movement of particles in gases, liquids and solids.
3. Complete the statements with the words from the following list: attraction, compress, compressed, easily, expand, faster, hard, heated, space, weak, widely.
   a. It is difficult to _____ a solid because there is so little _____ between the particles.
   b. Solids are usually _____ materials because there is a strong _____ between the particles.
   c. When a solid is _____, the particles move _____ and knock into one another more energetically. This causes the particles to move apart and the solid to _____ to a slightly greater volume.

d Only _____ attractions hold the particles of a liquid together and so they flow _____.
  e The particles in a gas are _____ spaced and so they are easily _____.
4 Use the moving particle theory to explain why gases are easier to compress than liquids or solids.
5 Compare the differences in attraction between the particles in a solid and the particles in a gas.
6 A liquid is heated until it turns into a gas. Explain what happens to the particles.

Change of state

Ice melts if it is left in the sunshine. Melting is called a **change of state**. The state of a substance depends on the environment that surrounds and affects it. What we know as natural gas on Earth is solid in other parts of the universe. Gold is a solid at normal temperature and pressure. In one sense, a gold ring is just 'frozen' liquid gold. When you heat gold it changes into a liquid that can be poured into moulds to make jewellery and gold nuggets (Figure 5.9).

FIGURE 5.9 Very hot gold is a liquid that can be poured into moulds to make gold bars.

Melting and boiling points

The **melting point** is the temperature at which a solid changes state to become a liquid. Heating a solid will cause its particles to vibrate faster. At a certain temperature, the particles will have (on average) enough energy to break away from their positions in the solid and move around inside a liquid.

If a substance is pure, then it will change state at precise temperatures. Ice melts at 0°C. Gold melts at 1064°C. Helium melts at −272°C, the lowest melting point of any substance. The melting point of a substance is the same as the **freezing point**. Can you see why?

FIGURE 5.10 Melting ice

The **boiling point** of a substance is the temperature at which it changes state from a liquid to a gas. At this temperature, the particles (on average) have enough energy to break away from the liquid. Water boils at 100°C. Alcohol boils at 78.5°C. Liquid oxygen boils at −183°C. When water boils to form steam, the volume of steam is very much larger than the volume of the liquid water. This can be dangerous, and can lead to explosions.

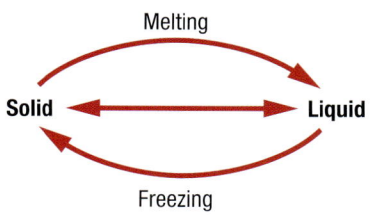

FIGURE 5.11 Flow chart showing melting and freezing

Go to http://mypsci1.nelsonnet.com.au and click on **Changing matter** to see an interactive simulation of changes of state.

ACTIVITY   Steam explosions

Carry out some research into where steam explosions can occur. Write a summary of the situation, and suggest ways the problem can be solved or avoided. Also discuss the reasons why effective possible scientific solutions are not always acted upon in this situation.

EXPERIMENT 5.2   Changes of state

AIM
To investigate the temperature changes during the changes of state of water.

MATERIALS
Per group of two students:
- crushed ice
- beaker
- hotplate
- data logger (or paper and a pen)
- temperature probe or thermometer immersed and then frozen in water

PROCEDURE
1. Place some crushed ice in the beaker.
2. Place the temperature probe, or thermometer, in the crushed ice.
3. Connect the probe or thermometer to the data logger and make sure it is on the graph function, with time on the *x*-axis and temperature on the *y*-axis.
4. Place the beaker on the hotplate.
5. Turn on the hotplate and wait for the ice to melt.
6. When the ice has melted, wait for a few minutes for the water to produce steam.

RESULTS
1. Record your results in a suitable table.
2. Use your results to plot a graph to show how the temperature changed over time.

CONCLUSION
1. What were the melting and boiling points of water?
2. Do you notice at some points in the graph that there is no change in the slope of the graph? Why might this be?

EVALUATION
Why might your temperature readings not have been very accurate?

EXTENSION
At the end of this experiment, you have produced steam. What will happen to the temperature of the steam if it is now heated further?

Go to http://mypsci1.nelsonnet.com.au and click on **States of matter** to access an interactive simulation to explore the idea of changes of state further.

Evaporation

Liquids can also change into gases below their boiling points – they evaporate. **Evaporation** requires energy. During evaporation, a liquid absorbs energy from its surroundings, which cool down. You might have experienced the cooling effect of a liquid, such as acetone or alcohol, evaporating on your hands. Your body can regulate its temperature by sweating. When you exercise, you get hot and sweat. The sweat then evaporates, causing cooling (Figure 5.13).

Water from oceans, lakes and other bodies of water is constantly evaporating to form water **vapour**. When air contains a lot of water vapour, we say the air has a high **humidity**. In very dry climates, low humidity (the lack of water vapour in the air) can be a problem for some people's skin and breathing. People often use humidifiers to increase the amount of water vapour in the air.

FIGURE 5.12 Clothes dry by evaporation.

FIGURE 5.13 Sweating helps cool you down by evaporation.

EXPERIMENT 5.3 Evaporation rates under different conditions

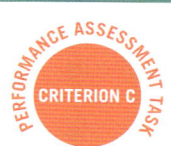

CRITICAL THINKING
Understand the importance of carefully considering the experimental data (evidence) before making a conclusion.

AIM
To compare the rate of evaporation under different conditions.

PREDICTION (HYPOTHESIS)
Write a prediction for how you think increasing the temperature will affect the speed of evaporation of a liquid. Explain your prediction.

MATERIALS
Each group of students will need:
- 1 cm^3 propanone (acetone)
- three microscope slides
- beaker of warm water
- three small sticks, such as splints
- stopwatch
- three droppers

SAFETY
Propanone is inflammable and an irritant. Do not use open flames, and make sure that the laboratory is well ventilated. Wear safety glasses.

PROCEDURE
1. Put a drop of propanone onto a microscope slide.
2. Measure the time it takes to evaporate.
3. Change the conditions and repeat the experiment. You could change the following variables.
   - Temperature: warm the microscope slide by placing it in warm water and then drying it.
   - Surface area: use the splint to spread out the drop more than it was originally.
   - Wind: use a fan to blow across the drop. If possible, try a fan giving both cold and hot air in turn.

RESULTS
Draw up a table to collate your results.

CONCLUSION
1. What did you learn from these results?
2. Explain the results by referring to the moving particle theory.
3. Did your results for increasing the temperature agree with your prediction?

EVALUATION
How well did the experiment work? Can you suggest any ways of improving the experiment?

EXTENSION
How do these results relate to the drying of wet clothes?

INVESTIGATION 5.1 The best drying conditions for clothes

CRITICAL THINKING
Think carefully about the variables involved in this investigation.

YOUR CHALLENGE
To design an investigation to show how clothes dry under different conditions.

THIS MIGHT HELP
You can use some of the ideas in Experiment 5.1. You will need to develop a scale to judge how dry the clothes are.

Carry out and write up the investigation by following the guide in Appendix 3 on page 169, or as advised by your teacher.

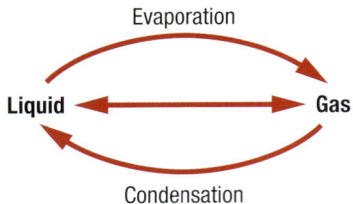

FIGURE 5.14 Flow chart showing evaporation and condensation

Condensation

Water vapour condenses to form liquid water (usually as droplets). **Condensation** is the opposite of evaporation. You are likely to have seen drops of water condensing on windows in your house, perhaps caused by water that evaporated when you cooked or had a hot shower (see Figure 5.15). When you breathe out on a cold day, you can see water in your breath condensing. Condensation can be a major problem in homes, leading to mould, mites, mildew on clothes, and the rotting of wood and other house materials.

Go to http://mypsci1.nelsonnet.com.au and click on **Condensation** to learn more about condensation problems around the home.

TA SOLVING CONDENSATION PROBLEMS IN HOMES

Do some research into the problems associated with condensation in homes that people in your neighbourhood experience. Design some possible solutions and explain them in a pamphlet to give to people. You might find the adjacent weblink useful.

FIGURE 5.15 Condensation occurs on a bathroom mirror after a hot shower.

Sublimation

When changing state, substances can sometimes miss a phase and go from a gas to a solid or a solid to a gas. This is called **sublimation**.

Sublimation is used in the entertainment industry to create 'smoky' clouds. Solid carbon dioxide, or dry ice, is dropped into hot water. The dry ice sublimes by turning directly into carbon dioxide gas. The cold carbon dioxide gas mixes with the warm, moist water vapour from the hot water. The water vapour then condenses. This produces lots of foggy water vapour that can be blown by a fan onto a stage.

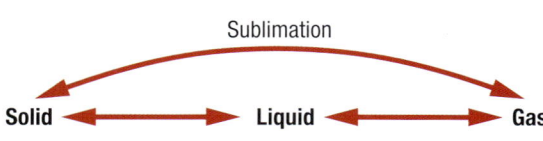

FIGURE 5.16 Flow chart showing sublimation

FIGURE 5.17 Sublimation is used to create special effects during rock concerts.

Changes of state and the weather

Condensation occurs when warm moist air comes into contact with either cooler dry air or a cooler surface. It occurs often in nature, resulting in clouds, fog and rain. Clouds are made of small droplets of water or ice. They form in three main ways.

1. The Sun shines, heating up the air. As air expands, it becomes less dense. Less-dense air rises. At higher altitudes, the hot moist air cools and the water vapour condenses into water droplets.
2. Moving air hits a mountain and is forced to rise. It cools and water droplets condense out.
3. Warm air meets a mass (front) of cold air. This forces the warm air to rise. The cooling produces water droplets.

If there are enough water droplets in a cloud, they can clump together into even bigger drops. Eventually, the drops become heavy enough to fall as rain. If the temperature is low enough, the small water droplets freeze and snow can form.

Mist and fog form when water vapour condenses close to the ground. This often happens as hot air is blown on top of cold water, such as lakes or the sea, or cold ground.

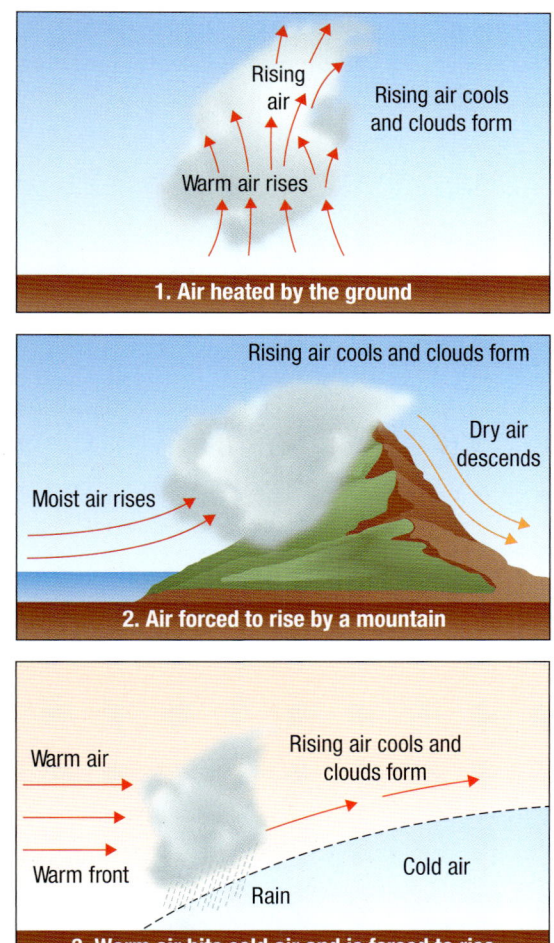

FIGURE 5.18 Three main ways for formation of clouds

FIGURE 5.19 Different types of clouds

REVIEW

1. Outline the difference between boiling and evaporation.
2. Outline why dogs stick out their tongues and pant.
3. Outline a situation in which condensation can cause a problem.
4. Dry ice (carbon dioxide) sublimes. State what this means.
5. What are clouds made of?
6. Outline two different ways that clouds can form.
7. Why do some clouds produce rain but others do not?
8. Outline why we often see clouds at the top of mountains.

ATL

COMMUNICATION
Use a variety of media to express ideas. Visual diagrams are a powerful way of helping people understand ideas. 'A picture is worth a thousand words.'

Expansion

When we heat up metals, liquids or gases, they expand (Figure 5.20). This means they become bigger. If you put a glass into very hot water, there is a risk it might crack because the glass expands quickly in the hot water. We can explain this **expansion** using the moving particle theory.

We know that when a substance is heated, the particles move faster. This extra movement means the particles need more space, so the substance expands. Have you ever noticed your shoes feel tighter on a very hot day? Can you explain this now using the moving particle theory?

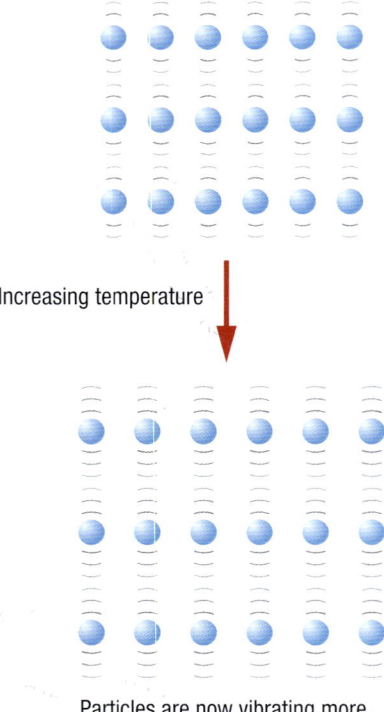

Particles are now vibrating more. The particles separate a little. This causes expansion.

FIGURE 5.20 Substances expand when they are heated.

Expansion of solids

Sometimes the expansion of metals can be useful. For instance, some thermostats in heaters contain a bimetallic strip (Figure 5.21). This strip is made of two different metals joined together. One of the metals expands more quickly when heated. As they are joined, this causes them to bend. This bending can be used to turn off the heating, so the temperature of the room, or an oven, doesn't go too high.

The expansion of metals can also be a nuisance. On hot days, metal train tracks can expand and move out of place (Figure 5.22). This can cause delays on train networks.

Go to http://mypsci1.nelsonnet.com.au and click on **Bimetallic strips**. View the interactive simulation of simultaneous expansion and contraction using the bimetallic strips.

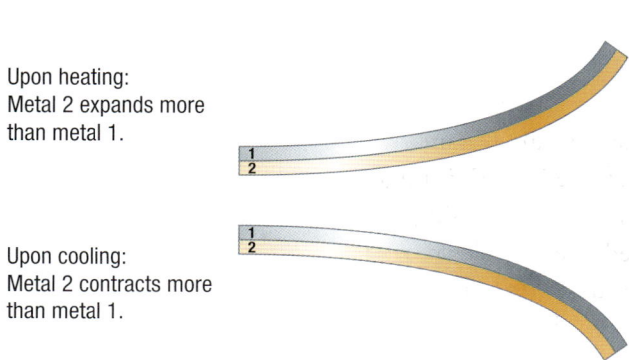

Upon heating:
Metal 2 expands more than metal 1.

Upon cooling:
Metal 2 contracts more than metal 1.

FIGURE 5.21 A bimetallic strip works because the two metals expand by different amounts on heating.

FIGURE 5.22 Train tracks can warp in the heat.

ACTIVITY Researching expansion

Choose one of the following topics to research with a partner.
1. How do we stop expansion damaging a bridge or railway line?
2. Why is it important not to use water heating pipes in long, straight lengths?
3. Why do metal window frames need a rubber spacer around their edges?

Discuss your findings with the class, with each student from each pair sharing something they have learnt.

Expansion of liquids

Liquids generally expand more than solids. If you heat a saucepan filled to the top with water, the water will expand and overflow. The water in a house's hot-water system expands as it is heated up. This can cause problems, so most hot-water systems have an extra expansion tank or use overflow pipes (Figure 5.23).

Climate change is causing the oceans to expand. This is partially responsible for rising sea levels around the world. Rising sea levels are threatening to flood low-lying countries (Figure 5.24).

FIGURE 5.23 Hot-water systems often have expansion tanks in case they overflow.

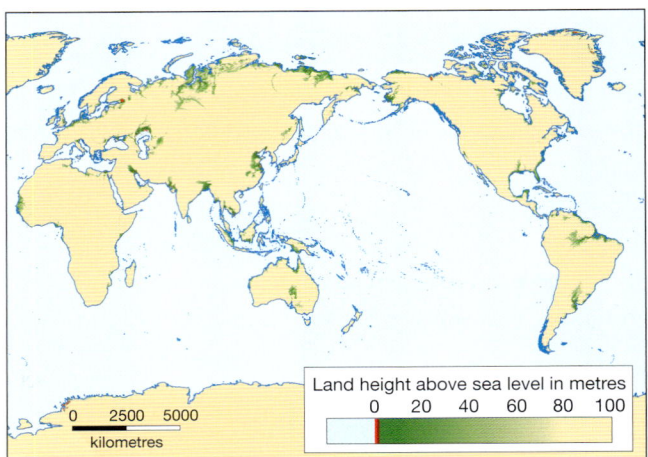

FIGURE 5.24 Low-lying areas of the world (shown in green and red) are under threat of flooding if global warming continues.

The contraction of liquids and gases as they cool can also be useful. When you open a new jar of jam or other food, it 'pops' as the lid's seal breaks for the first time. This is because when the jam was first added to the jar, it was hot. The lid was put on, and then the jam and air cooled down. This caused a partial vacuum, which 'pops' when the top is taken off.

Expansion of gases

Gases expand much more than solids or liquids. This is very useful for hot-air ballooning. Hot air is less dense than cold air, so a balloon filled with hot air rises from the ground into the sky.

Rising hot air also creates air currents called thermals. Birds use thermals to fly in a circle over the same place over and over again. As they ride the air current, they can climb to high altitudes without using much energy. Birds such as eagles and hawks use this method to extend their flying time as they search for food. Other birds use thermals to gain altitude and fly further during migration.

The uncontrolled expansion of gases can be dangerous and cause explosions. This is a particular problem in firefighting.

Go to http://mypsci1.nelsonnet.com.au and click on **Thermals** to read more about how birds use hot, rising air to help them fly. What other flying things take advantage of this effect?

FIGURE 5.25 An eagle uses thermals to extend its flying time.

EXPERIMENT 5.4 — Demonstrating expansion

AIM
To explain some examples of expansion.

PROCEDURE
Your teacher will instruct you on how to use the equipment shown in Figures 5.26–5.29.

FIGURE 5.26 Ball in a ring

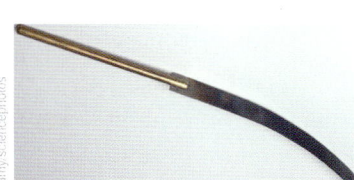

FIGURE 5.27 Bimetallic strip

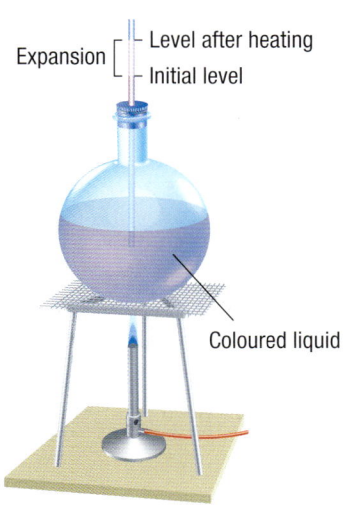

FIGURE 5.28 Expansion of liquids

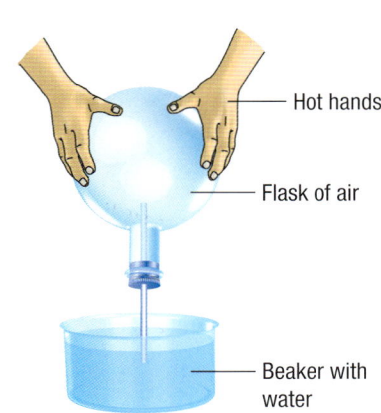

FIGURE 5.29 Expansion of gases

EVALUATION
Write a short explanation of what is happening in each of the situations in Figures 5.26–5.29, using your knowledge of expansion and the moving particle theory.

TA SUPPORTING OLDER OR DISABLED PEOPLE

In remote places with especially cold weather, older or disabled people can be at risk if the pipes in their homes freeze. How do you think local people can help look after these people? Create an awareness campaign to help people take action on behalf of older or disabled people.

Temperature and the moving particle theory

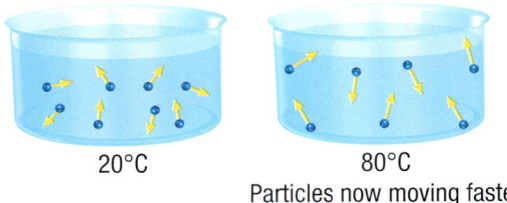

FIGURE 5.30 Particles in water move at different speeds at 20°C and 80°C.

You can use the moving particle theory to explain the difference between a beaker of water at 20°C and one at 80°C (Figure 5.30). At 80°C, the particles are moving faster on average than at 20°C. We can say that the average moving energy of the particles has increased. The energy is called kinetic energy.

People used to think that a substance called 'heat' would enter another substance as they heated it up. This was called the **caloric theory**. We now know this is not true. Heating up an object does not mean giving it a new substance called heat. It simply means we have caused the particles to move faster.

A thermometer is a measuring instrument used to find the temperature of something (Figure 5.31). A traditional thermometer comprises a hollow glass tube with a liquid such as mercury or coloured alcohol inside it. When the thermometer is put into a hot liquid, the moving particles in the liquid transfer heat energy to the particles in the mercury or alcohol, causing them to move faster and spread farther apart. The mercury or alcohol expands, and the volume of the liquid increases and reaches a higher level in the thermometer tube. The temperature we read off the scale on the side of a thermometer is related to the speed of the particles in the original liquid.

When the thermometer is cooled, the particles in the mercury or alcohol move slower and become closer together. The liquid contracts, its volume decreases and the level of the liquid in the thermometer falls.

Never use a thermometer as a stirring rod. Use only solid glass stirring rods. If you use a thermometer to stir a liquid, you can easily break the thin glass bulb at the end. The result is twofold. You make the thermometer useless, and you contaminate the liquid you are measuring with the thermometer's contents.

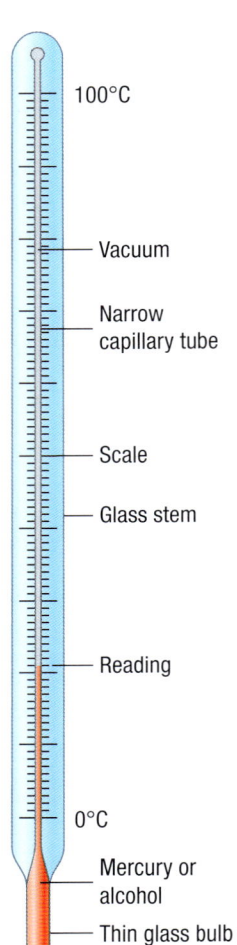

FIGURE 5.31 How a thermometer works: on heating, the mercury or alcohol expands and the volume of liquid rises up the capillary tube. On cooling, the liquid contracts and the level falls.

REVIEW

1. Use the moving particle theory to explain why a bimetallic strip bends when it is heated.
2. Explain why cold weather can result in broken water pipes.
3. State whether liquids or gases expand more when heated.
4. What do we mean by the term 'thermals'? Draw a diagram to show how they are useful to birds.
5. When making jam, outline why is it important to put the lid on the container when the liquid is still hot.
6. Outline how a thermometer works. Include a diagram in your answer.
7. State what is meant by the temperature of a substance.
8. Outline what is so unusual about the freezing of water to produce ice.
9. Draw a particle picture to show how the liquid in a thermometer rises as the temperature rises.

Diffusion: let's spread out!

If you have ever been in the same room as someone who has used a perfume or aromatic oil, you will have noticed that smells reach you after a while.

ACTIVITY Smelling distances

Place people around the room – under tables and on benches, as well as standing on the floor. Then open a bottle of something with a strong smell, such as perfume or eucalyptus oil. Get your classmates to raise their hands as soon as they smell it. Discuss your observations.

Gas particles, such as those of perfume, move through the air by a process called **diffusion**. The perfume particles move into the spaces between the air particles. We also can say that the perfume moves from a more dense collection of particles – that is, a high **concentration**, where it was just sprayed – to a less dense collection of particles – a lower concentration.

Diffusion is responsible for the spread of odours, even without any air disturbance, such as the smell of coffee when a jar is opened or the smell of petrol around a garage. The rate of diffusion increases with temperature because the particles have more energy and move faster.

Liquids also diffuse (Figure 5.32), although slower than gases.

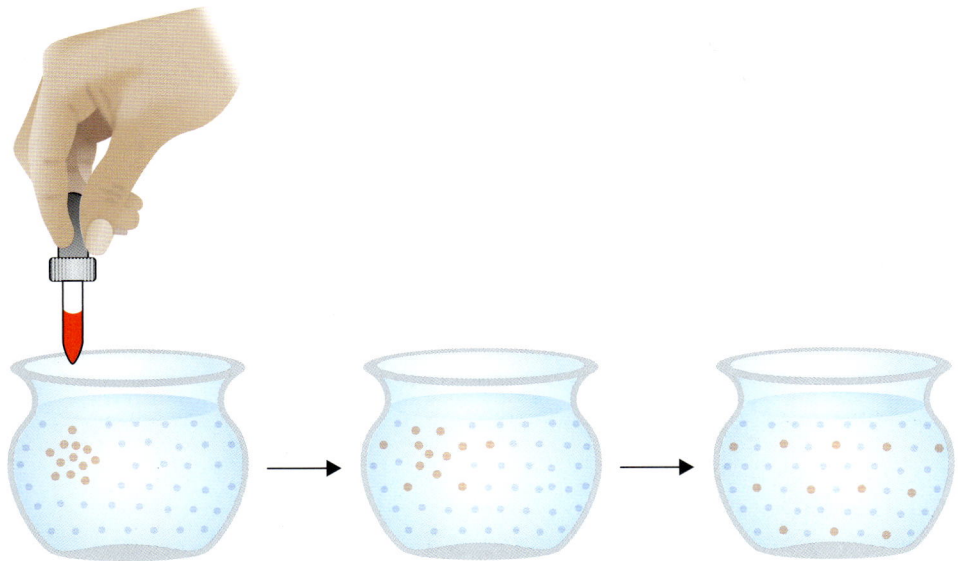

FIGURE 5.32 The red liquid slowly diffuses until it is evenly distributed throughout the water.

Diffusion

EXPERIMENT 5.5

TEACHER DEMONSTRATION 1
1. Place a few iodine crystals in the bottom of a beaker.
2. Carefully pour water over the crystals.
3. Leave the beaker for a few days and monitor what happens.

TEACHER DEMONSTRATION 2
Place cotton wool soaked in concentrated ammonia solution on one side of a diffusion tube, and cotton wool soaked in concentrated hydrochloric acid on the other side. Put the corks in place immediately.

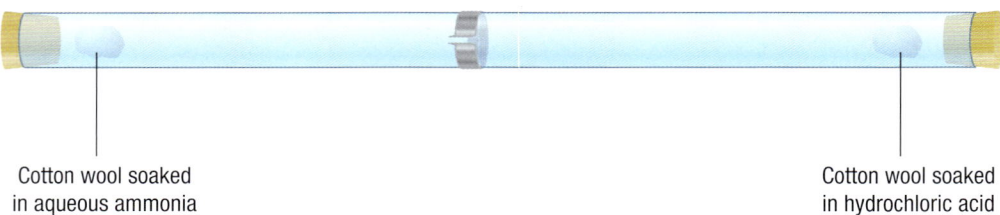

Cotton wool soaked in aqueous ammonia

Cotton wool soaked in hydrochloric acid

FIGURE 5.33 Diffusion tube with cotton wool soaked in ammonia on one side and cotton wool soaked in hydrochloric acid on the other

RESULTS AND CONCLUSION
1. Where have the two gases met in the diffusion tube?
2. How do you know when the two gases have met? (Hint: Think back to Unit 4 'Everyday acids and bases'.)
3. Explain why they do not meet in the middle.

SAFETY
The chemicals in this experiment are corrosive and toxic. Make sure you do not touch them. The room needs to be well ventilated.

Air pressure

As particles in a gas move around, they sometimes bump into each other. At other times, they collide with the walls of the container. These collisions of the particles with the walls cause **pressure**. When you blow air into a balloon, you are putting more moving particles into the balloon. This causes more collisions with the walls of the balloon. The balloon expands because the pressure of air particles is greater on the inside than on the outside. This pushes the sides of the balloon out and inflates it. The same idea can be used to explain how we can use a pump to inflate car tyres.

As you drive up a mountain, the number of air particles around you decreases. This means the air pressure on you is less, and this affects your body. Your ears might 'pop', which is the result of the air inside your ears adjusting to the new lower pressure.

Pressure and weather

On a weather map (Figure 5.34), you will see 'H' for areas of high (air) pressure and 'L' for areas of low (air) pressure. In areas of high pressure, the air is more dense and falls. As it falls, it warms up. The warmer air can hold more water vapour, so it is less likely that clouds or rain will form. The weather tends to be dry and cloudless. In areas of low pressure, the air is less dense and rises. As it rises, it cools. The cooler air can hold less water vapour and clouds are likely to form. This can cause rain.

Weather maps use **isobars** to connect areas of the same pressure. Wind is caused by differences in pressure. The wind will go from a high pressure to a lower pressure. Because of the spin of the Earth, the wind tends to follow the isobar lines. The closer the isobars are together, the stronger the winds.

Go to http://mypsci1.nelsonnet.com.au and click on **Weather**. Learn more about high- and low-pressure systems, and how to read a weather map.

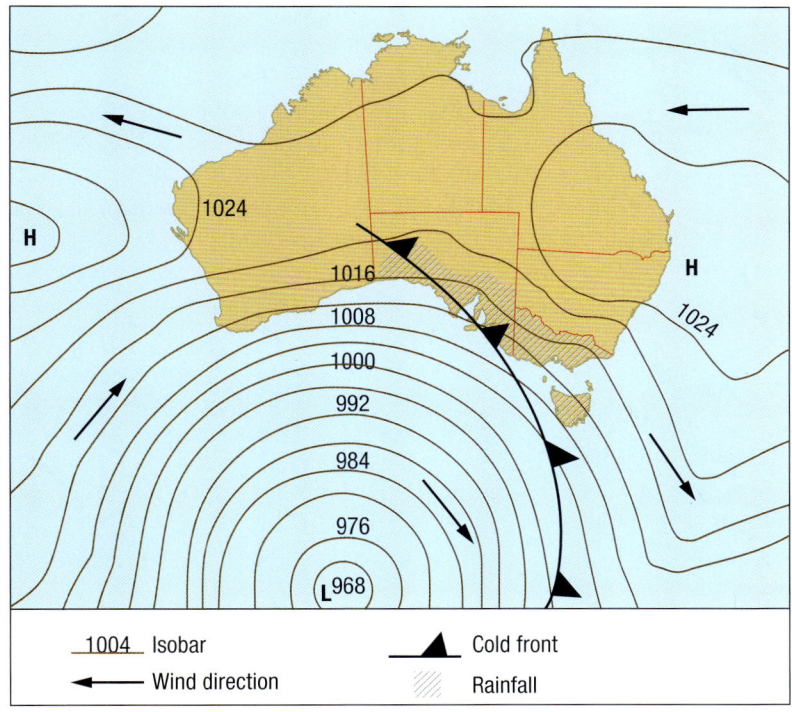

FIGURE 5.34 Isobar lines connect areas of the same pressure. The wind direction is from high to low pressure.

REVIEW

1. How would you explain diffusion using the moving particle theory?
2. Using the moving particle theory, suggest a reason why diffusion takes place faster in gases than in liquids.
3. Suggest a reason why diffusion happens faster at higher temperatures.
4. Are we more likely to have bad weather in an area of low or high pressure?
5. Outline why the tyres of a car seem more inflated in hot weather.
6. Suggest the possible consequences consequences on the body of living at higher altitudes, where the air is less dense.

UNIT QUESTIONS

CRITERION A

EXPLAINING SCIENTIFIC KNOWLEDGE

1. Explain what is meant by: (Level 1–2)
   a. melting
   b. boiling.
2. Explain why you can smell food cooking from another room. (Level 3–4)
3. Describe a:
   a. use for the expansion of metals
   b. problem caused by the expansion of metals. (Level 5–6)
4. Copy and complete the following table. (Level 7–8)

Characteristic	Solid	Liquid	Gas
Particle theory diagram			
Does it have a definite shape?			
Does it have a definite volume?			
Arrangement of particles			
Distance between particles			
Is it compressible?			
Attraction between particles			

APPLYING SCIENTIFIC KNOWLEDGE AND UNDERSTANDING TO SOLVE A PROBLEM

5. Some nights after cooking with gas, you find a lot of water on and around the windows. Suggest a reason for this. (Level 1–2)
6. You live near a mountain that often has a cloud near its top. Give a scientific reason for this. (Level 3–4)
7. Which of the diagrams A–D in Figure 5.35 represents the change of state as the lavender oil is evaporated? (Level 3–4)
8. On extremely hot days, railway tracks can twist and bend. Suggest a reason for this, and also suggest a way this problem could be solved. Explain your answer. (Level 5–6)
9. If you blew up a balloon and placed it in a refrigerator, would it become bigger or smaller? Explain your answer using the moving particle theory. (Level 7–8)

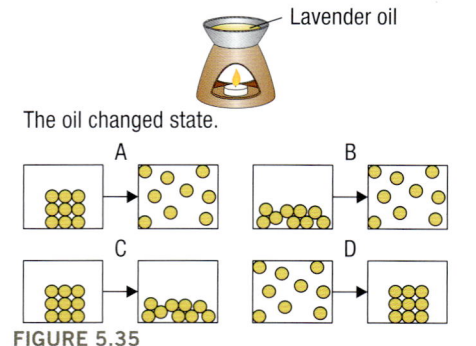

FIGURE 5.35

10. If you get out of the sea after swimming on a windy day, you feel colder than when you were in the sea. Suggest a reason for this and explain why, using ideas about moving particles. (Level 7–8)

INTERPRETING INFORMATION

11. You heard on a weather forecast that there would be high pressure over where you live. What kind of weather would you expect? (Level 1–2)
12. You went to a rock concert with a friend and she was amazed by the special effects of a lot of smoke on the stage. What explanation would you give her for how this was created? (Level 3–4)
13. In some countries, milk is delivered in glass bottles. In winter, freezing conditions can cause the glass bottles to crack. Suggest why the bottles crack. (Level 5–6)
14. The following table shows the results of an experiment comparing the evaporation of two different liquids. The two liquids were put in a wide container and a hair dryer was used to blow air across them. The temperatures of the liquids were measured every 5 minutes. (Level 7–8)

Time (minutes)	Temperature (°C) Liquid A	Temperature (°C) Liquid B
0	60	60
5	54	57
10	50	54
15	46	52
20	43	50

a. Show this information in a graph.
b. Explain why the temperature of both liquids falls.
c. Write a conclusion based on this data about the evaporation of the two liquids.
d. Invent an evaluation of this experiment. What errors could there be in the results? Was it a fair test? How could the experiment be improved?

REFLECTION

1. Has using models changed your view or understanding of scientific concepts?
2. Discuss the relationship between science and creativity.
3. How is the concept of change allowing us to understand changes in state?

UNIT 6
FORCES AND SAFETY

KEY CONCEPT
Change

RELATED CONCEPTS
Balance

Movement

Evidence

GLOBAL CONTEXT
Identities and relationships: an exploration into how knowledge of forces can be used to improve safety in sports and our daily lives

STATEMENT OF INQUIRY
Understanding forces can improve safety in sports and in our lives generally.

INQUIRY QUESTIONS

FACTUAL
1. What types of forces exist?
2. What effect does friction have on our lives?
3. How is speed calculated?

CONCEPTUAL
4. How does knowledge of gravitational forces help us understand sports?
5. How is knowledge of forces used when designing safety equipment for sports or our daily lives?
6. How do balanced and unbalanced forces relate to the movement of objects?

DEBATABLE
7. Should safety gear be compulsory when playing contact sports?
8. Why do many people think a force is needed to keep an object moving at constant speed?

Introduction

FIGURE 6.1 Safety gear should be worn when participating in challenging sports.

Being active is important for your physical and mental health. From leisure activities to pick-up games and organised sports teams, more people are participating in sports than ever before. Preventing injuries can be a challenge. Each year, more and more people try challenging and potentially dangerous sports such as free skiing, hang gliding, rafting, bungee jumping and motocross racing. People taking part in these sports can improve their performance and reduce the risk of injury by understanding the forces involved.

The use and design of safety helmets for cyclists | INVESTIGATION 6.1

YOUR CHALLENGE
Carry out an investigation into the use and design of safety helmets. Follow these steps.
1 Research how bicycle helmets are made and designed.
2 Research the incidence of bicycle accidents, and the head injuries they cause, in your country or city.
3 Make an official report on how the incidence of bicycle accidents and head injuries can be reduced.
4 Carry out a scientific investigation into how best to make helmets for Ed the Egg (see Figure 6.2).

THIS COULD HELP
The weblink on this page might be useful for your research.

There are a number of ways to carry out tests on the effectiveness of helmets. A simple method is to use an egg inside a polystyrene cup. This models your head inside your helmet.

Plan your basic method, consider how to make it a fair test, and decide on the materials to put inside the polystyrene cup.

Carry out and write up the investigation by following the guide in Appendix 3 on page 169, or as advised by your teacher.

ATL

CRITICAL THINKING Consider the evidence carefully. It will probably be difficult to gain reliable data during this investigation. Be very reflective before making any definite conclusions. You might need to repeat your experiments a number of times.

Go to http://mypsci1.nelsonnet.com.au and click on **Bicycle helmets** to find some sites that provide information about bicycle helmets.

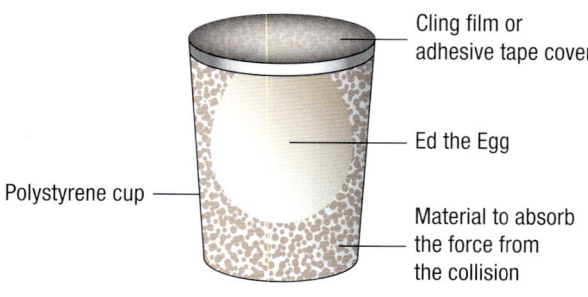

FIGURE 6.2 How to place the egg in the polystyrene cup helmet

Forces

The word **force** is used very carefully in science. A force acts on an object, or you can exert a force on something. An object does not 'have' a force. Most forces can be generally described as a push or a pull. Forces can make things speed up, slow down or change direction. They are measured in **newtons** (N). We measure forces using a newton meter.

Many forces act on us all the time. We have become so used to them that we often ignore them. **Contact forces** require contact between objects; **non-contact forces** act without contact.

Different types of forces

There are different types of forces, including:
- gravitational force
- frictional force
- electrostatic force
- magnetic force
- buoyancy force
- air resistance.

Think about where these forces exist around you. Which of these forces act on a person running on a football field? Which act on you as you swim laps in a pool? Which forces do you need to be able to walk?

Gravitational force

When you are learning how to high jump or pole-vault, you are trying to overcome **gravitational forces**. Gravity is the force of attraction between any two objects as a result of their masses. It is a non-contact force. The amount of gravitational force is related to the masses of the two objects and the distance between them. Objects with larger masses and objects that are closer together attract each other with a larger gravitational force. The region where the force is experienced is called a **field**. The Earth has a gravitational field. Scientists still don't fully understand why gravitational forces exist.

FIGURE 6.3 What forces are in action as this girl swings?

FIGURE 6.4 A pole-vaulter has to overcome gravity to jump over the bar.

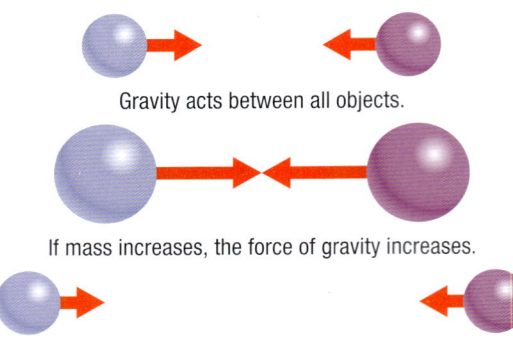

FIGURE 6.5 Gravity is a force that acts between any two masses. Two factors affect the gravitational attraction between objects: mass and distance.

You are attracted to the Earth by a gravitational force. This force is called weight. The Earth is attracted to us with the same force, but as the Earth is so large your weight is not significant. Theoretically, two people are attracted to each other by gravity, but the force is so small, they never notice it.

The Sun's gravitational field is very strong and is what keeps the planets in their orbits. The Earth's gravitational field keeps the Moon in orbit. The Moon is a large object and so its gravitational field affects the Earth – it attracts the oceans and causes tides.

Physical movement means coping with the Earth's gravity. A basketball player must be an expert in gravity to score a three-pointer. Free skiers use gravity to pull them down to go fast. And bungee jumpers have a very obvious relationship with gravity!

Mass and weight

Go to http://mypsci1.nelsonnet.com.au and click on **Gravity, mass and weight**. Play the game to learn more about how mass and weight are related to gravity.

The terms 'mass' and 'weight' are often confused, but there are some key differences between them. Mass describes how much matter is in an object. It can also be understood as a measure of how difficult it is to get something to move. The mass of an object is the same no matter where the object is located. Mass is measured in kilograms (kg). An object with a mass of 50 kg on Earth has a mass of 50 kg on the Moon and 50 kg on Jupiter.

FIGURE 6.6 Astronauts find it easy to jump on the Moon, where the force of gravity is less than on the Earth.

As weight is a force, it is measured in newtons (N). Weight depends on the strength of the gravitational field. Since the magnitude of gravity depends on the mass of the objects, objects smaller than Earth, such as the Moon, exert less gravitational force than Earth. Jupiter and the Sun exert much more gravitational force. You would weigh less on the Moon and more on Jupiter than you do on Earth. You could jump higher on the Moon.

The gravitational field on Earth exerts a force of approximately 10 newtons on a mass of 1 kilogram. So a person of 45 kilograms will experience a gravitational force of 45 × 10 = 450 N. This force of gravity is referred to as the weight of the object. We often say someone has a weight of 45 kilograms, but this is scientifically incorrect. Weight is a force and should be measured in newtons. It should also specify a direction — that is, downwards (towards the Earth). The next time someone asks you how much you weigh, tell them your weight in newtons. It will be interesting to see how they react.

The equation is:
weight (N) = mass (kg) × 10

Go to http://mypsci1.nelsonnet.com.au and click on **Mass vs. Weight** to watch a video from specialists aboard the International Space Station.

EXPERIMENT 6.1 Mass and weight

AIM
To establish the difference between mass and weight.

MATERIALS
- newton meter
- variety of objects of known and unknown mass
- scale balance (optional)

PROCEDURE
Use the newton meter to measure the weight (pull of gravity) of all the objects.

RESULTS
1 Do the results obtained for the weights of the known masses agree with the following equation?
weight (N) = mass (kg) × 10
2 From your results with the objects of known mass, calculate the masses of the unknown objects. Check their masses on a scale balance if you have one.

EVALUATION
Explain any differences you may have found in your results between the recorded weight and the calculated weight of the known masses. How accurate was your newton meter? How could its accuracy be improved?

Using ramps to help overcome gravitational forces

Ramps are merely inclined planes that make moving from one level to another easier. Pushing an object up a ramp takes less force than lifting it vertically. For example, using a ramp is an easier way for people in wheelchairs to access buildings with different levels than lifting the person and wheelchair upwards. The wheelchair and person travel further on the ramp, but less force is required.

FIGURE 6.7 The force needed to push the wheelchair up the ramp is less than the weight.

Go to http://mypsci1.nelsonnet.com.au and click on **Ramps** for fun interactive simulations using ramps.

FIGURE 6.8 Can you identify all the protective gear this snowboarder is wearing?

Ramps in sports

Many sports use ramps or slopes to enable participants to increase their speed in a controlled way. In downhill and free skiing, athletes use the slope, the low frictional force between their skis and the snow, and the effect of gravity to increase their speed. Going too fast down a hill can lead to serious injury. Downhill and free skiers must counteract the effects of low friction and high gravitational force by using turns to create more friction and help them slow down.

Skateboarders and snowboarders use ramps to help them gain the speed needed to perform tricks. The very fast speeds and high ramps can also make the stunts very dangerous. Participants in these sports wear safety gear to protect themselves and minimise the risk of injury.

EXPERIMENT 6.2 Ramps and gravity

AIM
To investigate the effect of increasing the height (slope) of a ramp on the speed of a moving object as it reaches the end of the ramp.

PREDICTION (HYPOTHESIS)
Predict what will happen to the speed of the trolley as you increase the slope of the ramp. Explain your reasons for this prediction.

MATERIALS
- ramp
- several textbooks
- trolley or other object that can roll down the ramp
- metre measuring stick
- speed sensor (optional)

PROCEDURE
Note: You can measure the speed of the trolley with a speed sensor. If a speed sensor is not available, then simply measure the time it takes to go down the ramp and the length of the ramp, and calculate the speed from this equation: speed = distance/time. You will study this equation later in the unit.

1. Use textbooks to give the ramp a suitable slope.
2. Measure how high the top edge of the ramp is from the floor. This is the height of your ramp. Record your results in a data chart.
3. Place your trolley at the top of the ramp and let it go. Be careful not to push it.
4. Measure the speed either with a speed sensor or using the speed equation.
5. Repeat steps 2–5, adding a textbook for each successive attempt until the slope of the ramp is about 45°.
6. Create a table to record your results.

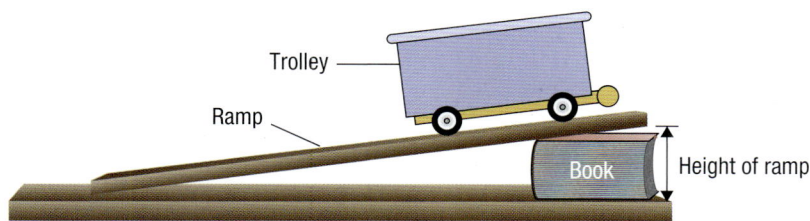

FIGURE 6.9 Experimental set-up

RESULTS
1. Complete your results table.
2. Draw a bar graph or line graph showing these results.

CONCLUSION
1. Describe the patterns you see in your results. Describe the relationship you see between the height of the ramp and the speed.
2. Discuss whether or not your prediction was supported.

EVALUATION
Discuss the validity of your method in carrying out this experiment by considering the following.
- Describe any unusual results.
- Evaluate how accurate your measuring was during the experiment.
- What errors do you see in this experiment?
- How could you improve your experiment?

CRITICAL THINKING
Reflectively analyse and evaluate evidence before making conclusions.

> **REVIEW**
>
> 1. State what is meant by a gravitational force.
> 2. Describe how mass and weight are different.
> 3. Calculate the weight of an object of mass 65 kg.
> 4. What is the mass of an object of weight 1200 N (on Earth)?
> 5. Outline the relationship between the gravitational force between two objects and
>   a. the distance between them
>   b. their masses.
> 6. Explain why you would weigh more on Jupiter and less on the Moon compared to on Earth.
> 7. Explain the advantages of using ramps to lift up people in wheelchairs.

Frictional forces

A **frictional force** is a contact force that acts when two surfaces rub against each other. A frictional force will slow you down by opposing (working against) your motion. It also produces heat and sound. You can see this when you rub your hands rapidly together. The amount of frictional force depends on the textures of the surfaces in contact with each other. Smooth or slick surfaces provide much less friction than rough or bumpy ones. Wet surfaces will normally provide less friction than dry surfaces. Friction can be a nuisance when it slows moving things or causes large amounts of heat that can destroy machines. But friction is also useful. You could not walk without friction.

FIGURE 6.10 The cleats on the boots of soccer players help them run faster. They allow the boots to grip the ground rather than sliding. They are also designed to protect players' feet from injury.

Friction in sports

Sports gear makers consider friction when designing their products. If the sport involves travel over rough terrain, tyres or shoes might need extra grip. This means knobby treads on tyres or cleats on shoes. Tyres for long bicycle races such as the Tour de France or Tour Down Under are specialised for the type of road they will travel on a particular day. These tyres are very different from the tyres of a mountain or town bike. Compare the racing tyres and cross-country tyres in Figure 6.11.

FIGURE 6.11 (a) Egoitz Garcia races in the Tour de France using very narrow tyres. (b) A cross-country bicycle.

Some athletes want to reduce friction to increase their speed. Ice skaters use very thin blades on their skates. The narrower the point of contact between the two objects, the less frictional force there is. As the skater moves, the ice melts slightly at the point where the blade meets the ice. This further reduces friction and allows the skater to glide over the surface.

Snow skiers wax the underneath of their skis to make them slide more easily over snow. This enables them to go faster. In contrast, surfers use a special wax on the top of their surfboards to increase friction and help them stay on the board.

FIGURE 6.12 The narrow blades of ice skates make very little contact with the ice.

Cars are also a good example of friction at work. Car tyres are much wider than bicycle tyres because the mass of a car is greater. Friction is increased when there is more contact between the surfaces. The safety of tyres is measured by the amount of tread present. New tyres have deep grooves that create a lot of tread. Very worn tyres have almost no tread and can be very dangerous to drive with. Driving on wet roads with worn tyres is very risky.

FIGURE 6.13 New tyres have deep groves that create tread to increase friction with the road.

How much friction?

INVESTIGATION 6.2

ATL

COMMUNICATION
Consider how best you should present your data from experiments, your results table and also the graphs to show the results.

YOUR CHALLENGE
Investigate how much friction there is between different surfaces.

THIS MIGHT HELP
Your teacher will give you some blocks of different materials, and some different surfaces for these blocks to move over. Develop a method to measure the amount of friction. For example, you could use a newton meter to measure the force needed to make the block move. Or you could investigate whether changing the slope of the surface would be another way to measure the amount of friction.

Carry out and write up the investigation following the guide in Appendix 3 on page 169, or as advised by your teacher.

FIGURE 6.14 A protective helmet showing the safety absorbers

Collisions in sports

Most accidents in sport occur when a person's body collides with a large object. This is especially serious if your head is involved in the collision. Such a collision is more likely in sports such as cycling, rugby and boxing. Large impact forces can damage your body. The large forces happen because your body is forced to slow down quickly. We protect our bodies against these large impact forces by using a form of insulation such as a helmet. The insulation absorbs some of the impact force by decreasing the rate at which the body slows down. Crumple zones and seat belts in cars also act in this way. They decrease the rate that a car or passenger slows down and so reduce the impact of a collision.

Even with helmets, many players in sports such as gridiron still suffer from concussion and long-term brain damage.

FIGURE 6.15 Collisions between gridiron footballers can result in concussion and long-term brain damage.

TA THE IMPORTANCE OF BICYCLE HELMETS

Each year, many children are hurt when riding bicycles without wearing helmets. A main reason for not wearing one is the family cannot afford to buy one. Many local police units, hospitals and some department stores offer free helmets for children. Research whether free helmets are available in your community and create a public service announcement that could be shared. You could also initiate a road safety campaign to educate young people about the importance of wearing helmets.

REVIEW

1 Outline the cause of friction between two surfaces.
2 Outline how friction between two surfaces can be reduced.
3 Would a cross-country racer want more or less frictional force between their tyres and the track? What sort of tyres would you recommend?
4 Describe why playing tennis on an icy surface would be dangerous.
5 Outline features of basketball shoes that help players move quickly on the waxed gym floor.
6 Explain why friction is important to motorists.
7 Describe the function of helmets in some sports.
8 Outline why seat belts in cars help protect you in an accident.

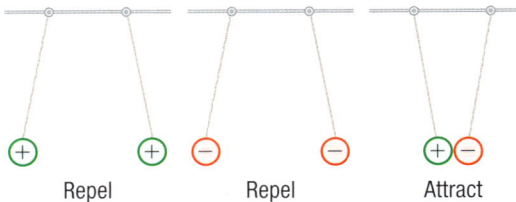

FIGURE 6.16 Electrostatic forces

FIGURE 6.17 Lightning is a dramatic example of electricity created in nature.

Electrostatic forces

Zap! You reach for the door handle and get a nasty shock. Or you hear crackling noises when you take off clothing made from synthetic materials. If you've experienced either of these, you've experienced **static electricity**. This is caused by electrostatic charges that usually build up because of friction. An **electrostatic force** is the force between objects that have an electrical charge. Electrical charge can be positive or negative. Electrostatic forces are non-contact forces.

Charged objects repel and attract in the following ways.
- Negative charges repel negative charges.
- Positive charges repel positive charges.
- Negative charges and positive charges attract.

When the amount of charge becomes very large, the charge can jump from one object to another. This produces sparks, which can be very dangerous. For instance, a spark in a flour factory can cause the flour dust to explode. People who work with flammable liquids must be especially careful. These liquids can build up a charge when poured or flow through hoses. A single spark from a **discharge** can cause a fire or an explosion.

Lightning is an enormous spark that occurs when clouds become highly charged as they move over each other (Figure 6.17).

Electrostatics　　ACTIVITY

1. Experiment with rubbing a balloon against your hair. What happens to your hair?
2. Place the balloon on a wall. What happens?
3. Rub some plastic rods or rulers against a variety of cloths. Will the plastic rod or ruler now pick up pieces of paper? Which cloth worked best?
4. Place a charged plastic ruler next to a trickle of water from a tap. Explain what happens.
5. Your teacher might be able to show you a Van de Graaff generator in action.
6. Discuss situations in your life where electrostatic charge can be a nuisance.

Go to http://mypsci1.nelsonnet.com.au and click on **Balloons** to see electrostatic charges in action.

FIGURE 6.18 A charged balloon attracting a stream of water

Magnetic force

Many toys and tools rely on magnets. Magnetic putty can seem to come alive as a magnet comes near it. A magnetic screwdriver is useful when working in cramped places with small screws. The screw is attracted to the screwdriver, which keeps it in place as the job is completed.

Magnets can **attract** or **repel** one another. They can attract other objects as well. A **magnetic force** is the force of attraction or repulsion between a magnet and another object. It is a non-contact force. You will learn more about magnets in Unit 7.

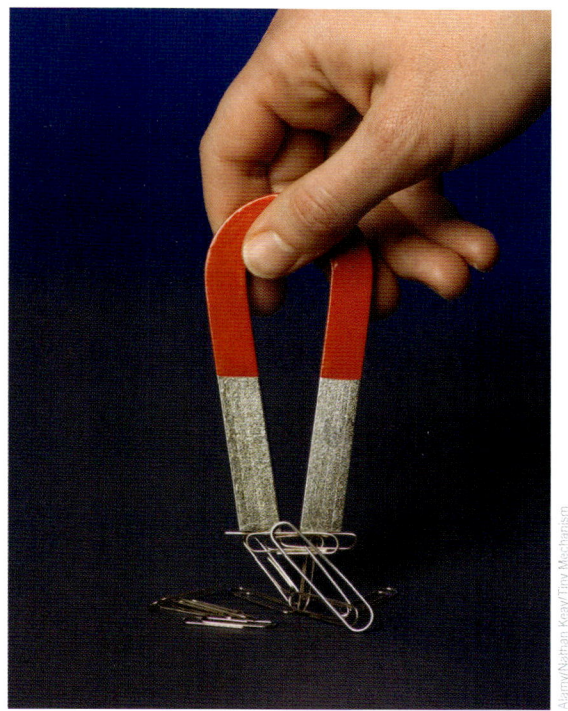

FIGURE 6.19 Magnets attract paperclips.

Buoyancy force

If you stop swimming in a deep pool, you don't sink to the bottom because the water exerts an upward force on your body. This force is called **buoyancy force** and it helps you stay near the top of the water (Figure 6.20). You can feel this force in action if you try to push a balloon under water.

Swimmers must use buoyancy to find the right technique to swim efficiently. Buoyancy force acts differently upon bone, muscle and fat. Rapid growth spurts change how the body floats and require changes in swimming technique. This can be frustrating for competitive swimmers.

Scuba divers use a special buoyancy control device. The device uses low-pressure air to increase the buoyancy force on the diver and the diver can add weights to go deeper. The buoyancy device also enables the diver to achieve neutral buoyancy to remain at one level for a period of time. If the buoyancy force is less than the force of gravity on the object, then the object will sink. If two forces are the same, then the object will float.

FIGURE 6.20 The buoyancy force acts upwards.

Buoyancy force also helps those who are recovering from injury or surgery. Water therapy provides a low-impact environment to strengthen muscles. Athletes recovering from injury can do exercises in water that they would not be able to do on dry land. You will learn more about buoyancy in *Science 2 for the international student*.

FIGURE 6.21 (a) An inflatable ring provides buoyancy in a swimming pool. (b) A scuba diver uses a special buoyancy control device to remain under water.

Air resistance

When parasailing, a person with a parachute is attached to a speedboat. The parachute provides **air resistance**. The driver of the boat will notice this, as the boat will slow down. Air resistance is the force that air exerts on you as you move. It slows you down, which is why it is sometimes called a drag force. There is less drag force as the boat slows down and the person lands in the water. Other sports that use a parachute, such as hang gliding or skydiving, depend on air resistance so the athlete can regulate speed and direction. Losing control can mean serious injury or death.

In contrast, other racing sports require athletes to work on reducing this drag force. Downhill snow skiers will get into a tight crouch, which minimises this force. Ski jumpers crouch tightly on the way down the ramp, then straighten and use air resistance to help them glide down the mountain. Elite bicycle racers use special handlebars and elongated helmets during time trials to reduce air resistance, enabling them to go faster.

Car designers use wind tunnels to test air resistance on new designs. The less air resistance a vehicle has, the less fuel it will use. This can save the consumer a lot of money.

There are many other instances where air resistance either helps or hurts performance.

Go to http://mypsci1.nelsonnet.com.au and click on **Adventures in skydiving** to see how gravity and air resistance work in skydiving.

FIGURE 6.22 This parasailer is using air resistance to rise into the air.

FIGURE 6.23 This ski jumper is crouching to minimise air resistance to build up speed.

EXPERIMENT 6.3   It's a drag!

AIM
To investigate how shape affects air resistance.

MATERIALS
- four sheets of printer paper per group

PROCEDURE
1. Collect your four sheets of paper. Leave one sheet flat, lightly crumple another, crumple one into a sphere and wad one into a ball.
2. Drop the four pieces of paper together to compare how each falls.
3. Repeat step 2.

RESULTS AND CONCLUSION
1. Describe how each piece of paper falls; for example, straight down or drifting side to side.
2. Do you get the same result when you repeat the experiment?
3. List your shapes in order from fastest to slowest.
4. List your shapes in order from least air resistance to most air resistance.
5. Which shape experienced the most air resistance? How is it different from the other shapes?
6. Which shape experienced the least air resistance? How is it different from the other shapes?
7. If you were skydiving, discuss whether you would want a smaller or larger parachute.

REVIEW
1. Outline a situation in which you would find electrostatic forces in your daily life.
2. Describe how you could use balloons to demonstrate electrostatic forces.
3. Buoyancy affects bone, muscle and fat differently. This is because of their different densities. Outline how growing taller but not heavier might affect a swimmer's buoyancy.
4. How does a scuba diver control their buoyancy?
5. Describe air resistance and how it affects an object's movement.
6. Explain how the shape of an object affects the amount of air resistance that acts on it.

Balanced and unbalanced forces

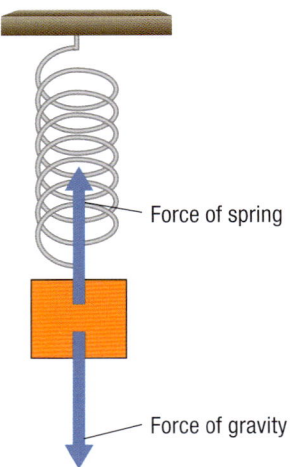

FIGURE 6.24 An example of balanced forces

Imagine an object hanging on a spring. It is not moving. The force of gravity downwards is equal to the force upwards caused by the stretched spring (Figure 6.24). This is an example of **balanced forces**. We say the object is at **equilibrium**.

Another example of balanced forces is a helicopter hovering in the air. The weight of the helicopter is balanced by the upward thrust of the engine. This keeps it stationary. The forces are balanced. If the helicopter pilot reduces the upward thrust, gravity will pull the helicopter down towards the ground (Figure 6.25).

A game of tug-of-war is a good example to show the difference between balanced and **unbalanced forces**. If the two teams pull with equal strength, then the forces are balanced and no one moves. If one team is stronger than the other, then the forces are unbalanced, and the teams move. This is shown in Figure 6.26.

FIGURE 6.25 This helicopter must hover in place in order to perform a rescue. The force of the weight is balanced by the upward thrust of the engines.

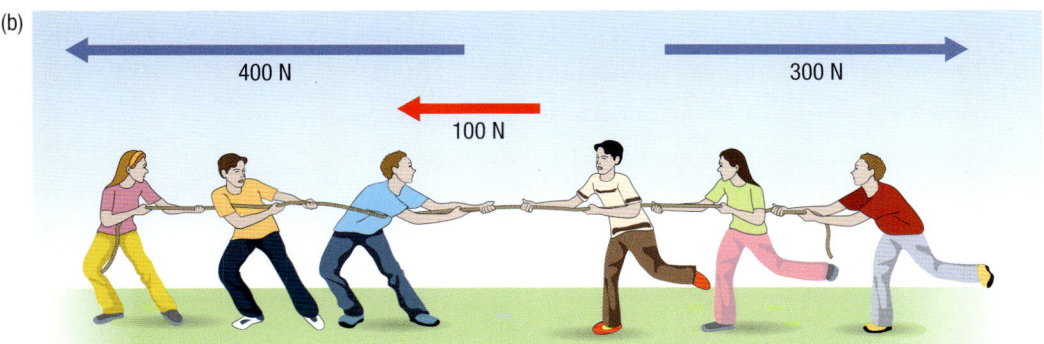

FIGURE 6.26 The outcome of a game of tug-of-war depends on whether forces are balanced or unbalanced.

Resultant forces

When two forces are unbalanced, there is a **resultant force**. You can see this in Figure 6.26b. The resultant force is 100 N to the left. This is the result of the mathematical calculation:

400 N − 300 N = 100 N

If the forces are in opposite directions, we subtract them. If the two forces are in the same direction, we add them (Figure 6.27).

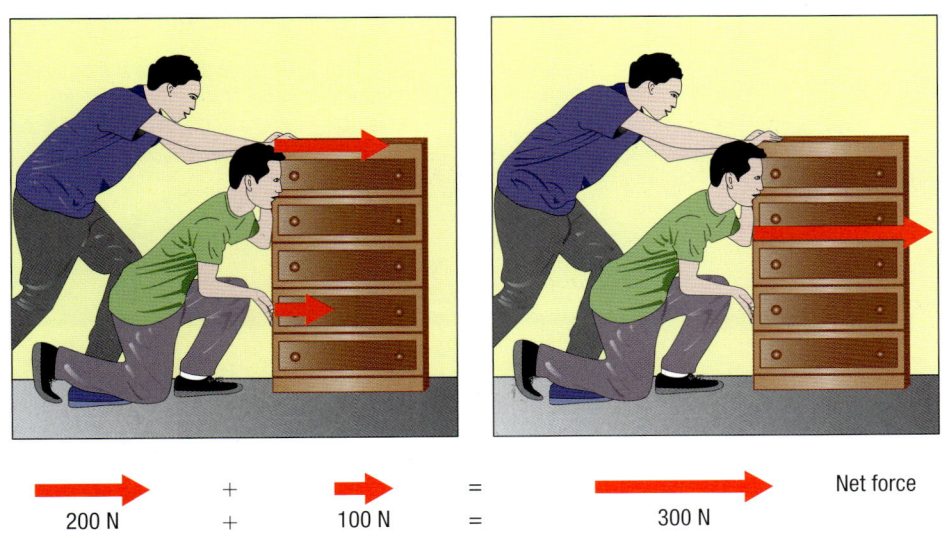

FIGURE 6.27 Resultant forces when the two forces are in the same direction

Unbalanced forces and movement of objects

Go to http://mypsci1.nelsonnet.com.au and click on **Forces**. Watch the interactive simulation on frictional force, applied force and resultant (total) force.

When forces are unbalanced, the resultant force will cause an object to move faster and faster. This is called acceleration.

Consider the car towing the caravan in Figure 6.28. Many forces are acting on the caravan at the same time. There is the pulling force exerted by the car as it goes forwards, as well as the frictional force acting in the opposite direction where the tyres touch the ground. If you combine their effects, the total force is the resultant force. If these forces are unequal in size, then a change in motion will result. The caravan will start to speed up (**accelerate**) or slow down (**decelerate**), depending on which force is greater.

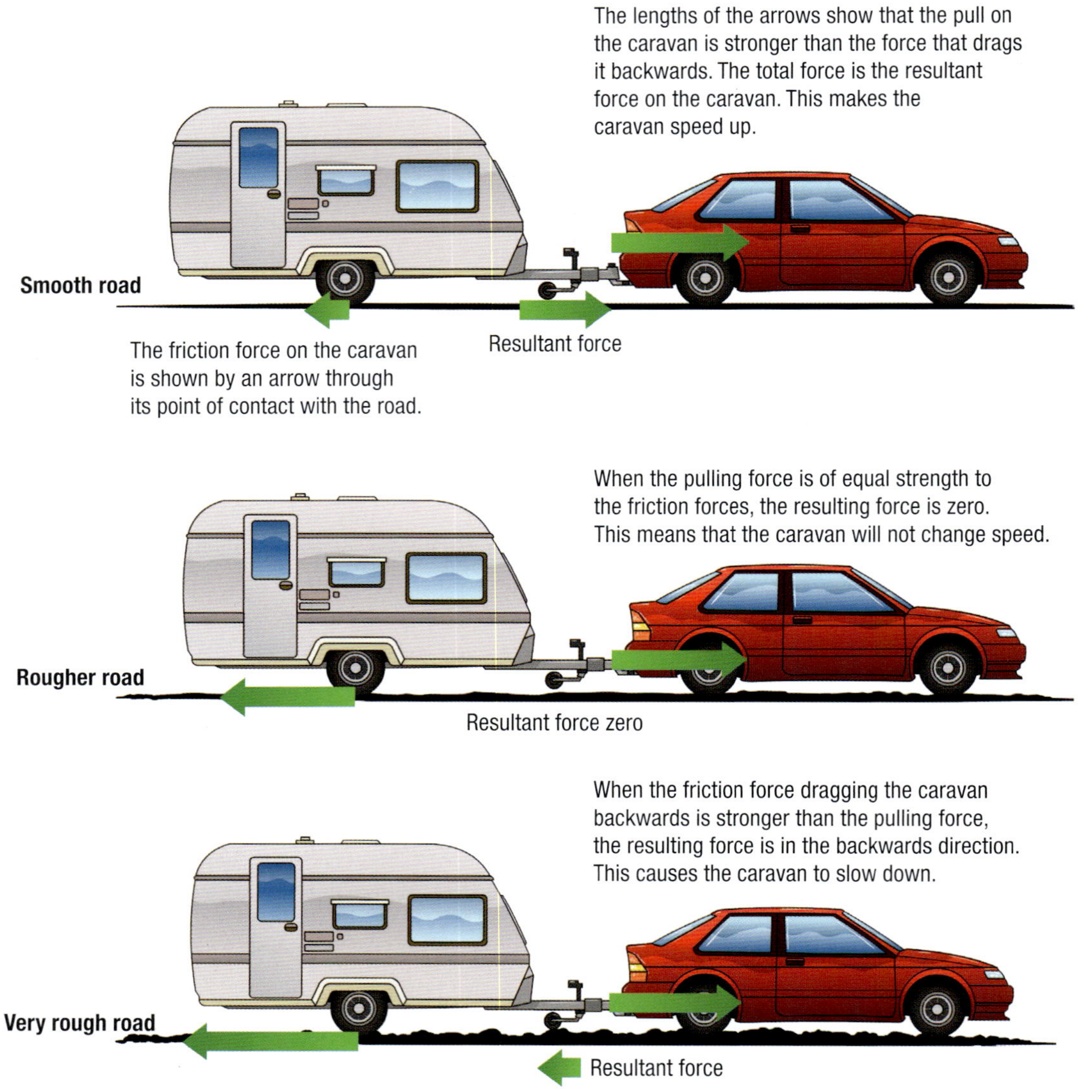

The lengths of the arrows show that the pull on the caravan is stronger than the force that drags it backwards. The total force is the resultant force on the caravan. This makes the caravan speed up.

Smooth road

The friction force on the caravan is shown by an arrow through its point of contact with the road.

Resultant force

When the pulling force is of equal strength to the friction forces, the resulting force is zero. This means that the caravan will not change speed.

Rougher road

Resultant force zero

When the friction force dragging the caravan backwards is stronger than the pulling force, the resulting force is in the backwards direction. This causes the caravan to slow down.

Very rough road

Resultant force

FIGURE 6.28 Unbalanced forces cause a change of motion.

To summarise:
- A resultant force on an object in the same direction as that in which it is moving causes it to speed up (accelerate).
- A resultant force on an object in the opposite direction to which it is moving causes it to slow down (decelerate).
- An object that experiences no resultant force, such as a spacecraft in space with its motors turned off, will carry on moving at the same speed forever.

A moving object does not need to have a resultant force acting on it to continue moving.

REVIEW

1. Draw a picture of two tug-of-war teams in each of the scenarios listed below. Use stick figures and label the pictures with longer arrows to show more force, and shorter arrows to show less force. Suggest a size for each force in newtons, calculate the resultant forces and draw arrows to show the resultant forces.
    a. Both teams pulling with the same force
    b. Team A pulling more strongly than team B
    c. Team B pulling more strongly than team A
2. Sam drew some force diagrams as shown in Figure 6.29.
    a. Only one of Sam's diagrams includes arrows that obey the conventions for drawing forces. Which one is correct?
    b. Copy Sam's incorrect diagrams and show how the forces should have been represented.

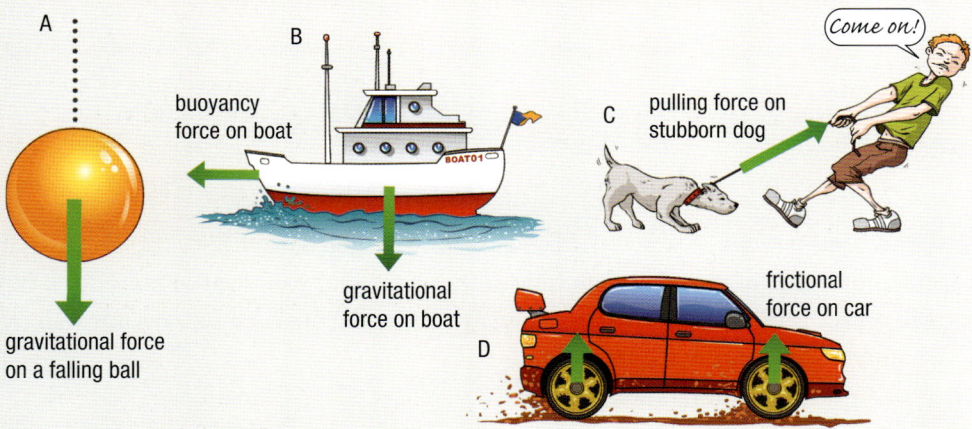

FIGURE 6.29 Sam's force diagrams

3. a. Suggest a reason why a spacecraft continues to move through space at constant speed even after its engines are turned off.
   b. Draw a diagram to show the forces on a helicopter hovering above the ground.

Calculating speed

We are all familiar with road signs telling us the maximum **speed** at which we can drive. In science, speed describes how far we travel in a certain time period. To calculate average speed, divide the distance travelled by the time it takes to get there. The formula for average speed is:

$$\text{Average speed} = \frac{\text{total distance travelled}}{\text{total time travelled}}$$

Speed is always expressed as a ratio of distance per time measurement. The distance and time travelled will depend on the object you are observing.

Calculating average speed

1 You have driven 120 kilometres in 2 hours. To find your speed, divide the distance travelled by the time travelled:

$$\text{Speed} = \frac{\text{distance travelled}}{\text{time travelled}}$$
$$= \frac{120 \text{ km}}{2 \text{ h}}$$
$$= 60 \text{ km/h}$$

Your average speed is 60 kilometres per hour.

2 A person has run 35 metres in 5 seconds. What as the person's speed?

$$\text{Speed} = \frac{\text{distance travelled}}{\text{time travelled}}$$
$$= \frac{35 \text{ m}}{5 \text{ s}}$$
$$= 7 \text{ m/s}$$

The runner's average speed was 7 metres per second, which is very fast!

To decide upon the most appropriate unit of measurement, you need to consider how quickly or slowy the object is moving. Is it fast or slow? For example, the pace of a person walking is usually measured in metres per second. The movement of a glacier might be measured in centimetres per day or, for very slow-moving ones, in metres per year. A snail might move centimetres per minute. A Maglev train moves more than 500 kilometres per hour!

Distance–time graphs

You use a distance–time graph to show speed over a period of time. In Figure 6.30, you can see that the object moved at a constant speed from A to B. From B to C, the object stopped moving. From C to D, the object moved again.

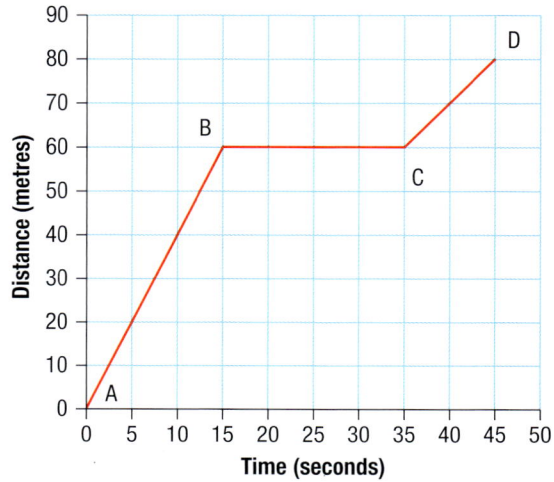

FIGURE 6.30 A distance–time graph

The slope of the graph tells you the speed of the object. You can see the slope of A–B is greater than the slope of C–D. This means the speed over A–B is greater than over C–D.

Calculating speed from a distance–time graph

You can calculate the speed from a distance–time graph by using the equation:

$$\text{Speed} = \frac{\text{distance}}{\text{time}}$$

In Figure 6.30, from A to B:

$$\text{Speed} = \frac{\text{distance}}{\text{time}} = \frac{60 \text{ m}}{15 \text{ s}} = 4 \text{ m/s}$$

TRANSFER (OF SKILLS)
Use of mathematical skills in science. Consider how your mathematics teacher has taught you to carry out calculations of this kind. Have you been taught about line graphs and the slope of lines in mathematics?

REVIEW

1 Calculate the speed of an object travelling:
   a 24 metres in 6 minutes
   b 720 kilometres in 8 hours
   c 96 metres in 0.5 hour
   d 120 kilometres in 4 hours.
2 Calculate the speed involved in the distance–time graph in Figure 6.31.
3 Calculate the speed of a caterpillar that travels 18 centimetres in 4 minutes.
4 What type of vehicle would travel 850 km/h?

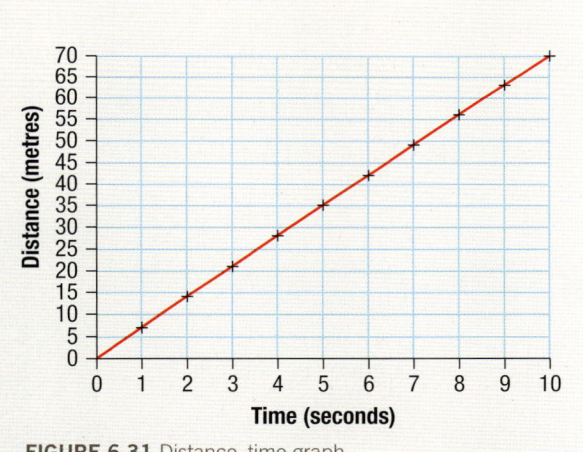

FIGURE 6.31 Distance–time graph

UNIT QUESTIONS

CRITERION A

EXPLAINING SCIENTIFIC KNOWLEDGE

1. Select the forces at work in the following statements from this list: gravitational, frictional, electrostatic, buoyancy, air resistance. (Level 1–2)
   a. If you rub an ebony rod with nylon, it will pick up pieces of paper.
   b. When you jump into a deep swimming pool, you struggle to get to the bottom.
   c. When you stop pedalling a bicycle along a road, it eventually stops.
2. State the effect of friction on moving objects. (Level 3–4)
3. Use the Earth and the Moon to explain the difference between mass and weight. (Level 5–6)
4. Mallika is combing her hair and notices the following. (Level 7–8)
   a. After combing, her hair is attracted to the comb.
   b. On removing the comb, her hair is still standing up a little.
   c. After a while, her hair lies as normal, close to her head.
   Explain her three observations by outlining your knowledge of electrostatic forces. You may use diagrams to help you.

APPLYING SCIENTIFIC KNOWLEDGE AND UNDERSTANDING TO SOLVE A PROBLEM

5. Mateo says his backpack is very heavy. Outline whether he should measure it in kilograms or newtons. (Level 1–2)
6. Calculate the speed of a: (Level 3–4)
   a. person who travels 840 kilometres in 6 hours
   b. ladybug that crawls 72 centimetres in 30 minutes
   c. car that travels 180 kilometres in 30 minutes.
7. Calculate the resultant force for a: (Level 3–4)
   a. drag racing car with an engine pulling it forwards with a force of 2350 N and a parachute slowing it down with a force of 3000 N
   b. falling skydiver experiencing a force due to gravity of 598 N and air resistance of 578 N.
8. You see someone struggling to lift a box up the stairs to a house. Explain to them the science of the advantages of using a ramp. (Level 5–6)
9. A friend does not want to wear a cycle helmet. Outline how you would make a scientific argument to try to convince them that a helmet is important for their safety. (Level 7–8)

INTERPRETING INFORMATION

10. A friend says frictional force is involved as a line of dominoes fall. Is he correct? (Level 1–2)
11. Someone says to you that roller-skating is a sport with few risks. How do you respond? (Level 3–4)
12. Here are some results from an experiment to investigate the speed of a model car down a ramp.

Height of ramp (cm)	Time to go down the ramp (s)
10	12.0
20	4.0
30	1.5

   a. Draw a graph to show these results.
   b. Interpret what these results show you.
   c. Suggest ways this experiment could be improved. (Level 5–6)
13. Figure 6.32 shows the scene after a terrible motor vehicle accident. Discuss reasons why this accident might have occurred, and why the people involved survived such a dreadful accident. (Level 7–8)

FIGURE 6.32

REFLECTION

1. In this unit, you studied the idea of balance. Where else in science and life is the idea of balance important?
2. Suggest some situations in other units where you have studied the idea of movement of particles or objects.
3. Why is it important to consider evidence very carefully in experiments?
4. Do people take safety seriously enough when they play sport? Discuss whether it should be compulsory for people to use appropriate safety equipment.
5. What would life be like without friction?

UNIT 7

MAGNETISM AND ELECTRICITY

KEY CONCEPT
Systems

RELATED CONCEPTS
Creativity
Energy
Models

GLOBAL CONTEXT
Scientific and technical innovation: an exploration into the uses of magnetism and electricity to improve our lives

STATEMENT OF INQUIRY
The quality of our lives has been improved by the creative applications of our knowledge of magnets and electricity.

INQUIRY QUESTIONS

FACTUAL
1. What is electrical current?
2. What are the properties of magnets?
3. What are the main uses of electricity and magnetism?

CONCEPTUAL
4. How do we explain series and parallel circuits?
5. How do ideas about potential difference, current and resistance link together?
6. How do we explain the properties and uses of magnets?

DEBATABLE
7. Are we as careful as we should be with our use of electricity and magnets?
8. Why can electricity be difficult to understand?

Introduction

Magnetism and electricity are two of the most engaging topics to learn about. Magnets have intrigued people for thousands of years. In ancient times, it was thought that magnets had magical powers and could heal the sick. Today, magnets have an incredibly wide range of uses, from toys and amusement park rides to computers and medical equipment. It has been known since ancient times that rubbing objects together produces static electricity. The transmission of electricity to people's homes started in some countries around the end of the 19th century, with enormous benefits for their lives. Unfortunately, about 20% of the world's population still do not have electricity in their homes.

Creative use of magnets or electricity

Carry out some research into toys or devices for the home that use magnets or low-voltage batteries. Brainstorm to generate some creative (even if crazy) possibilities. Choose the idea most likely to succeed and design on paper the toy or device. Include a scientific explanation of how it would work. If possible, make a prototype. Evaluate the prototype and suggest how it could be improved.

CREATIVE THINKING
Consider how best to carry out brainstorming and why it is such an important aspect of creativity.

Electricity

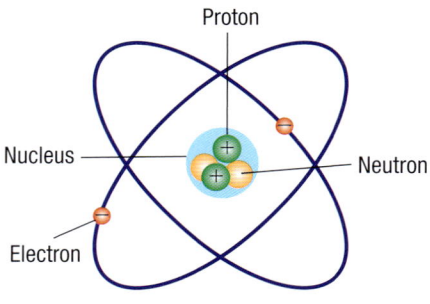

FIGURE 7.1 The three types of particle in an atom are protons, neutrons and electrons.

To understand electricity, you must first understand some basic information about atoms. All matter is made of atoms. Atoms contain protons, neutrons and electrons.
- Protons have a positive charge.
- Electrons have a negative charge.
- Neutrons have a no charge (an therefore are neutral).

Protons and neutrons make up the nucleus of the atom. Circling around this nucleus are one or more electrons.

Understanding charges

When an atom has an equal number of protons and electrons, their charges cancel each other out. The atom has a neutral charge. When two surfaces move across each other, sometimes some electrons move from one surface to another. This creates a negative charge on one of the objects and a positive charge on the other. This happens when you rub a plastic rod on a cloth.

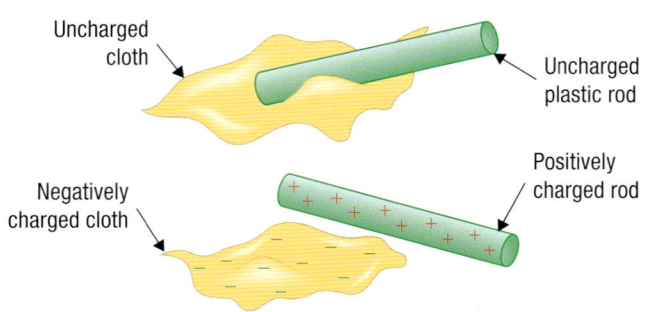

FIGURE 7.2 Electrons are transferred as the rod is rubbed by the cloth.

Creating electricity

The movement of electrons creates electricity. Some materials allow this movement more easily than others. These materials are called **conductors**. Metals are particularly good conductors of electricity. Materials that hold on to their electrons and do not allow easy movement from atom to atom are called **insulators**. Most non-metals are good insulators. Rubber and plastic are such good insulators that many electrical cables are wrapped in them for protection.

EXPERIMENT 7.1 Can you feel electrons?

AIM
To understand electrical current

MATERIALS
- 2 cm × 10 cm paper strip
- aluminium foil
- AA battery
- C or D battery (for Extension)

PROCEDURE
1. Hold the ends of the paper strip to the terminals of the battery, one on each end.
2. What do you notice? Record your observations.
3. Tear off 15 cm of aluminium foil and fold it lengthwise until you have a thick strip about 2 cm wide.
4. Cut the strip of foil to make one 20 cm strip and one 10 cm strip.
5. Bend the 10 cm strip to connect the top and bottom terminals. Hold it with your fingers for 10–15 seconds.
6. What do you notice? Record your observations.
7. Repeat step 5 with the 20 cm strip. Record your observations.

CONCLUSION
1. Did you feel a difference between the lengths of foil? Outline why or why not.
2. Did you feel anything when you attached the paper strip to the positive and negative terminals? Outline why or why not.

EXTENSION
Repeat the experiment with a C or D battery. Compare your results. Based on what you know so far about electricity, explain what is happening. Include scientific terms such as 'conductor', 'insulator', 'electrons' and 'transfer'.

REVIEW

1. Outline the three parts of an atom and their characteristics.
2. Outline what you know about electrons in an atom.
3. a Describe why rubbing a balloon against your hair causes both the balloon and hair to become charged.
   b State whether the balloon and hair have the same charge. Explain your answer.
4. Compare conductors and insulators in regard to electricity.
5. Think of a common appliance that uses electricity, such as a computer. Outline ways conductors and insulators are used in this appliance.

Electrical circuits and currents

Go to http://mypsci1.nelsonnet.com.au and click on **Electricity** to view simulations of moving electrons and how electricity works.

A common method of making an electrical circuit is to connect a cell or battery to a device such as a light globe. Batteries are a common way to provide electricity to a portable appliance. Game controllers, mobile phones and torches are a few of the many items that use batteries. A battery has a positive end, the **cathode**, and a negative end, the **anode**.

When the circuit is complete, the electrons can flow from the negative end of the battery, through the wire, through the light globe, then back to the positive end of the battery. This flow of electrons is called an electric current (Figure 7.3). The electrons carry electrical charge. The wires are made of good conductors such as copper. Figure 7.4 shows a simple circuit.

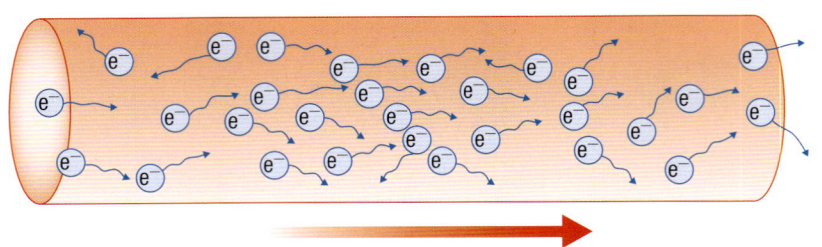

FIGURE 7.3 An electrical current is the movement of electrons through a wire.

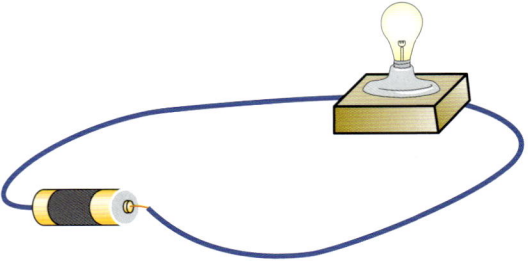

FIGURE 7.4 This simple circuit consists of a battery, wires and a light globe.

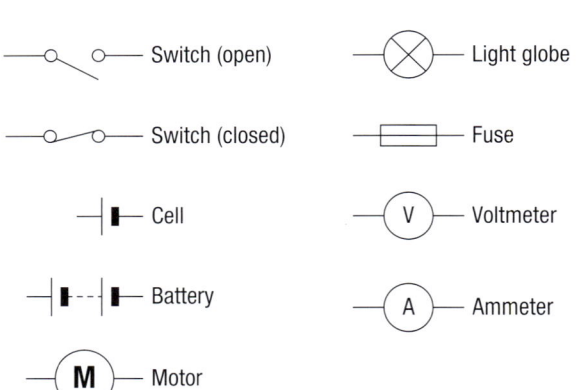

FIGURE 7.5 Circuit symbols

Drawing electrical circuits

Scientists use special symbols to show a circuit. This is easier and clearer than using realistic drawings. Some common symbols are shown in Figure 7.5.

The electrical circuit for a torch is shown in Figure 7.6. The correct scientific term for a battery you would buy in a shop is a cell. In science, a battery is actually a number of cells joined together.

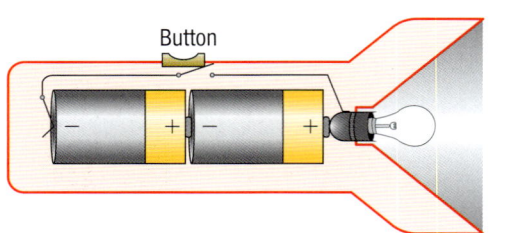 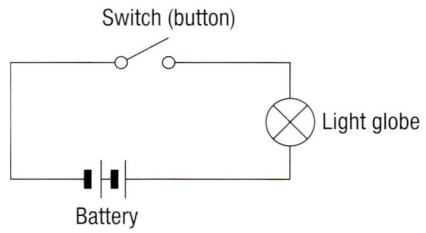

FIGURE 7.6 A hand-drawn circuit for a torch, and the corresponding scientific circuit diagram.

A model for an electrical circuit

A model can help you to understand how electricity works. In this example the model is water being pumped around a closed system by a pump. The central heating system in your house may use this type of system. Table 7.1 compares the two systems.

TABLE 7.1 A model for an electrical circuit

Central heating system model	Electrical circuit
The pump gives energy to the water to make it move through the system.	The battery gives energy to the electrons, which 'pushes' them around the circuit.
The pipes let the water flow around the system.	The wires are good conductors and let the electrons flow through them.
The water will only flow through the radiator if there is a closed loop. If the pipe becomes blocked at one point, then the water stops flowing everywhere in the loop.	The electrons will only flow if the circuit is complete. If you break one of the wires going into or out of the light globe, then the globe will go out.
The radiator has thin tubing, which slows down the flow of water.	The globe has a thin filament, which slows down the flow of electrons. This is called resistance. The electrons have to 'fight' their way through the globe and in the process lose energy as light and heat.

An **electric circuit** is a closed loop in which the electrons travel. It is a pathway of conductive material, usually copper. When the loop is closed, the electrons can travel without interruption. When there is a break in the circuit, the electrons cannot flow. A switch is inserted into the loop to control the flow of electrons. When the switch is closed, the electrons can flow. When the switch is open, electrons cannot flow. The rate of flow of electrons (electrical charge) is called the **electric current**. Electric current can be measured with an **ammeter** (Figure 7.8). The SI unit of current is the **ampere** (amps, for short).

If the electric current in a circuit is increased, then a light globe in the circuit will become brighter. So we can also use the brightness of a light globe to give an indication of the electric current.

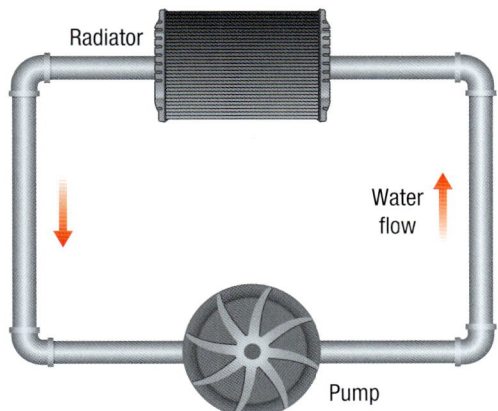

Water flows only when the pipe makes a closed loop.

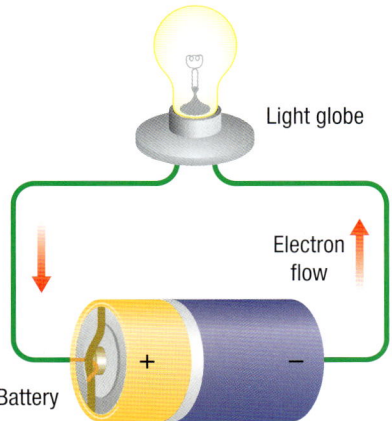

Electric charge flows only when the wire makes a closed loop.

FIGURE 7.7 A model to help us understand electricity

🅣🅐 HELPING STUDENTS IN THEIR LEARNING ABOUT ELECTRICITY

One reason that many people, including adults, find it hard to understand electricity is that they don't know a good model (or theory) for the flow of electricity around a circuit. Create a well-labelled and attractive poster showing electrons moving around an electrical circuit using the ideas from Figure 7.7. You are trying to help people understand circuits better. Think of a number of questions to test their understanding. For example, you could ask them what happens to the electrical current if two light globes are added to the circuit.

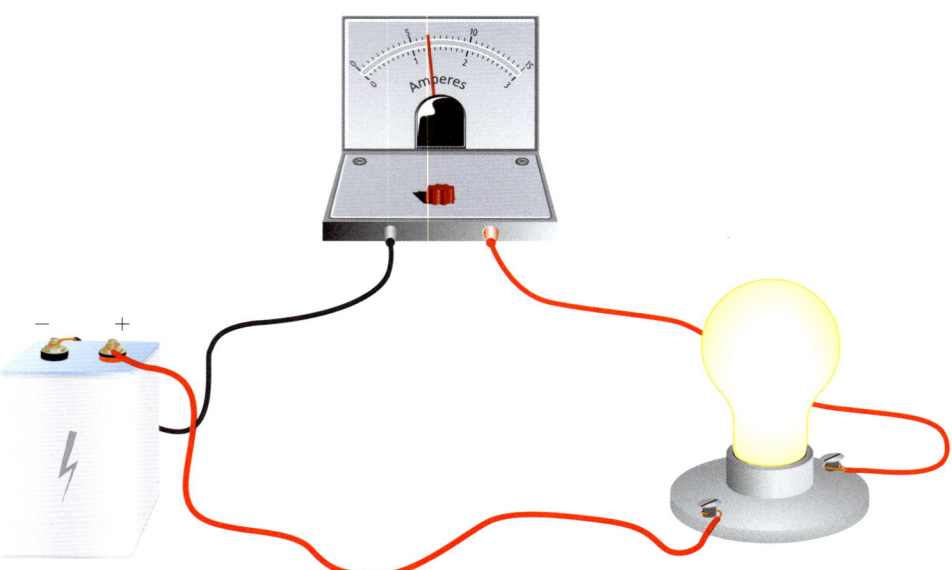

FIGURE 7.8 An ammeter is used to measure electric current.

Series and parallel circuits

There are two kinds of circuit. A circuit with all the components in the same loop is called a series circuit. A circuit with the components in separate branches of the circuit is called a parallel circuit. These two types of circuit are shown in Figure 7.9.

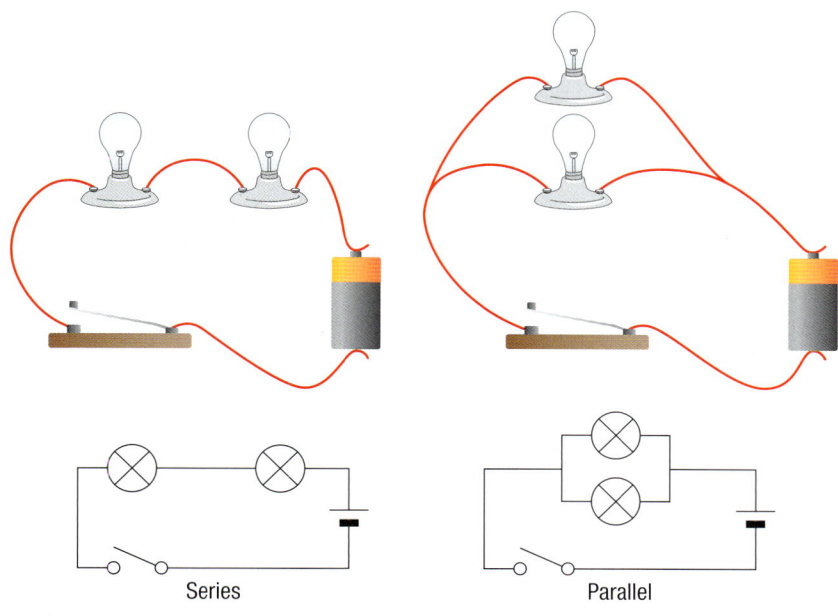

FIGURE 7.9 Series and parallel circuits

ACTIVITY: The difference between series and parallel circuits

1 Look at the two circuits in Figure 7.9. What differences do you see? How might the circuits behave differently?
2 If one of the wires to one of the light globes was to fall off, what would happen? Would the other light also go out? Would it be the same in both circuits?
3 Would the globes in the two circuits have the same brightness? Use the central heating model to help you answer this. It is not an easy question.
4 Redraw the two circuits to show how you could add a third globe to each. What difference might this make to the brightness of the globes?
5 Which type of circuit would be best for using in our houses?
6 Explain why the current (in amps) going through each of the two light globes in the series circuit will be the same.
7 Draw a circuit diagram for each of the circuits in Figure 7.10.

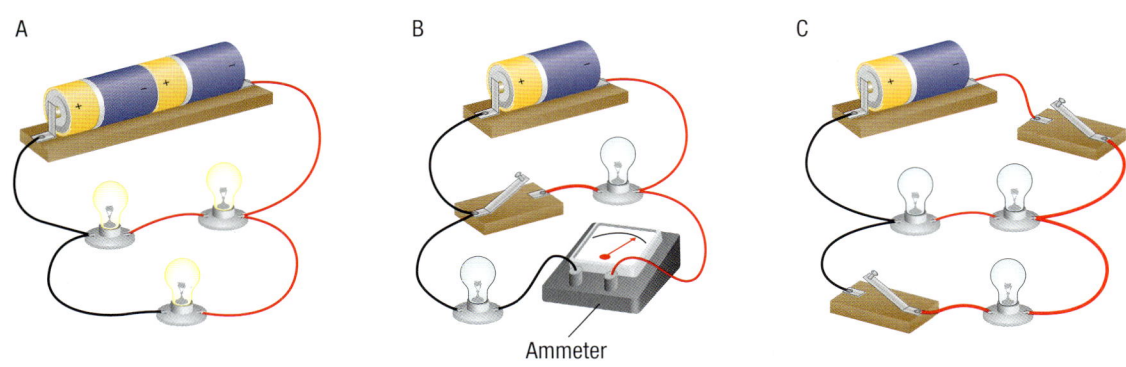

FIGURE 7.10

Go to http://mypsci1.nelsonnet.com.au and click on **Circuits**. Practise creating series and parallel circuits using this interactive simulation.

Measuring current in series and parallel circuits

EXPERIMENT 7.2

AIM
To make sense of the measurements you obtain when you measure the current in series and parallel circuits.

MATERIALS
Each group will need:
- two 1.5 V cells or a suitable power pack
- two holders for the cells
- ammeter (0–1 amp)
- six leads (4 mm)
- three lamps with holders

PROCEDURE
A Series circuits
1. Working in your group, make the circuits shown in Figure 7.11.

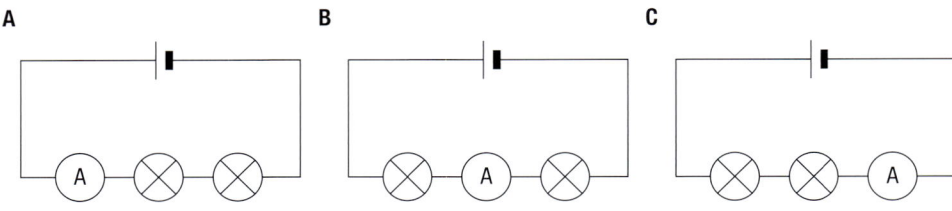

FIGURE 7.11

2. Take the readings on the ammeters.
3. Make a table to record your results.

B Parallel circuits
1. Working in your group, make the circuits shown in Figure 7.12.

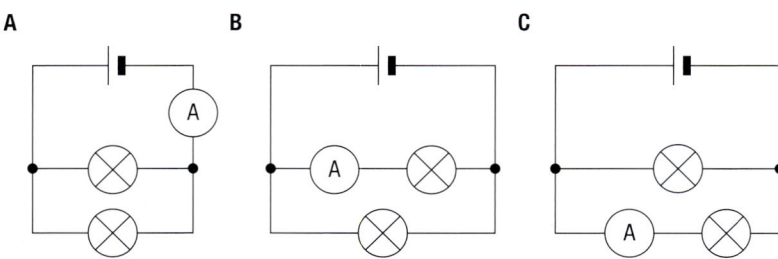

FIGURE 7.12

2. Take the readings on the ammeters.
3. Make a table to record your results.

CONCLUSION
Series circuits
Compare the measurements of current you obtained in circuits A, B and C. Interpret and explain the results.

Parallel circuits
Compare the measurements of current you obtained in circuits A, B and C. Interpret and explain the results.
Comparison
1. Compare the results for series circuit A with those for parallel circuit B. Explain the difference.
2. Compare the results for series circuit A with those for parallel circuit A. Explain the difference.

EXTENSION
Add a third light globe to circuit A for both the series and parallel circuits. Compare the differences this makes in each case.

Voltage (potential difference)

Batteries give energy to the electrons and 'push' them around the system. This push is usually called the **voltage** of the battery. Voltage is measured in volts. For example, many batteries have a voltage of 4.5 volts.

We use a voltmeter to measure the voltage of a cell. Voltmeters are used differently from ammeters. They always go in parallel with the device you are measuring the voltage of, as shown in Figure 7.13. This is why the push of electrons is better called 'potential difference' rather than voltage. We are measuring the difference in potential across the device.

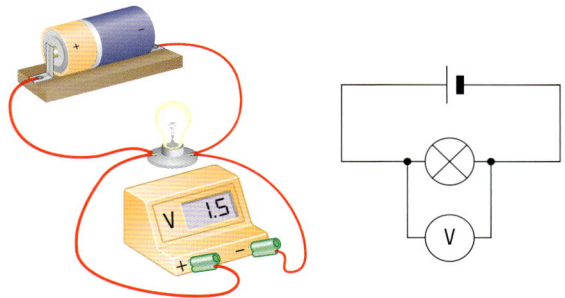

FIGURE 7.13 Placing a voltmeter in parallel allows you to measure the voltage (potential difference) across a light globe.

Another model for voltage

Look carefully at Figure 7.14. It is showing the idea of batteries 'lifting up' the electrons in terms of their energy. Then the electrons move around the circuit and lose this energy when they move through a device such as a lamp or a motor. This is because these devices resist the flow of electrons, and the electrons have to use up energy to get through them. In this circuit with two light globes, the electrons use up half the energy getting through the first globe, and the other half getting through the second globe. If the battery is 4 volts, then you can see that the voltage (potential difference) across each of the globes is 2 volts (2 + 2 = 4).

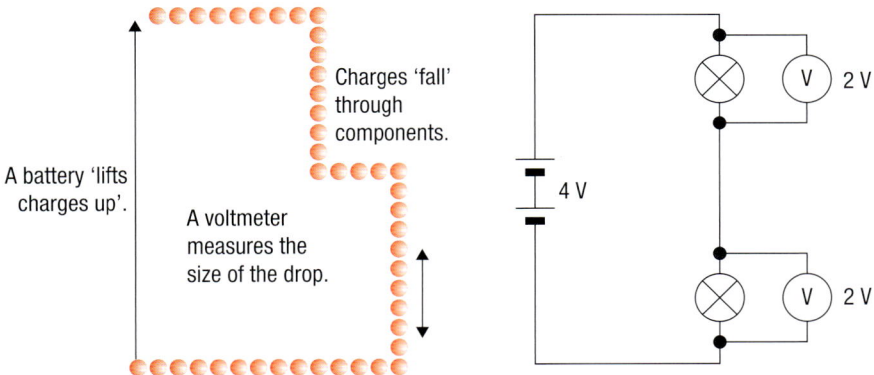

FIGURE 7.14 A model of a battery as a 'lifting' device

Figure 7.15 is a circuit diagram in which the voltmeters are in parallel with the device they are measuring the voltage of.

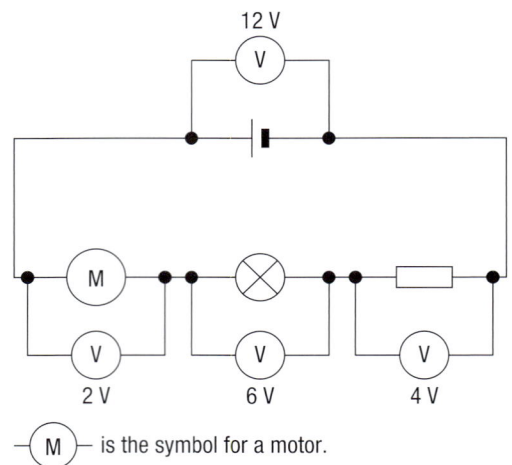

FIGURE 7.15 The voltages around a circuit

Voltage calculations

ACTIVITY

Complete the unknown voltages in the circuit diagrams in Figure 7.16.

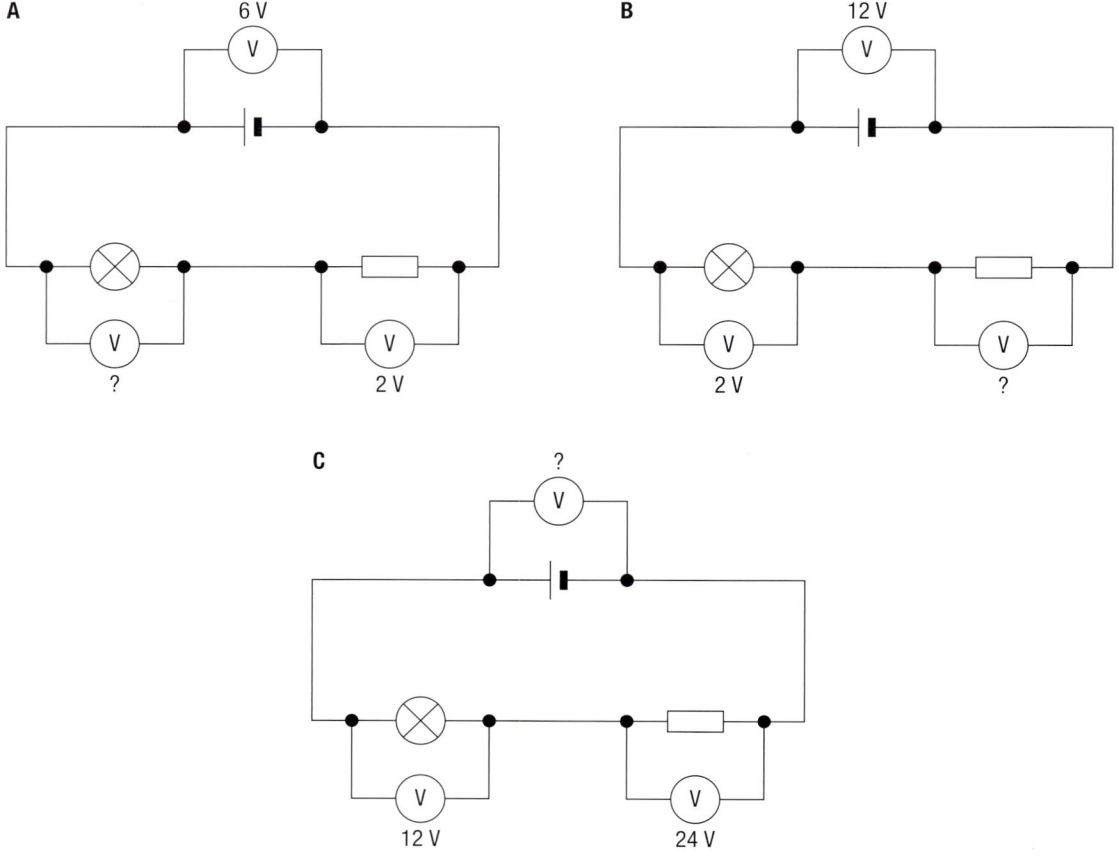

FIGURE 7.16 More series circuits

EXPERIMENT 7.3 Measuring voltages (potential differences)

AIM
To measure voltage at different points around a circuit.

MATERIALS
- two 1.5 V cells and holders
- three light globes (1.5 V)
- voltmeter
- six leads

PROCEDURE
Make the series circuit in Figure 7.17 and measure the voltage between points:
a   A and B
b   C and D
c   D and E
d   E and F.

CONCLUSION
Interpret your results based on the previous discussion about voltage.

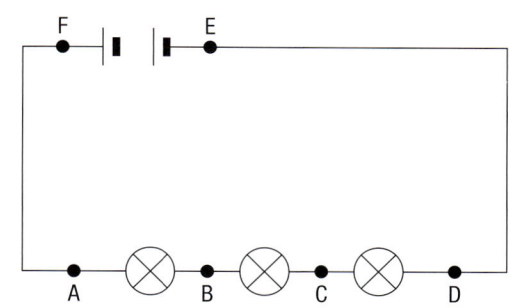

FIGURE 7.17 A series circuit

EXTENSION
Construct a parallel circuit, and measure the voltage at various points. What differences do you note compared with the series circuits? Can you explain these differences?

REVIEW

1 State the name of the charged particle that moves in an electric current.
2 Outline the role of the battery in an electric circuit.
3 We say that a light globe resists the flow of current. What does this mean?
4 Draw a series circuit to show two light globes in a circuit with two cells and an ammeter.
5 Draw a circuit to show three light globes in parallel with a cell, and a switch associated with each light globe.
6 Would you choose a series or a parallel circuit for a set of 20 lights for a celebration? Explain your answer.
7 Many students have difficulties with the idea of voltage. How would you explain the idea of voltage to a student of your age?
8 Find the unknown currents A_1–A_5 in the circuits in Figure 7.18. Assume all the light globes are the same.

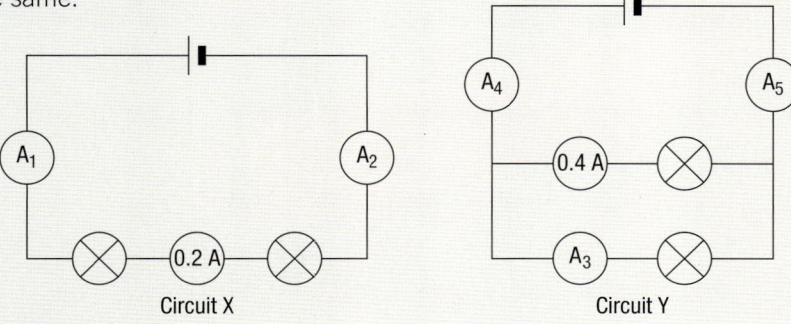

FIGURE 7.18

Go to http://mypsci1.nelsonnet.com.au and click on **Simulations**. Use these interactive simulations to learn more about different concepts of electricity, including building circuits, magnets and electromagnets, conductivity, capacitors and more.

Magnets

Magnets are objects that have a magnetic field and attract certain materials. They are attracted to objects containing iron, cobalt or nickel. Magnets and these materials pull towards each other. Magnets can be any shape or size. They vary in strength – some are weak, while others are strong enough to lift hundreds of kilograms. The effect that magnets have on other objects is said to be caused by their magnetic force.

FIGURE 7.19 Magnets can be any shape or size.

FIGURE 7.20 A horseshoe magnet with iron filings

What magnets are made of

Magnets can be found in nature or be made by humans. **Magnetite**, sometimes called lodestone, is very common (Figure 7.21). Magnetite is a kind of iron ore, and is the most magnetic mineral found in nature. Most magnets contain iron.

Sometimes, materials are combined to make magnets. **Neodymium** is a rare earth element. (You will learn more about elements in *Science 2 for the international student*.) When neodymium is mixed with iron and boron, it makes the strongest permanent magnet available. For example, a neodymium magnet the size of a penny can lift up to 10 kilograms. You must be very careful when handling these magnets. The tip of a person's finger was accidentally removed when it was caught between two of these very strong magnets! Neodymium magnets are used today in many industries. They are found in magnetic jewellery, name tags and electric motors of hybrid cars, and are even used to collect dust from the surface of Mars.

Ceramic magnets are the most common type of magnet used today. They are made of iron in a ceramic mix, and can be shaped in many ways – from comical-shaped refrigerator magnets to ring, bar or horseshoe magnets used in science classes. Ceramic magnets are generally not very strong.

Flexible magnets, such as those given out by stores for advertising, are made when magnetic powder is mixed with plastic or rubber (Figure 7.22). When cooled, they can be cut, twisted, stamped, painted and more without losing their magnetism.

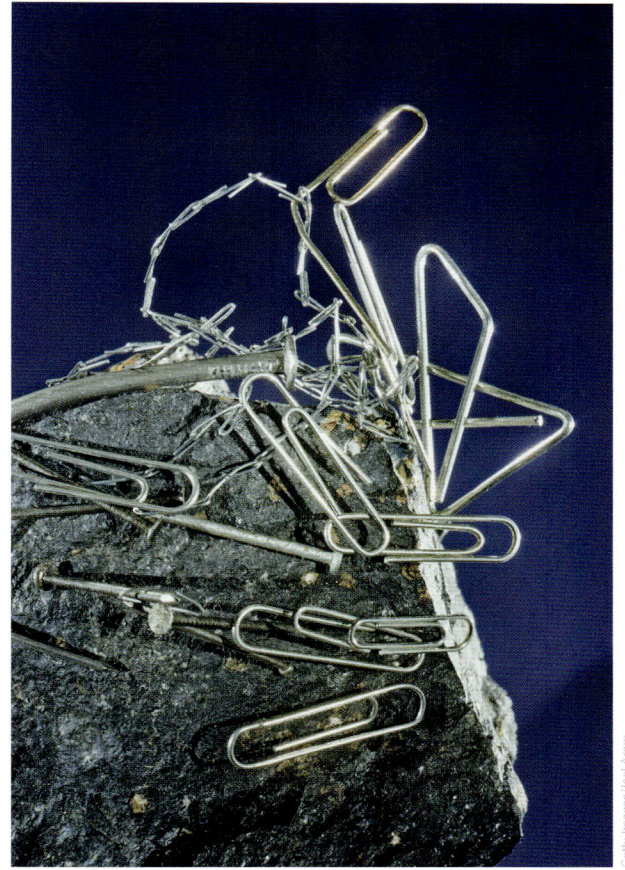

FIGURE 7.21 Lodestone is a naturally occurring magnet.

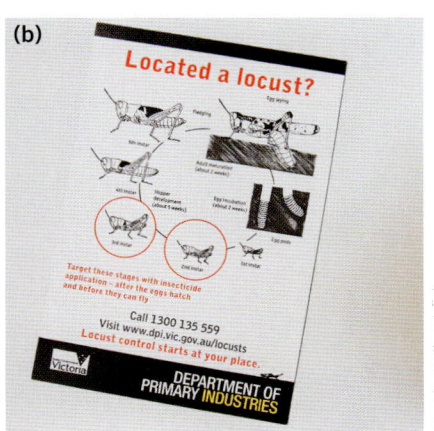

FIGURE 7.22 (a) Magnets on a fridge and (b) a flexible plastic magnet with advertising are just some of the many forms magnets can take.

Magnets have poles

FIGURE 7.23 A bar magnet has north and south poles at either end.

A magnet has two poles: a north pole and a south pole. For a simple bar magnet, this is often represented as shown in Figure 7.23. Although the poles are usually at the ends of the magnet, this is not always the case. Figure 7.24 shows a magnet that has its poles in the centre and outside of a circular shape.

FIGURE 7.24 This cylindrical magnet has its poles on the inside and outside of the circular shape.

FIGURE 7.25 A levitation toy. The rings appear to float due to the magnets repelling each other.

Flexible magnets typically have the north pole on one side and the south pole on the other.

The poles of a magnet demonstrate the **force of attraction** and the **force of repulsion**. When poles have the opposite magnetic force, they are attracted. When they are attracted, they pull towards each other. When they have the same magnetic force, they are repelled. When objects are repelled, they push away from one another.

A fun activity to try is to make a toy by placing a series of ring magnets on an unsharpened pencil (Figure 7.25). When opposite poles are brought near to each other, they will be attracted and stick together. When like poles are brought near each other, they are repelled. This can cause levitation.

Magnets have fields

Poles are not the only places on a magnet that exert force. Magnets don't need to be touching an object to attract it. Each magnet has an area where you can observe a force, called the **magnetic field**. This is the region around the magnet that can attract materials towards it. Magnetic fields are usually represented by **field lines**.

One easy way to study a magnetic field is to sprinkle iron filings on a piece of paper or glass that has a magnet underneath. The iron filings form a pattern of lines. The field lines created show where the magnetic field is located. The closer the field lines are to one another, the stronger the magnetic field is at that point.

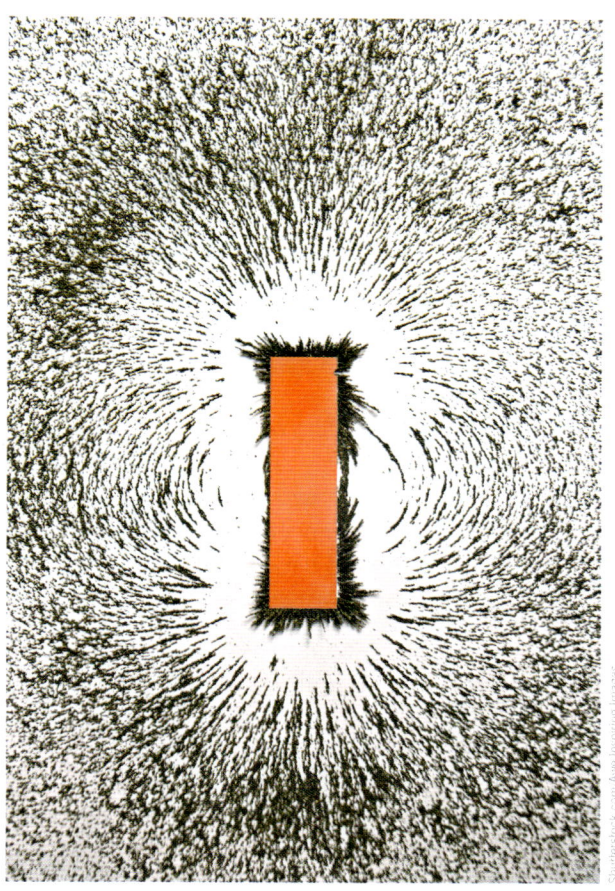

FIGURE 7.26 Scattered iron filings show the magnetic field around a bar magnet.

EXPERIMENT 7.4 Magnetic poles and fields

AIM
To identify magnetic poles and fields around different-shaped magnets.

MATERIALS
- two bar magnets
- circle magnet
- horseshoe magnet
- large white paper
- iron filings
- safety goggles
- record sheet

SAFETY
Iron filings are lightweight and can easily get blown around. Their sharp ends can embed in eyes and fingers and be very painful. Always wear safety goggles when using iron filings.

PROCEDURE
1. Put your safety goggles on before you begin and make sure you have a clean area to place your white paper.
2. Sprinkle the iron filings in an even layer on the paper, leaving wide empty margins around the edge.

COLLABORATION
Carry out your roles and accept responsibility when working in groups/teams.

3 Use the edge of the bar magnet to make a place for it in the centre of the iron filings layer.
4 Sketch your observation on your record sheet.
5 Carefully lift the magnet and remove any filings attached.
6 Shake the paper gently to rearrange the filings into a layer.
7 Place the two bar magnets on opposite sides of the paper with north poles facing each other. Slowly slide the magnets towards each other. Stop sliding them when they are about 6 cm apart.
8 Sketch your observation on your record sheet.
9 Shake the paper gently to rearrange the filings into a layer.
10 Place the two bar magnets on opposite sides of the paper with opposite poles facing each other. Slowly slide the magnets towards each other. Stop sliding them when they are about 6 cm apart.
11 Sketch your observation on your record sheet.
12 Shake the paper gently to rearrange the filings into a layer.
13 Place the horseshoe magnet on the iron filings and sketch your observations.
14 Place the circle magnet on the iron filings and sketch your observations.
15 Follow your teacher's directions to clean your area safely.

CONCLUSION
1 Describe each sketch you created, using scientific terms.
2 Outline how this experiment related to magnetic fields.

EVALUATION
How could you have done this experiment differently or improved it?

REVIEW
1 Outline what is meant by the poles of a magnet.
2 State when magnets attract and when they repel.
3 Explain what is meant by a magnetic field.
4 Suggest a use for magnets:
   a attracting
   b repelling.
5 List three types of magnets. Outline a benefit and limitation of each type.
6 State a type of magnet found in nature.

The Earth: a giant magnet

The Earth is a giant magnet. It is surrounded by a magnetic field (see Figure 7.27). The **magnetic north pole** and **magnetic south pole** are the natural poles of the Earth's magnetic field. They are located near, but not exactly at, the 'true' (or geographic) North and South Poles. A **compass** needle points to the Earth's magnetic north and south. At these magnetic poles, the field lines point directly into or out of the ground. At the equator, the field lines are horizontal to the ground.

While scientists can observe the effects of the Earth's magnetic field, they cannot explain how it came about. They think the movement of the outer core is involved. The outer core of the Earth is made of liquid iron and nickel. As the Earth rotates, the liquid spins and creates electrical

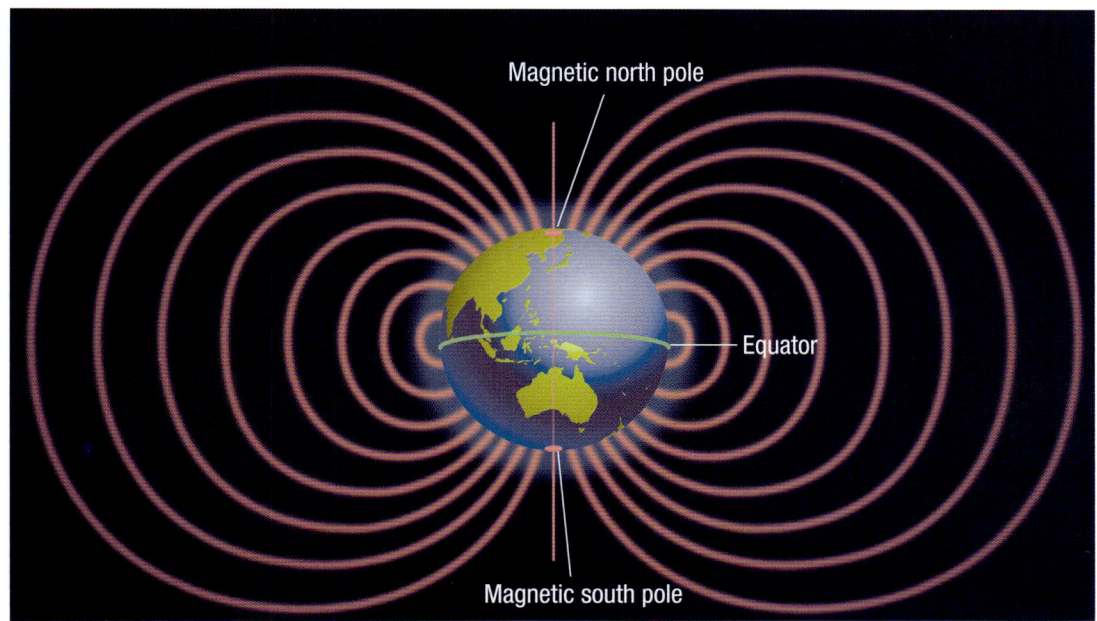

FIGURE 7.27 The Earth's magnetic field

currents. These electrical currents are associated with magnetism.

When the Earth's magnetic field traps solar particles, the brilliant Aurora Australis and Aurora Borealis are formed (Figure 7.28). These **auroras** are also known as the Southern Lights and Northern Lights. The solar particles interact with the Earth's atmosphere and make colourful displays.

Scientists have used evidence from new crust that has formed along the Mid-Atlantic Ridge to show that the magnetic north and south poles do not stay in the same place. In fact, the magnetic poles of the Earth have reversed a number of times. It seems to happen about once every one million years.

FIGURE 7.28 The colourful display of an aurora

Magnets can be permanent or temporary

A **permanent magnet**, such as a bar magnet, is one that always keeps its magnetic properties. Inside permanent magnets, **domains** (or mini-magnets) are always lined up. The domains in **temporary magnets** can be made to line up when placed next to a permanent magnet. When the permanent magnet is removed, the domains return to their random positions. The magnetism from the temporary magnet is then lost.

If you bring a steel paperclip near a bar magnet, it will be attracted to the magnet. If you put another steel paperclip next to the first, it will be attracted too. You can create a chain of paperclips in this way. The paperclips are acting as temporary magnets because they only attract one another while they are next to a permanent magnet. They come apart when the permanent magnet is moved away.

Electromagnets

Electromagnets are a special type of temporary magnet that use electricity. When the ends of a wire are attached to an electrical source, such as a battery, a magnetic field is created. To make it stronger, the wire can be coiled.

Electromagnets can be switched on and off. When both ends of the wire are attached to the battery, an electromagnet is created. When one end is removed, the magnet stops working. The mini-magnets in the object line up their north and south poles when an electric current runs through it. This creates magnetism.

Electromagnets are mainly used in industry. Large electromagnets can be attached to cranes. When the electricity is turned on, the crane can pick up and move very heavy metal objects, such as scrap metal (Figure 7.30). When the magnet is turned off, the mini-magnets return to their random order and the scrap metal is dropped in its new location.

Danish scientist Hans Christian Ørsted (1777–1851) showed that a moving electric current creates a magnetic field. English scientist Michael Faraday (1791–1867) was interested in this electromagnetism. Faraday discovered that moving a magnet over a wire produced electricity. The larger the magnet, the stronger the current. He could also make a stronger current if he coiled the wire around the magnet and moved the magnet. In this way, magnetism and electricity are uniquely related. This discovery has led to numerous technology breakthroughs in use today.

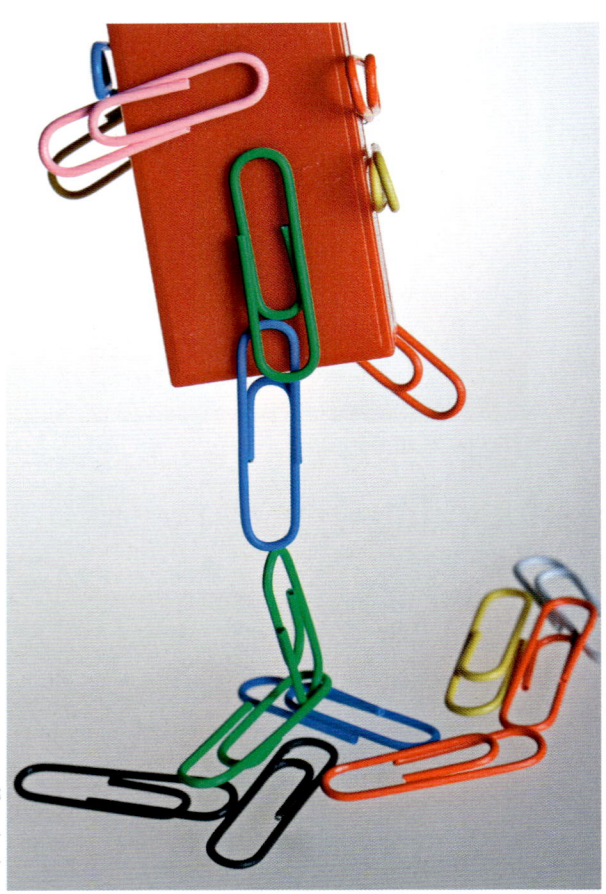

FIGURE 7.29 A bar magnet attracting a line of steel paperclips

FIGURE 7.30 Electromagnets are used to pick up scrap metal.

Electric motors and generators are based on this concept. Most of the electricity we use is created this way. Wind, solar, water, nuclear or fossil fuel energy is used to spin large coils of wire around or inside a magnet.

INVESTIGATION 7.1 — Electromagnets

YOUR CHALLENGE
To create an electromagnet and investigate a variable that affects its strength.

THIS MIGHT HELP
Your teacher will provide you with the following materials: compass, 9 V battery or suitable high-current power supply, insulated copper wire, large iron nail, paperclips.

You could measure the strength of your electromagnet by the number of paperclips it picks up or its effect on a compass.

Carry out and write up the investigation by following the guide in Appendix 3 on page 169, or as advised by your teacher.

CRITICAL THINKING: ANALYSING DATA
Understand the importance of considering whether you have any anomalies (outliers) in your data. Also consider the idea of looking for patterns or trends in your data.

Using magnets

Many everyday items use magnets. The hard drive on your computer uses tiny magnets to store and read data. Speakers for stereos, mobile phones and hearing aids; electric motors; doorbells; headphones; and the strips on debit, credit and ID cards all use magnets. Electromagnets are used as magnetic sweepers at construction sites and airports. Food industries use them to separate metal items from their products. Some amusement park rides use magnets in their braking systems. An example is the Giant Drop on the Gold Coast, in Queensland, Australia, the tallest tower drop ride in the world. Without magnets, our lives would be less entertaining and less convenient.

FIGURE 7.31 The strip on the back of a debit or credit card contains tiny magnetic particles.

Magnets in medicine and health

Magnets are used in medicine. A doctor might use a magnet to remove tiny iron splinters from your eye. The health industry uses magnets in wheelchair motors and **magnetic resonance imaging (MRI) machines**. MRI uses electromagnets, permanent magnets and superconducting magnets to create a detailed picture of the tissues in your body. Superconducting quantum interference devices (SQUIDs) are electromagnets that use tiny electrical impulses to aid in mapping brain activity without surgery.

Magnets in transportation

Modern transportation would not be possible without electromagnets. Electric motors in cars use them. Maglev trains in Asia do not have a regular train engine. They rely on powerful electromagnets to move along quickly and smoothly.

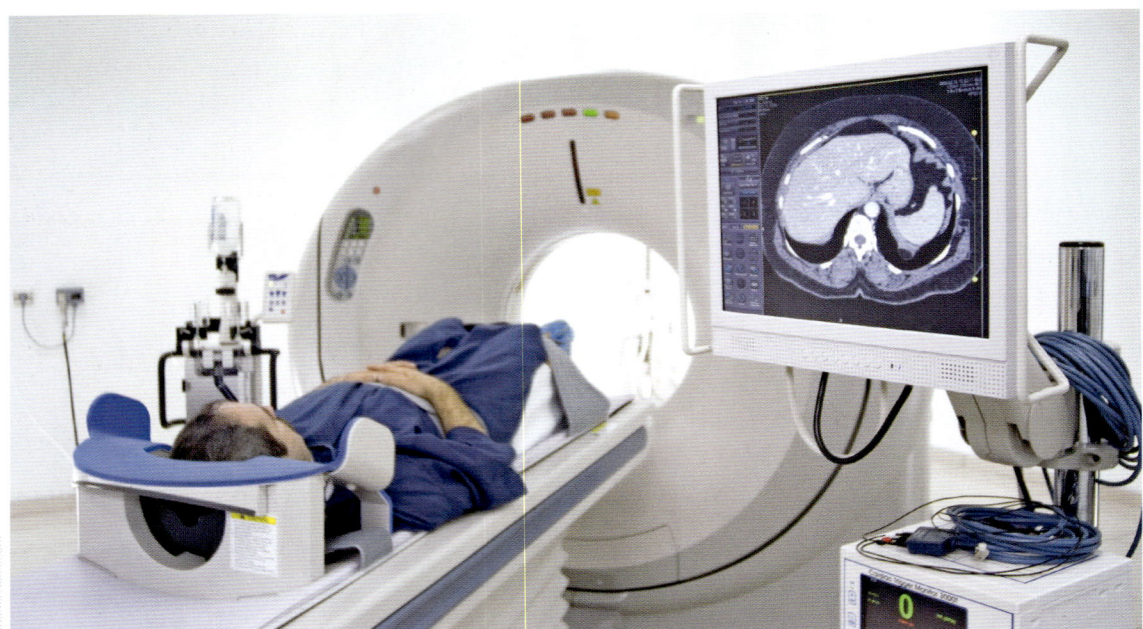

FIGURE 7.32 An MRI machine uses magnets to create a detailed picture of the tissues in your body.

Maglev is short for **magnetic levitation**. A magnetic field suspends the train up to 10 millimetres (1 centimetre) above the tracks. Powerful magnets are attached underneath the train and along the tracks. Maglev trains use the magnetic properties of attraction and repulsion for movement and braking. Because it does not touch the ground, a maglev train experiences less friction. At a recent test run in Japan, a maglev reached a speed of 603 km/h!

FIGURE 7.33 A maglev high-speed train uses magnets to reduce friction.

New uses for magnets

Scientists at Carnegie Mellon University in the USA have created a **nanomagnet**, which is only nanometres in size. A nanometre is one-billionth of a metre. The scientists mixed these nanomagnets with petroleum oil. This mixture was poured over an existing patch of petroleum oil. When a strong magnet was placed nearby, all the petroleum oil was attracted.

Scientists think this will provide an eco-friendly way to clean up oil spills in the ocean. Unfortunately, the nanomagnets are expensive to make and many would be required to clean up a spill. The scientists are also unsure what to do with the oil/nanomagnet mixture once it is removed from the ocean.

Future of magnets

Scientists from all over the world travel to Florida in the USA to use the National High Magnetic Field Laboratory. Here, scientists use powerful magnets to discover new things. Some of their research includes developing a magnet for the International Space Station, improving MRI machines and creating new ways to analyse chemicals.

The Large Hadron Collider is a research facility near Geneva, Switzerland. It has 27 kilometres of **superconducting magnets**. Superconducting magnets are a type of electromagnet that must be cooled to temperatures colder than in outer space. This creates a 'super' strong magnet. Scientists want to find out more about the nature of the universe with their research in this facility.

There are thousands of different magnets that scientists use to carry out different experiments. Who knows what the next new use of marvellous magnets may be!

FIGURE 7.34 The Large Hadron Collider uses superconducting magnets, which are cooled with liquid helium. In 2012, scientists using the Large Hadron Collider discovered the elusive Higgs boson particle.

ACTIVITY   Large Hadron Collider

The Large Hadron Collider has been one of most successful and well-known science developments in recent times. Visit the weblink to learn more about this facility. Discuss the reasons for building it, and some of the factors involved in a project of this kind; for example, economic, political and ethical. Give your opinion about whether this project was worth spending all this money on.

INFORMATION LITERACY
Critically evaluate information from the internet. Are you using primary or secondary sources?

Go to http://mypsci1.nelsonnet.com.au and click on **Large Hadron Collider**. Will scientists be able to answer the question of dark matter?

REVIEW

1. Outline what you know about permanent magnets.
2. Outline the benefits of electromagnets over permanent magnets.
3. Describe how scientists want to use nanomagnets to aid in oil spills.
4. What are four everyday objects that use magnets?
5. What are two ways in which the health industry uses magnets?
6. How does the maglev train work?
7. Outline how scientists think auroras are formed.
8. Outline why the Earth is called a giant magnet.
9. Describe how an electromagnet works.
10. In which direction do compasses point?

UNIT QUESTIONS

CRITERION A

EXPLAINING SCIENTIFIC KNOWLEDGE

1. Compare a permanent magnet with a temporary magnet. (Level 1–2)
2. Draw diagrams showing two magnets repelling each other, and two magnets attracting each other. (Level 1–2)
3. What is actually moving in an electrical current? (Level 3–4)
4. Outline what happens when you bring an electric current near the needle of a compass. (Level 3–4)
5. Describe how to make an electromagnet. (Level 3–4)
6. Draw a circuit showing a battery and two light globes in a circuit, with both an ammeter and voltmeter in appropriate places. (Level 5–6)
7. Explain how magnetic levitation works in a maglev train. (Level 5–6)
8. Explain how electromagnets work, how their strength can be increased, and their advantages compared to normal magnets. (Level 7–8)
9. a Draw circuit diagrams to show how two light globes can be placed in both series and parallel circuits with a cell.
   b Compare the different brightnesses of the globes in the two circuits.
   c Explain why the brightnesses of the globes are different. (Level 7–8)

APPLYING SCIENTIFIC KNOWLEDGE AND UNDERSTANDING TO SOLVE A PROBLEM

10. You dropped a box of sewing pins on the floor and they scattered. Outline how you could pick them up without hurting yourself. (Level 1–2)
11. Explain how scientists want to use nanomagnets to benefit the environment. (Level 3–4)
12. A person has connected a buzzer to a cell and an ammeter. She finds the buzzer is too quiet. Explain what she could change to produce more noise from the buzzer. How would the reading on the ammeter change? (Level 5–6)

13. What are the unknown values in the circuits in Figure 7.35? (Level 7–8)

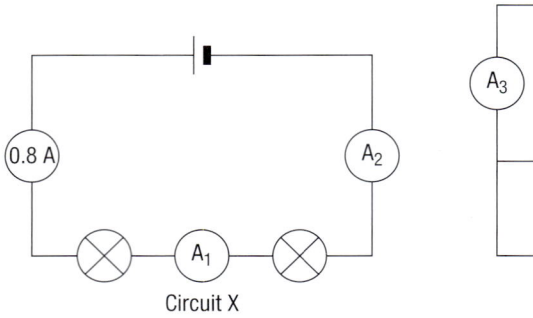
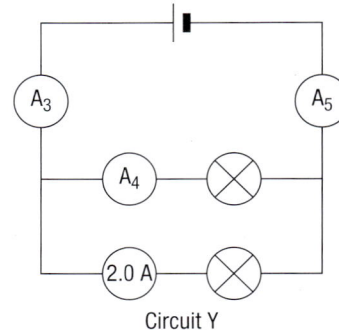

FIGURE 7.35

INTERPRETING INFORMATION

14. Your brother says aluminium is magnetic. Outline how you could test his statement. (Level 1–2)
15. Your television is often covered in dust. Suggest a reason for this. (Level 3–4)
16. Modern drink cans are made of both iron and aluminium. What complications would this cause for recycling? (Level 5–6)
17. Your Christmas tree lights do not work. None come on at all. From your knowledge of circuits, suggest a reason for this. Also suggest how you could make the lights work. (Level 7–8)

REFLECTION

1. Why might people in ancient times have viewed magnets as having magical properties? Justify your answer.
2. Explain how the use of models can help students understand electricity.
3. Electricity is one way energy can be transferred to our homes. Name some other ways energy can reach our homes.
4. Discuss some of the creative ideas that you see in our use of devices that use magnetism and electricity.
5. Outline the main dangers associated with electricity and the use of magnets.
6. Suggest reasons why people find electricity difficult to understand.

UNIT 8
OUR DYNAMIC EARTH

KEY CONCEPT
Change

RELATED CONCEPTS
Development

Scale

Cycles

GLOBAL CONTEXT
Orientation in space and time: an exploration into how the Earth has changed over time

STATEMENT OF INQUIRY
The surface and atmosphere of the Earth are the result of billions of years of gradual cycles of change.

INQUIRY QUESTIONS

FACTUAL
1. What is meant by plate tectonics?
2. What is the structure of the Earth?
3. What are the main three classes of rocks and how are they formed?

CONCEPTUAL
4. Why is the theory of plate tectonics important to our understanding of the Earth?
5. How is knowledge about fossils helpful to scientists studying the past?
6. How does the idea of the rock cycle help us understand the landscapes around us?

DEBATABLE
7. Do we fully understand all the changes over the geological time scale, from 650 million years ago to the present?
8. Is the impact of humans on landscapes positive or negative?

Introduction

The Earth has a number of amazing and unique features: Uluru in Australia, the Grand Canyon in the USA, the Himalayas in Asia, the Karst Caves in Slovenia, the Petra Gorge in Jordan and the Sahara Desert in Northern Africa to name a few. Humans have tried to explain the natural world since ancient times. Before science could explain the local natural forms, people created stories and passed them down from one generation to the next. Scientists can now describe the likely conditions millions of years ago. In this unit, you will study cycles of change in our planet and how they led to what we see and experience today.

FIGURE 8.1 (a) Petra Gorge in Jordan, (b) Bryce Canyon in Utah and (c) the Himalayas are just some of the Earth's unique rock formations.

The rock cycle

Create a presentation about two famous rock formations – for example, Wave Rock in Western Australia, the Grand Canyon in Arizona, the Giant's Causeway in Northern Ireland, The Wave in Arizona, or a formation in your locality. Use the rock cycle to explain how these formations were formed. Your chosen formations should be based on two different types of rock. Be sure to document the sources of information you used.

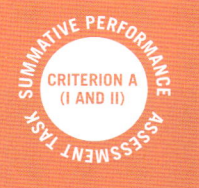

CRITERION A (I AND II)

ATL

COMMUNICATION
Use a variety of media to communicate with a range of audiences, expressing your ideas clearly and correctly and using scientific language.

FIGURE 8.2 (a) Wave Rock, Western Australia, (b) the Giant's Causeway, Northern Ireland

From the beginning

FIGURE 8.3 Formation of our solar system

FIGURE 8.4 The Barringer Crater, in Arizona, USA, is evidence of an asteroid collision with the Earth 50 000 years ago.

Go to http://mypsci1.nelsonnet.com.au and click on **Earth**. Learn from different perspectives about the Earth's early formation and what scientists think about where our water comes from. With which do you agree?

Scientists know from dating meteorites that the solar system is about 4.5 billion years old. Interstellar dust and gas, or **solar nebulae**, were drawn together by their gravitational forces. Solar nebulae are formed mainly from hydrogen and helium atoms left over from the initial formation of the universe (often referred to as the Big Bang). Other heavier elements such as iron were also present from previous stars and their supernova explosions. These particles became asteroids as more collided and collected. More mass meant greater gravity and the process accelerated. Eventually all material in the object's gravitational field was combined and this area mostly cleared. In this way, the planets formed. Early Earth would have been a mixture of hot solids and gases. The surface was molten rock and there would not have been much atmosphere.

The changing Earth

Over time, the molten surface of the Earth cooled and a solid shell formed. The Earth still collided with many other bodies such as asteroids. You can see the result of one such collision in Figure 8.4. Scientists think one such collision, relatively soon after the formation of the Earth, caused the formation of the Moon. They also think that this particular collision might be the reason why the Earth spins on an **axis** tilted at 23°. A number of scientists also believe that these colliding bodies brought much of the water presently on the surface of the Earth. Before that, the Earth's atmosphere would have been mostly made of the gases released in volcanic eruptions. Not a very hospitable place!

The Earth's gravity pulled the heaviest elements, such as iron and nickel, towards its centre. The lighter elements such as oxygen and silicon rose upwards to the surface. Eventually, the Earth formed the three different layers we know today – the core, mantle and crust as shown in Figure 8.7. (You will study elements further in *Science 2 for the international student*.)

It is difficult to find traces of the first rocks, but some still exist. The oldest complete rock formation, estimated to be about 3.8 billion years old, is at the Isua Greenstone Complex in Greenland. The oldest mineral found is a zircon **crystal**, dated at around 4.4 billion years old, which was found in Australia.

Early atmosphere

Scientists are not sure of the exact composition of the Earth's atmosphere at the beginning. But they think gas from volcanic eruptions would have created toxic fumes of sulfur dioxide, methane, water vapour, nitrogen and carbon dioxide. This is nothing like what it is today – it is more like something from a movie about aliens!

The first primitive life form began in the oceans around 3.5 billion years ago. This was in the form of **cyanobacteria**, simple one-celled organisms with no nucleus. The cyanobacteria have an extensive fossil record (Figure 8.5). Cyanobacteria contained chloroplasts, which used carbon dioxide, water and sunlight to synthesise their food. The by-product of this **photosynthesis** was oxygen. This gradually led to the formation of the atmosphere we have today: 78% nitrogen, 21% oxygen, 0.9% argon, 0.004% carbon dioxide and some water vapour (Figure 8.6).

Go to http://mypsci1.nelsonnet.com.au and click on **Oldest rock** to read about the discovery of the oldest rock on the planet.

FIGURE 8.5 Fossilised cyanobacteria nodes such as these are around 3.5 billion years old.

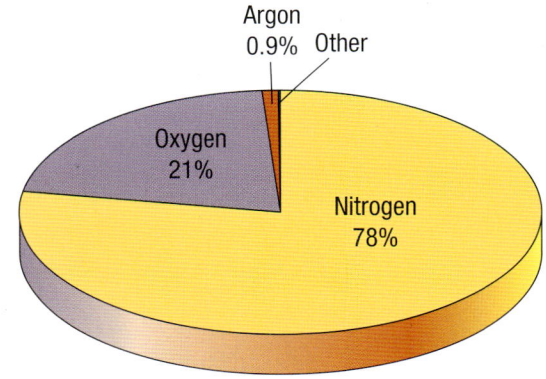

FIGURE 8.6 Composition of our present-day atmosphere

Geologic time

It is very difficult to imagine or visualise the evolution of the Earth since its formation 4.54 billion years ago. It was not until 85% of this time had passed that life in the oceans appeared (635 million years ago). It was not until 99.95% of this time had passed that humans, *Homo sapiens*, appeared (200 000 years ago). Scientists have labelled the different stages of geologic time, shown in Figure 8.7 (page 148). You can see how the last 650 million years have been split into **eras**, then subdivided into **periods**, and the events that occurred in each.

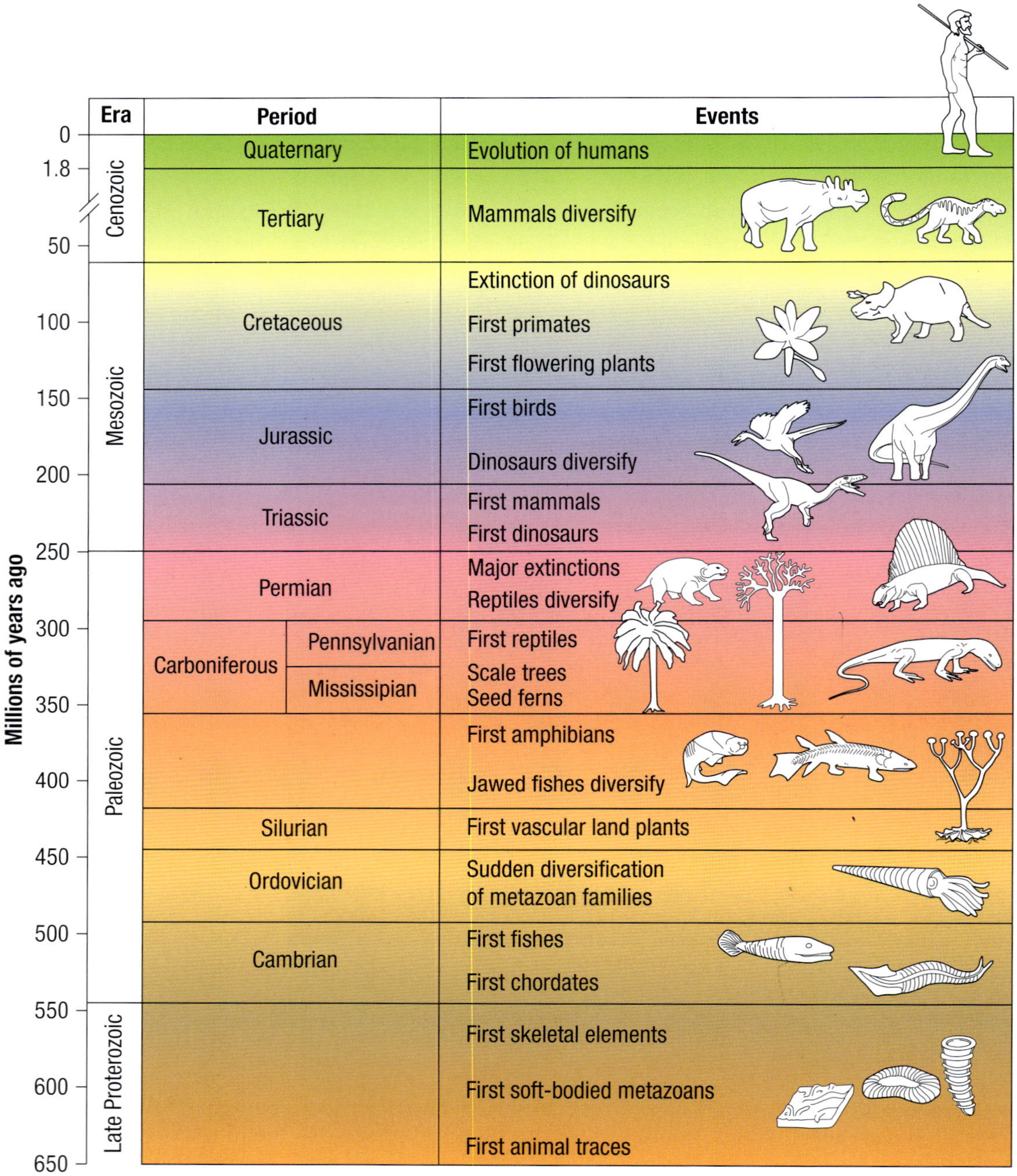

Era	Period		Events
Cenozoic	Quaternary		Evolution of humans
Cenozoic	Tertiary		Mammals diversify
Mesozoic	Cretaceous		Extinction of dinosaurs / First primates / First flowering plants
Mesozoic	Jurassic		First birds / Dinosaurs diversify
Mesozoic	Triassic		First mammals / First dinosaurs
Paleozoic	Permian		Major extinctions / Reptiles diversify
Paleozoic	Carboniferous	Pennsylvanian	First reptiles / Scale trees
Paleozoic	Carboniferous	Mississipian	Seed ferns
Paleozoic			First amphibians / Jawed fishes diversify
Paleozoic	Silurian		First vascular land plants
Paleozoic	Ordovician		Sudden diversification of metazoan families
Paleozoic	Cambrian		First fishes / First chordates
Late Proterozoic			First skeletal elements / First soft-bodied metazoans / First animal traces

FIGURE 8.7 Geologic time scale, 650 million years ago to the present

Go to http://mypsci1.nelsonnet.com.au and click on **Extinct organisms** to visit a website provided by the Smithsonian Institution and find out how scientists learn about extinct organisms.

The first evidence for establishing this geologic time scale came from the study of **fossils** in rocks. Fossils are traces of dead plants and animals found in sedimentary rocks. Different fossils are found in different layers of sedimentary rocks. Older fossils are found in deeper layers since that sediment was deposited first. From this, we can estimate how old the rocks are relative to each other. The evidence obtained from fossils was an important aspect of the development of the theory of evolution. New technology has enabled scientists to date samples more accurately. They use the rate of decay of radioactive elements in the rocks.

ACTIVITY: A geologic timeline

In this activity, you will construct a timeline from a roll of toilet paper. Each sheet will represent 4.5 million years. This will determine the placement of events on your timeline.

1. Take a roll of toilet paper that has 1000 sheets. Each sheet will represent 4.5 billion divided by 1000 years, i.e. 4.5 million years.
2. Roll out the toilet roll along a long corridor.
3. On the first sheet, indicate the formation of the Earth (4500 million years ago).
4. On the remainder of the sheets, indicate when the following events happened.
   - First appearance of simple life on the planet: 3700 million years ago
   - Oldest rocks: 3500 million years ago
   - Appearance of animal life: 700 million years ago
   - First fish: 500 million years ago
   - Plants on land: 400 million years ago
   - Animals such as lizards on land: 300 million years ago
   - Dinosaurs appear, and disappear: 225 and 65 million years ago
   - Monkeys appear: 35 million years ago
   - Grass appears: 15 million years ago
   - Humans appear: 200 000 years ago
5. What other events could you add?

Structure of Earth

Earth has three main layers: the crust, the mantle and the core (Figure 8.8). The **crust** is solid and the thinnest layer, an average of 40 kilometres thick. The crust under the ocean is thinner and denser than the crust under land.

The crust is relatively brittle, a little like the shell of a hard-boiled egg. It is mainly made of the lightest elements – silicon, aluminium and oxygen. These are often combined as **minerals**, such as feldspar and quartz. The crust is divided into gigantic pieces called plates. These plates 'float' on the upper portion of the next layer, the mantle. This idea of plates will be discussed in the next section.

The layer beneath the crust is the **mantle**, which is around 3000 kilometres of thick, dense rock. The mantle is mainly made of magnesium, silicon and oxygen. The mantle is similar in consistency to soft plastic or silly putty.

Rocks in the upper mantle are so hot that they are almost molten. Convection currents cause the rocks to churn around very slowly. The convection currents also make the crustal plates move. The lower mantle is more solid than the upper mantle and is very hot.

Deeper into the Earth is the dense **core**, mainly made of iron and nickel. The **outer core** is the only liquid layer of the Earth, an area of molten rock. The Earth's magnetic field is thought to originate from the movement of this layer. The **inner core** is solid due to the extreme pressure exerted by the upper layers and by gravity. Scientists think that the radioactive decay of elements in the inner core continues to produce enormous amounts of heat.

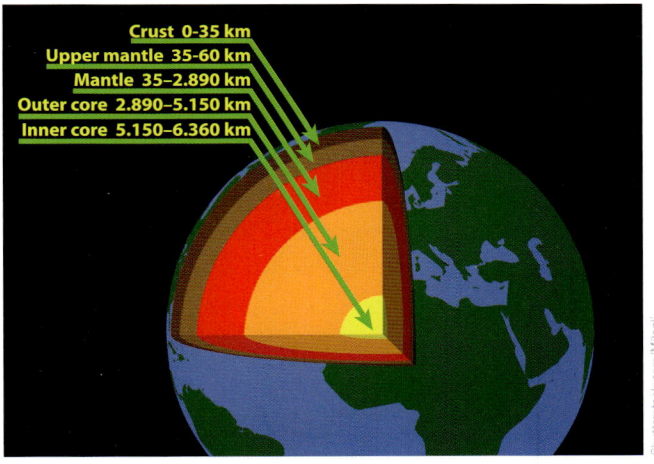

FIGURE 8.8 The Earth is made of three layers – the thin crust, mantle and core.

PERFORMANCE ASSESSMENT CRITERION A (I AND II)

A model of the layers of the Earth

ACTIVITY

Create a model of the Earth showing the relationship and scale of each layer to the others. This would be a good time to speak with your maths teacher about scale and ratios. Look at the depths of each layer. What ratios can you identify? How will you convert those? What will you create your model from – clay, Styrofoam, cake, or something else? How will you label and mark your model to show your understanding?

ATL

TRANSFER
Consider the importance of being able to transfer skills and knowledge from one subject to another.

REVIEW

1. Describe how the solar system and the Earth formed.
2. State what the solar nebula mainly consists of.
3. Outline where the heavier and lighter elements are in the Earth. Explain your answer.
4. Outline how the Moon formed and why the Earth spins on a tilted axis.
5. Outline how scientists think much of the water reached the Earth.
6. Explain how scientists think they know how old the Earth is.
7. Explain how fossils help us understand the history of the Earth.

Go to http://mypsci1.nelsonnet.com.au and click on **Earth's structure** to learn about Earth's structure, plate tectonics, and more!

Go to http://mypsci1.nelsonnet.com.au and click on **Centre of the Earth** to learn how far we've gone and what scientists think. Can we travel to the centre of the Earth?

Plate tectonics: a theory is born

Maps we have today include details that **cartographers**, or mapmakers, long ago would not have dreamed of (Figure 8.9). Satellites now orbit the Earth and are able to take pictures from space. We now have the ability to see the ocean floor. At one time it was thought the bottom of the ocean looked relatively flat like the bottom of a lake or pond.

Maps from the late 17th century showed that South America and Africa might fit neatly together. They almost looked like puzzle pieces. Alfred Wegener (1880–1930), a German scientist, was curious about this. His research found there were identical fossils in both South America and Africa. In 1912, he suggested that all the continents had once been part of one huge continent. He called it Pangaea, meaning 'all lands'. He thought that at some time in the past, Pangaea broke apart

Go to http://mypsci1.nelsonnet.com.au and click on **Historical perspective** to learn more about the development of the theory of continental drift and plate tectonics.

FIGURE 8.9 (a) The map of the world circa 1675–1710 shows little accurate detail compared to (b) maps of today.

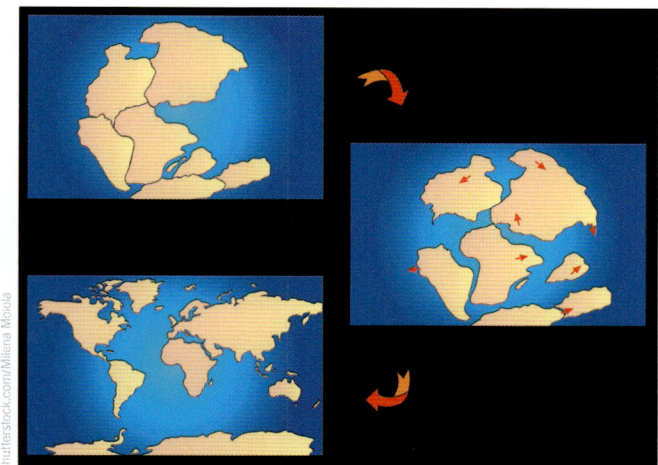

FIGURE 8.10 Pangaea (upper left) broke up and plates shifted over many millions of years.

and the continents drifted to their current positions (Figure 8.10). This idea of continental drift was controversial, but it caused others to start thinking. Many scientists disagreed, asking how he thought continents could move through the ocean.

In the 1950s, further evidence was obtained to support Wegener's idea. Especially important was evidence that the floor of the sea was spreading out in some places. This evidence included the Mid-Atlantic Ridge (Figure 8.11). This was the birth of the plate tectonic theory, a new theory that replaced previous theories and represented a key moment in science.

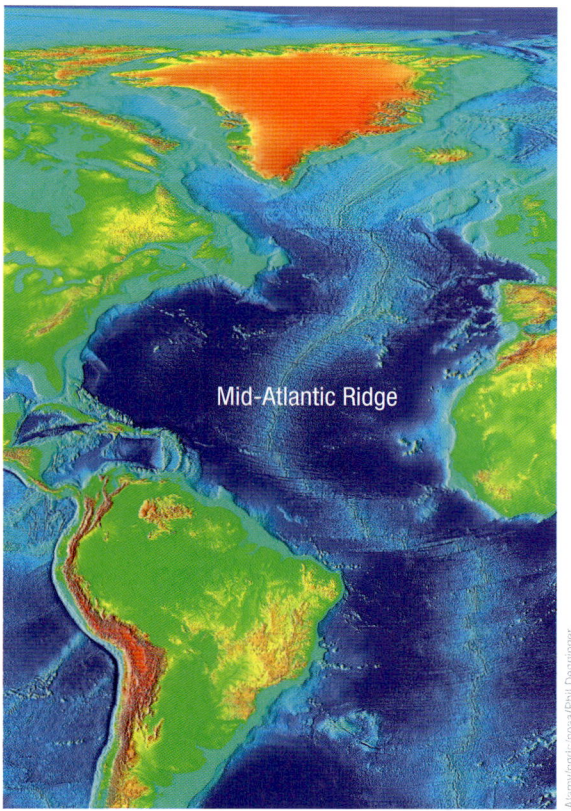

FIGURE 8.11 The discovery of the Mid-Atlantic Ridge system was evidence for seafloor spreading and led to the development of the theory of plate tectonics.

Tectonic plates and their movement

Imagine you drop a hard-boiled egg on the floor. When you pick it up, the shell is cracked into jagged pieces (Figure 8.12a). The Earth's crust is similar to the eggshell (Figure 8.12b). These jagged pieces of crust, **tectonic plates**, move as a result of forces deep below the surface. The solid layer of the Earth, the crust, moves on the semisolid layer of the upper

Go to http://mypsci1.nelsonnet.com.au and click on **Tectonics**. You can have fun with this interactive website as you learn about plate tectonics.

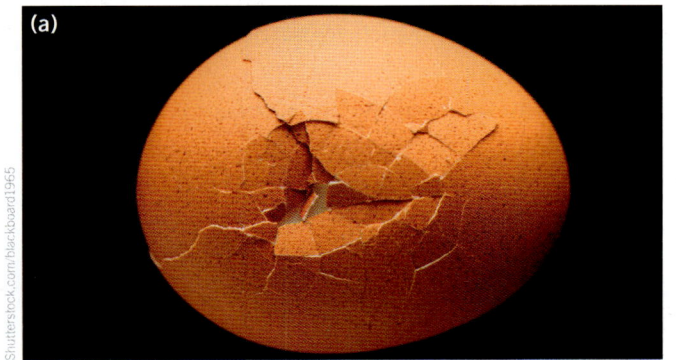
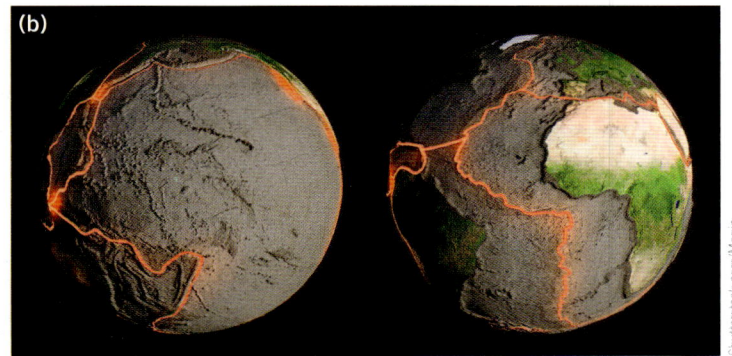

FIGURE 8.12 Cracks in an eggshell are similar to cracks in the Earth's crust, which make up tectonic plates.

mantle. The regions where plates meet are called **boundaries**. The plates generally move about as fast as your fingernails grow (4–11 cm/year). Over your lifetime, not much change can be seen. Over thousands or even millions of years, the change is remarkable!

Types of boundaries

There are three types of plate boundaries: divergent, convergent and transform. Each type of boundary has particular characteristics. Movement at some boundaries can cause earthquakes and volcanoes.

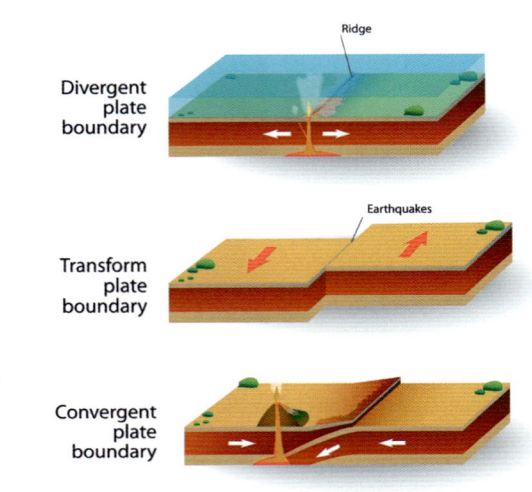

FIGURE 8.13 Three types of plate boundaries and their movements

Divergent boundaries

Some plates move away from each other, or diverge. The most-studied **divergent boundary** is the Mid-Atlantic Ridge, under the Atlantic Ocean. The North American Plate is moving west and the Eurasian Plate is moving east. This creates a **rift**, or tear in the crust. At the boundary, deep under the Atlantic Ocean, magma oozes up to create new crust. As the plates keep slowly moving apart, lava oozes and piles up to make a ridge on either side. This is typical of this type of boundary. The Mid-Atlantic Ridge can be seen on land in Iceland. Iceland is growing as an island as it is being slowly ripped apart. Rift volcanoes add huge amounts of lava when they erupt, which cools into new land.

Convergent boundaries

To converge means to come together. The areas where plates are coming together are called **convergent boundaries**. Oceanic crust is made up of dense igneous rock, such as basalt. Continental crust is made up of lighter rock, such as granite. When continental and oceanic crust collide, the denser oceanic crust is forced underneath the lighter continental crust (Figure 8.15). An example can be found where the Indo-Australian Plate collides with the Eurasian Plate, creating the Indonesian Island Arc. Here, some of the most powerful volcanoes in the world are found.

Sometimes, crust of about the same density collides. It could be continental crust crashing into continental crust or oceanic crust crashing into oceanic crust. In these instances, the plate edges are both forced upwards. This creates fold mountains, an example of which can be found where India

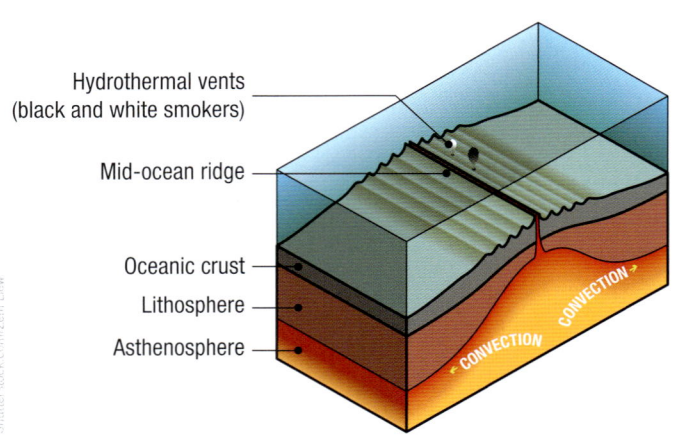

FIGURE 8.14 Magma oozes up where the North American Plate moves away from the Eurasian Plate, and creates new crust in the form of ridges.

runs into the Eurasian Plate. Very thick crust of up to 78 kilometres has been created, which has led to the formation of the highest mountains in the world, the Himalayas.

Transform boundaries

Most **transform boundaries** are found underwater. If you look at pictures of the Mid-Atlantic Ridge on Google maps, you will notice many horizontal lines spreading out from the vertical rift. Each line is a transform fault line. Transform faults can move in three ways: one side can slip upward, the sides can slightly pull apart with one side slipping downward, or the sides can try to slip horizontally past each other. The most famous transform fault is on land. It is the San Andreas Fault on the western coast of California (Figure 8.16). It marks the place where the Pacific Plate is moving north-west relative to the North American Plate. Transform boundaries mainly cause earthquakes.

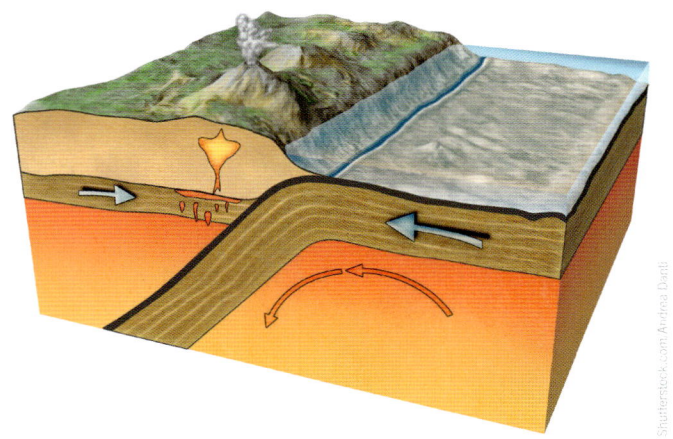

FIGURE 8.15 A trench is formed underwater as oceanic crust is forced below continental crust. Mountains and volcanoes can form at the edge of a continental plate.

Go to http://mypsci1.nelsonnet.com.au and click on **Plate boundaries** for a website that offers Flash simulations of the different types of plate boundaries.

FIGURE 8.16 The San Andreas Fault in California, USA, is along a transform boundary.

ACTIVITY Modelling movement at plate boundaries

1. Carefully twist the top off a sandwich cookie (biscuit) such as an Oreo. Break it in half.
2. Replace the pieces and pull them apart.
3. Sketch what your cookie looks like, noting the jagged broken edges. Describe how they are like the edges of tectonic plates at a divergent boundary. What are the limitations of this model?
4. Matching the broken edges, model a transform boundary, where plates try to grind past each other in opposite directions. Sketch what your cookie looks like and describe how this models transform boundaries. What are the limitations of this model?
5. Push the pieces towards each other, forcing one under the other. Sketch what your cookie looks like and describe how this models a convergent boundary. What are the limitations of this model?
6. Follow your teacher's directions on disposal of the cookie.

Go to http://mypsci1.nelsonnet.com.au and click on **Tectonic plates**. This web page will help you identify the different tectonic plates and where movements happen along plate boundaries.

Click on **Dynamic Earth** for in-depth information and interactive simulations to understand the three major types of movement.

Earthquakes

Earthquakes occur mostly along plate boundaries. Tectonic plates are moving very slowly all the time. In the broken eggshell model, the edges of the shell were jagged and rough. This is similar to plate boundaries. When plates try to move past each other, there is a problem. The jagged edges get stuck and do not allow the plates to move easily. Pressure builds up as the plates resist movement until there is a sudden jolt of movement. This is an earthquake. The longer pressure builds up, the greater likelihood of a major quake and damage. We measure the strength of earthquakes with the Richter scale, which goes from 1 to 10. The strongest earthquake on record was of a strength of 9.5 in Chile in 1960.

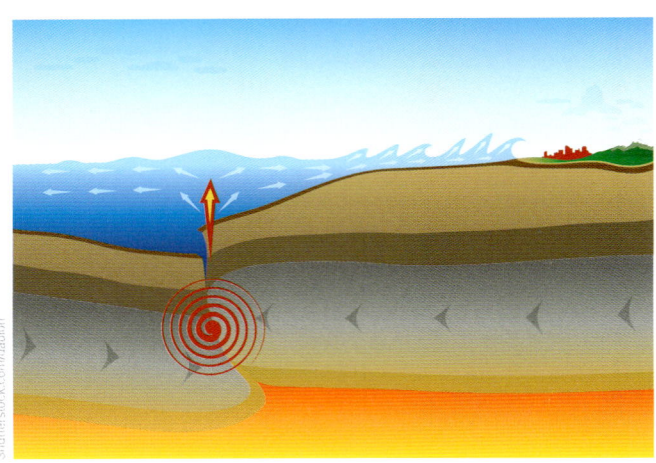

FIGURE 8.17 The Ring of Fire is named for the many volcanoes located at the edges of subduction zones in the Pacific Ocean.

Volcanoes

Many volcanoes result when friction builds up as plates grind past each other. The rock gets so hot that it melts. Gases are released and create pressure. If enough pressure is exerted, an eruption occurs. This is why most volcanoes occur around plate boundaries, particularly in **subduction** zones. Subduction occurs when denser oceanic crust is forced under lighter continental crust. This type of convergent boundary can be found around the edges of the Pacific Ocean. It is referred to as the Ring of Fire because of the high number of active volcanoes (Figure 8.17).

Volcanoes can also form over **hotspots**. A hotspot is an area under the crust with a huge column of magma beneath it. The islands of Hawaii were formed this way. The island of Iceland not only sits above a hotspot, but is being pulled apart by the Mid-Atlantic Rift. Because of this, enormous amounts of lava flow when Icelandic volcanoes erupt.

Tsunamis

Japan sits at the boundary of the Eurasian Plate and Pacific Plate. It experiences about 1500 earthquakes every year. The Japanese people are used to feeling minor tremors almost every day. Japan has stringent building codes and the people practice earthquake safety drills regularly.

In 2011, an extremely strong earthquake that measured 9.0 on the Richter scale occurred off the coast of Sendai, Japan. It was the fourth-most powerful earthquake ever recorded. The extreme movement of the plates (almost 50 metres) and length of time the ground moved (about 6 minutes) led to the formation of a **tsunami**. As the ground moved, almost 400 kilometres of island coastline dropped over half a metre. This displaced an enormous amount of water. The displaced water created a wave that reached almost 40 metres high and travelled as far as 10 kilometres

FIGURE 8.18 Underwater earthquakes cause tsunamis as massive amounts of water are displaced.

Go to http://mypsci1.nelsonnet.com.au and click on **Japan's natural disaster** to read more about Japan's incredible natural disaster.

inland. It severely damaged nuclear power plants and wiped out entire communities. Even today, more than 2500 people are still missing.

AID FOR PEOPLE AFTER A MAJOR EARTHQUAKE OR TSUNAMI

Carry out some research to find out how the country concerned and the international community responded to help people following a recent major earthquake or tsunami. How much damage was done? What aid agencies were involved? What kind of aid did they provide? How successful was the aid? You could organise some action in your school to help respond to a natural disaster of this kind.

REVIEW

1. Describe the three types of plate boundary and the three types of movement, and their consequences.
2. Outline where you are most likely to find a range of volcanoes and explain why.
3. Outline Wegener's idea of continental drift and how it developed into the theory of plate tectonics.
4. Explain what a tsunami is and how it is created.
5. State what is meant by the Ring of Fire.

The rock cycle

Scientists use the idea of the **rock cycle** to describe how rocks and landscapes have gradually changed over millions of years. The rock cycle is shown in Figure 8.19. Refer to this diagram throughout the next section to help you follow the various transformations. The main idea is that all rocks can be traced back to the cooling and solidification of the molten rock (**magma**) from Earth's formation.

Go to http://mypsci1.nelsonnet.com.au and click on **Rock cycle**. Play this interactive simulation to learn about the rock cycle with Rocky.

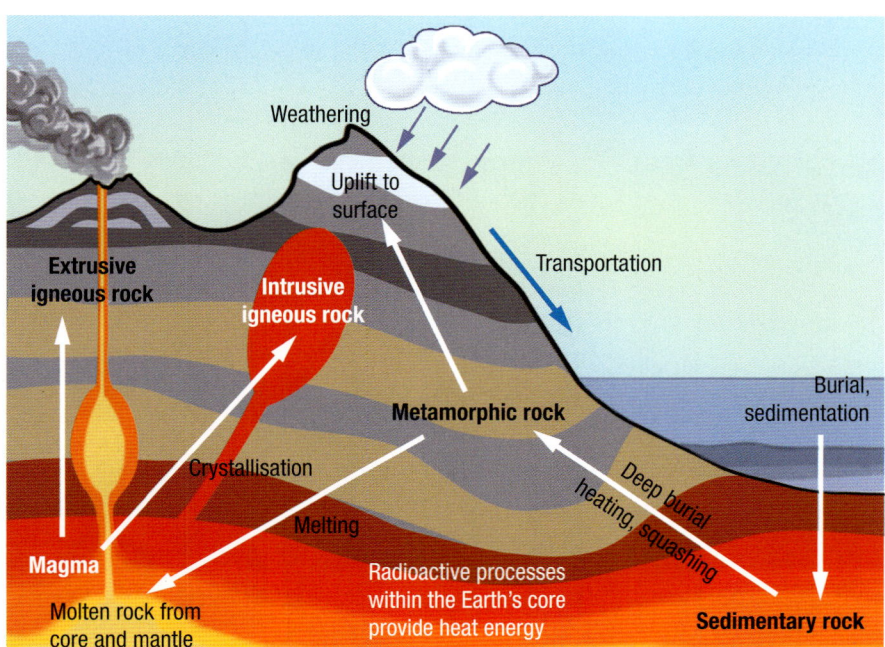

FIGURE 8.19 The rock cycle

Igneous rocks

Any rock produced from cooled and hardened molten rock is called **igneous rock** (from the Latin *igneus*, meaning fire). Sometimes there is not enough pressure for magma to erupt and make it to the surface. It cools and solidifies underground. It is still classified as igneous rock.

FIGURE 8.20 Example of igneous rock

Sedimentary rocks

Any type of rock can be broken down in nature into tiny parts. This process is called **weathering** and you will study weathering in more detail in the next section. As rocks are broken down into tiny pieces, water, wind or gravity will move them to a new location. This overall process is called **erosion**. For example, a river can transport the tiny pieces of rock (sediment) to the mouth of the river and out to sea where they will be deposited, or dropped to the sea floor, to form layers of sediment.

Another example is when wind carries the tiny particles to another location where they form layers of sediment. These layers are hardened into **sedimentary rocks** after being compacted, or squashed by pressure. Sometimes they are glued together by minerals in the sea. Sedimentary rocks can be formed from any type of rock that has been weathered, eroded, deposited and compacted. Examples are mudstone and sandstone. Some sedimentary rocks are almost entirely formed from minerals from sea life, such as limestone.

Sedimentary rocks:
- often contain fossils
- may react with acid (e.g. limestone)
- often have layers of different sediments
- are usually composed of small pieces cemented or pressed together
- have a great variety of colours from the different rocks that were eroded
- usually have pores between pieces.

FIGURE 8.21 Weathering and erosion of the Grand Canyon in Arizona, USA, exposes layers of sedimentary rock.

FIGURE 8.22 Some examples of sedimentary rocks

Metamorphic rock

Metamorphic rocks include any type of rock that has sunk back into the mantle, then been heated under pressure and recrystallised. They look different to and are generally harder than the original rock.

FIGURE 8.23 Metamorphic rocks include (a) gneiss, (b) slate, (c) pink marble and (d) quartzite.

Completing the cycle

Igneous rock can also be turned into metamorphic rock. If the Earth's plates move enough, then both metamorphic and igneous rock can be changed back to magma. Later, this magma can be reborn as igneous rock – and the cycle starts again. You can follow the different types of rock through the cycle in Figure 8.18.

Weathering: breaking down or dissolving rocks

As soon as rocks are exposed to the surface of the Earth, they begin to break down as a result of various processes. This process of breaking down or dissolving rock is called weathering. There are three types of weathering: physical, chemical and biological.

Go to http://mypsci1.nelsonnet.com.au and click on **Physical weathering** to see an animation of the freeze/thaw cycle of physical weathering.

Physical weathering

Physical weathering is a result of temperature change and the freeze–thaw cycle. Rocks can split when extreme temperature changes cause them to expand and contract. Water can also aid in weathering when it becomes ice. Some rocks allow water to enter through their surface. These are known as **porous rocks** (Figure 8.24). When water freezes, it expands and exerts pressure on the rock. More water enters the rock, more ice forms and more force is exerted on the rock. Over time, the rock breaks apart. You may have observed water expanding on freezing when a soft drink has been left in the freezer too long.

FIGURE 8.24 Porous rock, such as limestone, can be split from the cycle of water freezing and thawing over time. This is physical weathering.

EXPERIMENT 8.1

When rocks freeze

AIM
To investigate how freezing water causes physical weathering in porous rock.

MATERIALS
- freezer
- small beaker
- small piece of porous rock
- enough water to cover the rock

PREDICTION (HYPOTHESIS)
Predict what you think you will see after porous rock is covered in water and then frozen and thawed. Explain your reasons for your prediction.

PROCEDURE
1. Cover the rock with water in a beaker and place it in the freezer overnight.
2. Remove the beaker and allow the water to thaw. Count the number of pieces of rock that have fallen to the bottom. Record your results.
3. Repeat steps 1 and 2 at least six times.

RESULTS
1. Describe what happened to your rock.
2. Convert your results into a table. You may do this by hand or by using a spreadsheet.

CONCLUSION
1. What pattern did you see in your results?
2. Did the weathering of your rock increase over time?
3. Write a general conclusion to describe what you have learnt. Was your original prediction correct?

EVALUATION
How well did the experiment work? Can you think of any way to improve the experiment? Outline some further experiments you could carry out based on the effect of freezing water on rocks.

Chemical weathering

Chemical weathering occurs when chemicals break down rocks. Sometimes water alone will react with minerals in the rocks. Rainwater is usually naturally slightly acidic (approximate pH 5.6). This is because of dissolved carbon dioxide. This reacts with rocks such as limestone. Limestone caves are formed in this way. Pollution gases such as sulfur dioxide (from the burning of fossil fuels) and nitrogen oxides (from motor cars) can make rainwater even more acidic, as low as pH 3.5. Very acidic rain can cause even faster weathering of rocks and buildings. You might have noticed worn limestone statues in cities you have visited. Acid rain is a problem near many manufacturing cities and their surroundings. Natural and human-built environments are damaged when the wind blows toxic gases across state or international borders and acid rain forms. The choices some communities make can have serious consequences for others.

FIGURE 8.25 Chemical weathering of a statue caused by acid rain

INVESTIGATION 8.1

Investigating chemical weathering of a variety of rocks

YOUR CHALLENGE
Investigate a variety of types of rocks. Acids do not have to be strong to damage rocks. Your challenge is to test the effects of weak acids on different rocks.

THIS MIGHT HELP
Your teacher will provide you with cups, timers, pieces of rock and a choice of weak acids, such as vinegar and lemon juice, to use in your investigation. What is your main independent variable in this investigation? Perhaps you could investigate other variables as well. How will you compare how quickly different rocks react?

Carry out and write up the investigation by following the guide in Appendix 3 on page 169, or as advised by your teacher.

SAFETY
Use safe laboratory procedures at all times. Wear eye protection, clean up any spilt chemicals quickly, and dispose of materials as directed.

CRITICAL THINKING
Consider whether the experiment you carried out produced valid results.

Biological weathering

Plant and tree roots can cause rocks to break. When they are small, plant roots find their way into small cracks in the rock. As they grow, the roots become larger and force the crack open (Figure 8.26). Very small plants such as mosses and lichens can also cause this. Look around your school or neighbourhood. How many examples of **biological weathering** can you find?

Erosion

Erosion is the wearing down and carrying away of the Earth's surface (Figure 8.27). Erosion can be caused by water, wind or ice. Rock wears away when wind and water hurl sand at its surface at high speed. It happens to rocks in the river when they are knocked against each other and worn smooth (Figure 8.28). Waves continually crashing into cliffs eventually wear away the land. The eerie hoodoos of Bryce Canyon in Utah, USA, were formed when bits of sand in the wind carved out the softer rock. This left strange looking columns in their place. Ice from glaciers carve valleys as they grind downhill (Figure 8.29).

FIGURE 8.26 Tree roots can cause rocks to crack.

FIGURE 8.27 Soil erosion

Shutterstock/Steve Bower

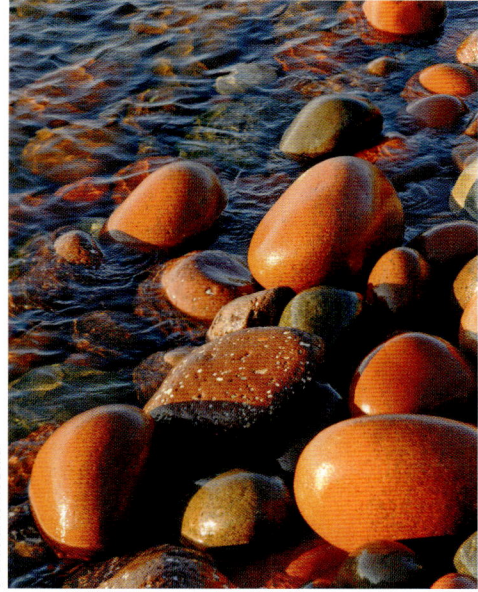

FIGURE 8.28 Moving water smooths rock surfaces.

Shutterstock.com/Asaf Eliason

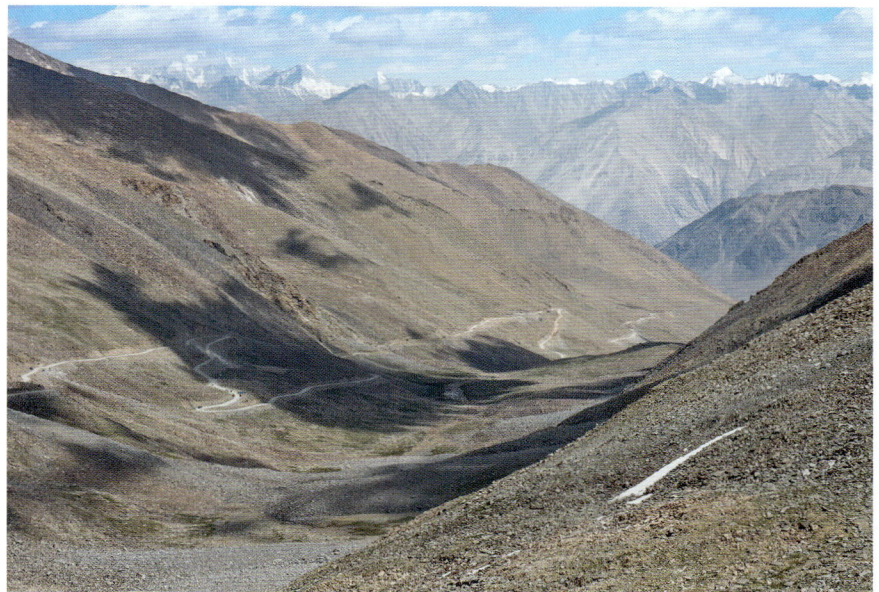

FIGURE 8.29 This distinctive U-shaped valley was caused by a glacier.

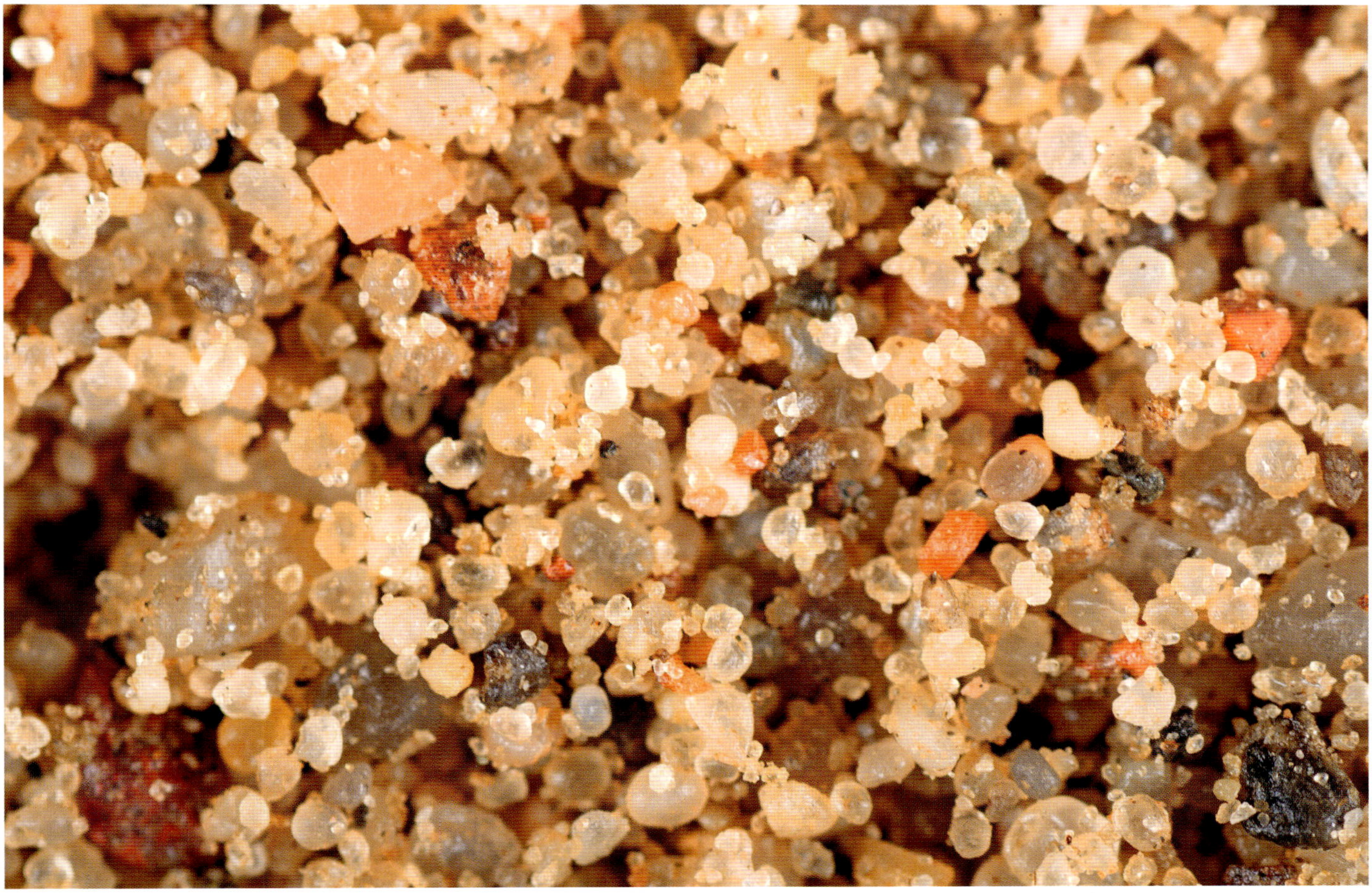

Shutterstock.com/Yury Smelov

FIGURE 8.30 Grains of sand are tiny bits of silicate rock, mainly quartz, broken down over time.

How do river rocks become round?

INVESTIGATION 8.2

YOUR CHALLENGE
Design and carry out an investigation into how quickly rocks are rounded during erosion.

THIS MIGHT HELP
Your teacher will provide you with sugar cubes to model the erosion of real rocks. The erosion you will study will be the shaking of these sugar cubes in plastic bottles. You will need to invent a method to measure how much of the sugar cube has been eroded. For example, you could weigh the amount of eroded sugar cube. How many shakes do you think you need to give the bottle? How many times will you repeat the shaking?

REFLECTION
Monitor your work. You are likely to have experienced some difficulties in developing your method for this investigation. Did you monitor your progress and consider revised experimental strategies?

Go to http://mypsci1.nelsonnet.com.au and click on **Erosion** to play an interactive game demonstrating types of erosion.

Our impact

Human activities can accelerate erosion to natural landscapes. Grasses and native plants secure the soil in place, so removing them has an impact on erosion. Tourism can be particularly hard on fragile areas.

Some human activities that increase erosion are:
- hiking, beach activities, skiing, mountain bike riding and driving off-road vehicles, which cause physical erosion
- intensive farming and deforestation, which can cause poor soil structure and consequent erosion of the land
- the introduction of new species of animals such as rabbits and deer, which can increase the erosion of mountains and hills when the animals consume all the available vegetation.

REVIEW

1. Outline how these factors can cause rocks to weather.
    a. Ice
    b. Tree roots
    c. Wind
    d. Changes of temperature
2. Suggest a reason why stones that are in windy places or running water become round and smooth.
3. Outline what chemical weathering does to minerals in rocks.
4. Outline how sedimentary rocks are formed.
5. State the difference between sedimentary rock and metamorphic rock.
6. Outline the stages in the rock cycle.
7. What is the difference between weathering and erosion?
8. Suggest a reason why sedimentary rocks often have layers of slightly different colours.
9. Discuss ways in which human activities can increase erosion.

UNIT QUESTIONS

CRITERION A

EXPLAINING SCIENTIFIC KNOWLEDGE

1. What layer of the Earth am I? (Level 1–2)
   a. I contain molten rock.
   b. The rocks in me are almost molten and they slowly churn about.
   c. I am solid and scientists think that I contain iron and nickel.
   d. I am solid and the thinnest layer.
2. Use the diagram in Figure 8.31 to answer the questions. (Level 3–4)

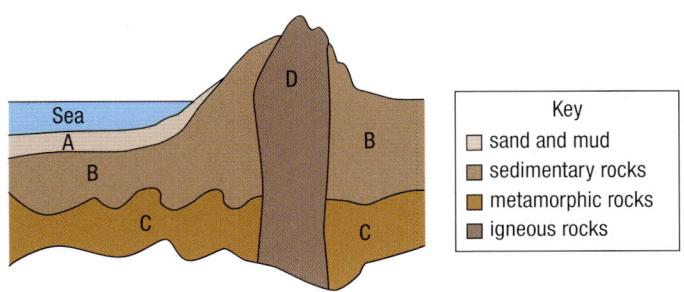

FIGURE 8.31

   Match a letter A–D from the diagram to each description a–e. You may write each letter more than once.
   a. Rock changed by heat and pressure
   b. Rock formed by magma cooling and solidifying
   c. The oldest rock shown in the diagram
   d. Region where eroded materials are deposited
   e. Region not being affected by erosion
3. Outline the scientific view of how the Earth was formed. (Level 5–6)
4. Summarise the theory of plate tectonics. Describe the evidence for it, and describe two situations on the Earth where we see these moving plates in action. (Level 7–8)

APPLYING SCIENTIFIC KNOWLEDGE AND UNDERSTANDING TO SOLVE A PROBLEM

5. Suggest a reason why countries such as Chile and New Zealand have many earthquakes. (Level 1–2)
6. Rainwater can damage rocks by both physical and chemical weathering (Level 3–4)
   a. Suggest one way rainwater causes physical weathering.
   b. Suggest one way rainwater causes chemical weathering.
7. Describe the conditions that would result in the most erosion to a mountain. (Level 3–4)
8. Construct a timeline across your workbook page and indicate the approximate timing of the: (Level 5–6)
   a. formation of the Earth
   b. appearance of the first simple life forms
   c. appearance of dinosaurs
   d. appearance of *Homo sapiens*.
9. Suggest the outcome of the following types of collisions between plate boundaries. (Level 7–8)
   a. One plate is forced under the other.
   b. Plates slowly pull apart and magma oozes to the surface.
   c. The jagged edges of plates are locked as in a puzzle. When enough pressure is exerted, they slip in opposite directions.
   d. Two plates collide and both edges are forced upwards.
10. You are hiking through a natural area and notice an unusual sedimentary feature. It almost appears as though someone has placed an enormous boulder on top of a tall thin column. Your guide assures you it is natural. Use your understanding of the rock cycle, weathering and erosion to explain how this formation could have formed. (Level 7–8)

INTERPRETING INFORMATION

11. Someone says that fossils can be found in all types of rocks. Outline why that person is or is not correct. (Level 1–2)
12. Outline why scientists can use a fossil's placement in rock to tell how old the rock is. (Level 3–4)
13. Some movies send submarines to the centre of the Earth. Explain how realistic you think this is using what you have learnt over this unit. (Level 5–6)

14 A community wants to open an undeveloped area for hiking. Another group wants this area opened for four-wheel off-road recreational driving. Create an argument using what you have learnt about erosion to support opening this area for one of these activities. (Level 7–8)

REFLECTION

1. When considering change in science, we need to consider the appropriate scales to use. Compare the scales used in this unit for time, and for movement of the tectonic plates. How are we able to measure these?
2. A big idea in this unit was how scientific theories develop over time. We learnt how a completely new theory about the Earth (the plate tectonic theory) was developed. Try to find out what people believed before the plate tectonic theory. A lot of scientists were not initially convinced by the plate tectonic theory and took a long time to be convinced. Why do you this might have been?
3. Another big idea in this unit was cycles, such as the rock cycle. What do we mean by cycles in science? Discuss with your teacher other cycles in nature.
4. Find out how complete the fossil record is. Are there any gaps in our knowledge? Are there still any disagreements about the fossil record? Why is the fossil evidence controversial for some people?
5. Did humans and dinosaurs ever inhabit the planet at the same time? This question is often asked of people to find out their knowledge of science. What do you think the answer is?
6. Discuss the idea that human activities have contributed positively to the development of landscapes. We often protect natural landscapes; should we also protect human-formed landscapes such as those formed by farming?

Appendices

Appendix 1: Approaches to Learning (ATL) framework in MYP Sciences

One of the main reasons the IB is so respected worldwide is that it places Approaches to Learning (ATL) in a central role in all IB programmes, thus encouraging the skills, habits and dispositions necessary to succeed in learning, both at school and for the rest of your life. Whenever you are learning in the MYP, you should remember that there are two things happening.
1. You are learning about the subject you are studying.
2. You are learning about learning.

The key attribute you need is to believe that you can continue improving as a learner over your life. Throughout the *Science for the international student* books, you will see reminders of ATL skills (from the list below) that are involved in the tasks we have set.

ATL skill categories and clusters	ATL skills
COMMUNICATION I Communication	1 Express ideas clearly, precisely and persuasively. 2 Use effective and correct scientific language. 3 Use appropriately a variety of media for communication, including 21st-century technologies. 4 Use appropriate forms and modes of communication for different purposes and audiences. 5 Use strategies skilfully for speaking in public, reading for meaning, and structured writing.
SOCIAL II Collaboration	1 Show empathy to others when working in diverse teams, be aware of cultural differences, and encourage and support all members of a team. 2 Show flexibility and willingness to make necessary compromises to accomplish a common goal when working in groups. 3 Carry out a variety of roles and accept responsibility when working in groups/teams; show negotiating, advocacy, consensus-making and leadership skills. 4 Listen effectively and use non-verbal communication/body language. 5 Use social networking to build relationships effectively.
SELF-MANAGEMENT III Organisation	1 Understand the importance of setting personal goals, both long term and short term. 2 Manage time well, establish priorities and meet deadlines, using a daily and longer-term planner. 3 Prepare for and sit examinations, prepare a study program, make summaries, revise actively and control emotions. 4 Be organised for learning, including preparing materials, books, notes, online resources and necessary equipment for class. 5 Establish good support systems through family and friends, and create a pleasant place to study.
IV Affective	1 Be self-motivated, have a positive attitude, and believe you can improve as a learner. 2 Be mindful of mental distractions and how to improve focus. 3 Be resilient: cope well with failure and unexpected challenges. 4 Persevere in achieving long-term goals (have grit). 5 Be emotionally intelligent: control emotions and stress.

ATL skill categories and clusters	ATL skills
V Reflection	1 Be self-aware as a learner; be able to discuss your strengths and weaknesses and make goals for improvement. 2 Be able to give and respond well to feedback. 3 Show self-awareness of your learning, and be able to strategically plan how to carry out a task. 4 Monitor your work to review the progress being made, the areas of difficulty and the need for revised strategies. 5 Be knowledgeable about aspects of learning such as multiple intelligences and learning styles.
RESEARCH **VI** Information literacy	1 Access information from a range of sources in an efficient and effective way; be skilled in summarising information and note-taking. 2 Evaluate information critically, be able to identify primary and secondary sources, and identify points of view and bias. 3 Use information selectively, accurately and creatively for the task at hand. 4 Understand the legal and ethical implications around the use of information, academic honesty and intellectual property rights; use citations, footnotes, referencing and bibliographies. 5 Develop the skills to function in a knowledge economy, using digital technologies such as networking tools and social networks.
VII Media literacy	1 Think critically about media to analyse, evaluate and understand how and why media messages are constructed and identify any bias, spin or misinformation that may be present. 2 Appreciate how individuals interpret messages differently. 3 Understand how media can influence our beliefs and behaviours, and culture and society generally. 4 Show an understanding of the ethical and legal issues surrounding the access to and use of media. 5 Understand and utilise the most appropriate media creation tools, characteristics and conventions to communicate information and ideas.
THINKING **VIII** Critical thinking	1 Use various types of reasoning, such as deduction and induction, as appropriate to the situation. 2 Be able to logically design scientific investigations to explore research questions, to develop an appropriate hypothesis and to control variables. 3 Reflectively analyse and evaluate evidence, data, arguments, alternative points of view, and claims and beliefs, to make valid judgments, conclusions, interpretations and decisions. 4 Synthesise and make connections between information and arguments to create new understandings. 5 Solve problems effectively, including in non-familiar situations; ask penetrating questions to clarify the problem.
IX Creative thinking	1 Show curiosity, a desire to dig deeper; enjoy novelty and uncertainty, and coming up with new ideas, products and solutions. 2 Be creative and imaginative, play with ideas; show divergent thinking, and be willing to let go and take risks; tolerate ambiguity; see mistakes as opportunities for learning. 3 Reason through metaphor and analogy; elaborate ideas; synthesise disparate bits of information; utilise knowledge in new contexts; formulate general concepts by abstracting common properties. 4 Design new products and technologies; be innovative and show entrepreneurial skills. 5 Create original works and ideas.
X Transfer (of skills and knowledge)	1 Show the motivation and meta-cognitive ability to support possible transfer of skills and knowledge within a discipline or across disciplines. 2 Be able to apply conceptual understandings and skills to new situations and across disciplines. 3 Appreciate the importance of interdisciplinary challenges and authentic problems, in which transfer of skills and knowledge is so important. 4 Be knowledgeable about recent developments in neuroscience and use information about the functioning of the brain to discuss learning (including the value of active, inquiry-based, contextual, collaborative and conceptual learning). 5 Understand how memory works and use techniques to improve memory.

Appendix 2: MYP Science 1 assessment criteria

	Achievement Level			
	1–2	**3–4**	**5–6**	**7–8**
Criterion A **Knowing and understanding**	i **Select** scientific knowledge. ii **Select** scientific knowledge and understanding to **suggest solutions** to problems set in **familiar situations**. iii **Apply** information to **make judgments**, **with limited success**.	i **Recall** scientific knowledge. ii **Apply** scientific knowledge and understanding to **suggest solutions** to problems set in **familiar situations**. iii **Apply** information to **make judgments**.	i **State** scientific knowledge. ii **Apply** scientific knowledge and understanding to **solve problems** set in **familiar situations**. iii **Apply** information to **make scientifically supported judgments**.	i **Outline** scientific knowledge. ii **Apply** scientific knowledge and understanding to **solve problems** set in **familiar situations** and **suggest solutions** to problems set in **unfamiliar situations**. iii **Interpret** information to **make scientifically supported judgments**.
Criterion B **Inquiring and designing**	i **Select** a problem or question to be tested by a scientific investigation. ii **Select** a testable prediction. iii **State** a variable. iv **Design** a method **with limited success**.	i **State** a problem or question to be tested by a scientific investigation. ii **State** a testable prediction. iii **State** how to manipulate the variables, and **state** how **data** will be collected. iv **Design** a **safe method** and **select appropriate materials and equipment**.	i **State** a problem or question to be tested by a scientific investigation. ii **Outline** a testable prediction. iii **Outline** how to manipulate the variables, and **state** how **relevant data** will be collected. iv **Design** a **complete and safe method** and **select appropriate materials and equipment**.	i **Outline** a problem or question to be tested by a scientific investigation. ii **Outline** a testable prediction using scientific reasoning. iii **Outline** how to manipulate the variables, and **outline** how **sufficient, relevant data** will be collected. iv **Design** a **logical, complete and safe method** and **select appropriate materials and equipment**.

	Achievement Level			
	1–2	**3–4**	**5–6**	**7–8**
Criterion C **Processing and evaluating**	i **Collect and present** data in numerical and/or visual forms. ii **Interpret** data. iii **State** the validity of a prediction based on the outcome of a scientific investigation, **with limited success**. iv **State** the validity of the method based on the outcome of a scientific investigation, **with limited success**. v **State** improvements or extensions to the method that would benefit the scientific investigation, **with limited success**.	i **Correctly collect and present** data in numerical and/or visual forms ii **Accurately interpret** data and **outline** results. iii **State** the validity of a prediction based on the outcome of a scientific investigation. iv **State** the validity of the method based on the outcome of a scientific investigation. v **State** improvements or extensions to the method that would benefit the scientific investigation.	i **Correctly collect, organise and present** data in numerical and/or visual forms. ii **Accurately interpret** data and outline results **using scientific reasoning**. iii **Outline** the validity of a prediction based on the outcome of a scientific investigation. iv **Outline** the validity of the method based on the outcome of a scientific investigation. v **Outline** improvements or extensions to the method that would benefit the scientific investigation.	i **Correctly collect, organise, transform and present** data in numerical and/or visual forms. ii **Accurately interpret** data and **outline** results **using correct scientific reasoning**. iii **Discuss** the validity of a prediction based on the outcome of a scientific investigation. iv **Discuss** the validity of the method based on the outcome of a scientific investigation. v **Describe** improvements or extensions to the method that would benefit the scientific investigation.
Criterion D **Reflecting on the impacts of science**	i **State** the ways in which science is used to address a specific problem or issue. ii **State** the implications of using science to solve a specific problem or issue, interacting with a factor. iii **Apply** scientific language to communicate understanding. iv **Document** sources.	i **State** the ways in which science is used to address a specific problem or issue. ii **State** the implications of using science to solve a specific problem or issue, interacting with a factor. iii **Sometimes apply** scientific language to communicate understanding. iv **Sometimes document** sources correctly.	i **Outline** the ways in which science is used to address a specific problem or issue. ii **Outline** the implications of using science to solve a specific problem or issue, interacting with a factor. iii **Usually apply** scientific language to communicate understanding **clearly and precisely**. iv **Usually document** sources correctly.	i **Summarise** the way in which science is applied and used to address a specific problem or issue. ii **Describe and summarise** the implications of using science and its application to solve a specific problem or issue, interacting with a factor.* iii **Consistently apply** scientific language to communicate understanding **clearly and precisely**. iv **Document** sources **completely**.

*Factors include moral, ethical, social, economic, political, cultural or environmental.

Appendix 3: Guidance on carrying out and writing up MYP 1 scientific investigations (criteria B and C)

Title
- Give the investigation a title; for example, ' Properties of Springs'.

Problem/Research question (criterion B I)
- Outline what you are trying to find out; for example, 'How does the weight on a spring affect its length? I am interested in the type of relationship and whether the amount of weight used makes any difference to the length of the spring.'

Prediction (Hypothesis) (criterion B II)
- Outline what you think is going happen in your investigation; for example, 'My hypothesis is that the spring will stretch as I put more weights on it.'
- Use your scientific knowledge to explain why you think this will happen; for example, 'I think it will stretch because a force will cause the particles of the spring to separate.'

Variables (criterion B III)
- To do a fair test, you must only change one variable at a time.
- Write down the variable you will measure (dependent variable); for example, length of spring.
- Write down the variables that you will change (independent variables); for example, weights put on the spring, length of spring.
- Write down the variables that you will keep the same while doing your investigation (control variables); for example, the spring you use.

Experimental method (criterion B III and IV)
- List all the materials and equipment you will use.
- Design a logical, complete and safe method, showing the materials and equipment you have selected. Include a special section on the safety issues. Drawing a diagram will often help you explain what you want to do.
- Include what range of measurements you will take and/or the size of the sample, and how often you will repeat readings.
- Your plan also needs to include an explanation of how you will control and manipulate the variables and how you will collect sufficient and relevant data. Describe how you will process the data.
- Sometimes you might need to carry out a preliminary experiment to check that your plan actually works. You might need to alter some aspects of your initial plan.

Results (criterion C I)
- Collect, organise and present all your observations or measurements (data) carefully and fully; use a well-labelled table, including correct column headings and units.
- Draw an appropriate graph of your results if they include numbers.

Conclusion and explanation (criterion C II and III)

- Accurately interpret your data; that is, what does your data tell you about your original research question? Comment on any patterns in your results. If you have numbers and a graph, discuss the shape of the line and the relationship it shows between the variables. This is your conclusion. Make sure you explain your conclusion, showing good scientific understanding.
- When writing your conclusion, construct a well thought out and reflective argument based on careful consideration of your evidence. Is your evidence good enough? If you feel your results don't really provide enough evidence to make a firm conclusion, then say so.
- Evaluate your prediction (hypothesis) – did it prove to be valid based on your results?
- Note: Where a result seems to be out of place and does not keep to the pattern, it is called an anomaly. (Perhaps a mistake was made in the reading.) You should discuss these results, and suggest reasons for their presence, but don't use them in making your conclusion.

Evaluation (criterion C IV and V)

- How well do you think your method worked? Did you have any problems you dealt with while carrying out the experiment?
- Validity: Did you collect sufficient valid data to answer the question? Did the instruments measure what they were meant to? What errors were there in your measurements? Was it truly a fair test? Did you repeat your readings enough times? Was your sample well chosen and large enough?
- Improvements: Write down how you might make your investigation better, especially to improve the validity or to obtain more reliable evidence. Write down any further experiments you could carry out to get more evidence or to extend this investigation.

Appendix 4: Articulating the conceptual framework in MYP Sciences

The MYP Science conceptual framework is defined by the key concepts of change, systems and relationships. These key concepts are further articulated through the use of related concepts. This conceptual framework will then be articulated in the curriculum via a series of integrating conceptual statements.

> In MYP Science, students develop their understandings about scientific **systems** and the **changes** that take place within these systems via the investigation of causal **relationships**.

The conceptual framework

Systems

Scientists use a systems approach to study the world. There are different kinds of systems, including the universe itself, the Earth, ecosystems, and closed systems in physics.

Related concepts	Integrating conceptual statements	Examples
Environment (biology)	The form, development and survival of an organism or a community is influenced by its surrounding **environment**, i.e. a combination of both abiotic and biotic factors.	In biology, we study the reasons for the changing populations of animals. In chemistry, we consider how pollution has affected fish life in lakes. In physics, we consider the impact of energy policies on the environment.
Interaction	Often there are **interactions** in science when two objects or more come together in a way that affects both of them.	In biology, we study the interaction between flowers and bees. In chemistry, we consider the interactions between water molecules. In physics, we study the interactions between electrostatic charges.
Models	Scientists use **models** to help them understand and to study some aspects of the world.	In biology, we use a model of the lungs to understand how breathing happens. In chemistry, we use models of chemical structures to understand the properties of salt (sodium chloride). In physics, we could use a model to simulate how particles move in a gas.
Cycles	To understand many systems, we need to consider **cycles** of energy and matter.	In biology, we consider cycles such as menstruation. In chemistry, we study cycles of elements in nature, such as carbon and nitrogen. In physics, we study cycles in the appearance of sunspots.
Scales	Different systems work at different **scales**, usually in relation to size, energy and speed. Scientists have developed the SI system of units to aid communication.	In chemistry and biology, we learn that different scales in size of particles of matter have an enormous effect on their properties. In physics, we consider speeds that range from a few centimetres per year (moving tectonic plates) to millions of metres per second (the speed of light).

Change

In science, change is viewed as the difference in a system's state when observed at different times. This change could be qualitative (such as differences in structure, behaviour or level) or quantitative (such as a numerical variable or a rate).

Related concepts	Integrating conceptual statements	Examples
Energy	**Energy** can be transformed from one form to another. Energy flows can be tracked through a system. The total amount of energy is conserved in closed systems.	In biology, we track energy flows through an ecosystem. In chemistry, we study how we can relate the heat given out in reactions to bond energies. In physics, we study how solar energy can be converted to electrical energy.
Transformation	Molecules, organisms, materials and energy can be **transformed** from one form to another.	In biology, we learn about genetic transformations in cells or the transformation as caterpillars change into butterflies. In chemistry, we learn about sand being transformed into glass. In physics, we study how energy can be transformed from one form to another.
Movement	Change and **movement** are at the heart of all natural systems, from the universe itself to the smallest cell.	The study of biology and chemistry depends on understanding the movement of particles. In physics, Newton's laws are used to explain the movement of objects.
Balance	Achieving a **balanced** state or equilibrium is an important idea in many sciences. Feedback loops are an important aspect of understanding many stable systems.	In biology, we consider how the body regulates its temperature. In chemistry, we learn about how reversible chemical reactions reach equilibrium. In physics, we consider how the forces on an object can be balanced.
Evolution	The natural world can be understood by considering **evolutionary** changes, some gradual, others sporadic.	We study the theory of biological evolution, which examines the changes in all forms of life over generations. We also can consider how technology evolves over time.
Conditions	Physical **conditions** influence chemical reactions and physical properties of materials.	In chemistry, we learn about the influence of factors such as temperature on the speed of reactions and how erosion of rocks is affected by changes in physical conditions.

Relationships

Relationships in science indicate the connections found among variables through observation or experimentation. These relationships also can be tested through experimentation. Scientists often search for the connections between form and function. Modelling is also used to represent relationships where factors such as scale, volume of data, or time make other methods impractical.

Related concepts	Integrating conceptual statements	Examples
Patterns	Recognising and seeking explanations for **patterns** in nature or collected data is the first step in scientific inquiry.	In biology, we consider the patterns in fossil records. In chemistry, we study patterns in the reactions of elements. In physics, we consider the patterns we see in the movement of the planets.
Cause and effect	The search for underlying causes of scientific phenomena is based upon establishing **cause and effect** relationships. We must always remember 'correlation does not necessarily imply causation'.	In biology, we could look for cause-and-effect relationships to help us learn how to reduce certain diseases. In chemistry, we consider the causes of increased erosion. In physics, we look for cause-and-effect relationships between force and changes in motion.
Evidence	Scientists use observations and data to develop **evidence** to support their claims, conclusions or answers to research questions. Scientists need to make careful arguments to justify their evidence.	In scientific investigations, we need to carefully consider the evidence when making conclusions; for example, did the results show that a heavier weight on the pendulum made it swing faster or slower or did it make no change?
Consequences	Making changes to systems (especially ecosystems) can have significant **consequences**; sometimes these can be predicted, other times they can be unexpected.	We consider the consequences of global warming, the possible consequences of nanotechnology, and the consequences of increased air traffic.
Form and function	The **function** (purpose, role, way of behaving) of a system or a structure is related to its **form** (the shape, relationships between the parts, composition and properties).	In biology, this is a crucial concept, with applications ranging from studying the arrangement of legs on an animal, to the shape of seeds, to the form and function of different cells. In chemistry, we consider how a substance's structure at the ionic or molecular level results in its actual properties. In physics, we discuss how to alter the design of a bike to improve its performance.
Development	Scientific understanding is being continuously **developed** via a continuous process of scientific investigation.	In biology, we consider how ideas about the cause and spread of diseases developed, and also the theory of biological evolution. In physics and chemistry, we study how ideas about the atom developed, especially in the late 19th and early 20th centuries.

Related concepts	Integrating conceptual statements	Examples
Creativity	The scientific endeavour is associated with a high level of creativity.	We experience the importance of creativity by studying the contributions of many truly creative scientists, such as Rutherford, Darwin and Mendeleev, through designing and carrying out our own experiments, and in the way we use our ideas in science to develop higher-level understandings.

Note: The following diagram has limitations. There are many other relations between key and related concepts, and between different related concepts, not shown in this diagram. However, we feel it could help teachers and students start developing a mental map of how the conceptual framework for Sciences links together.

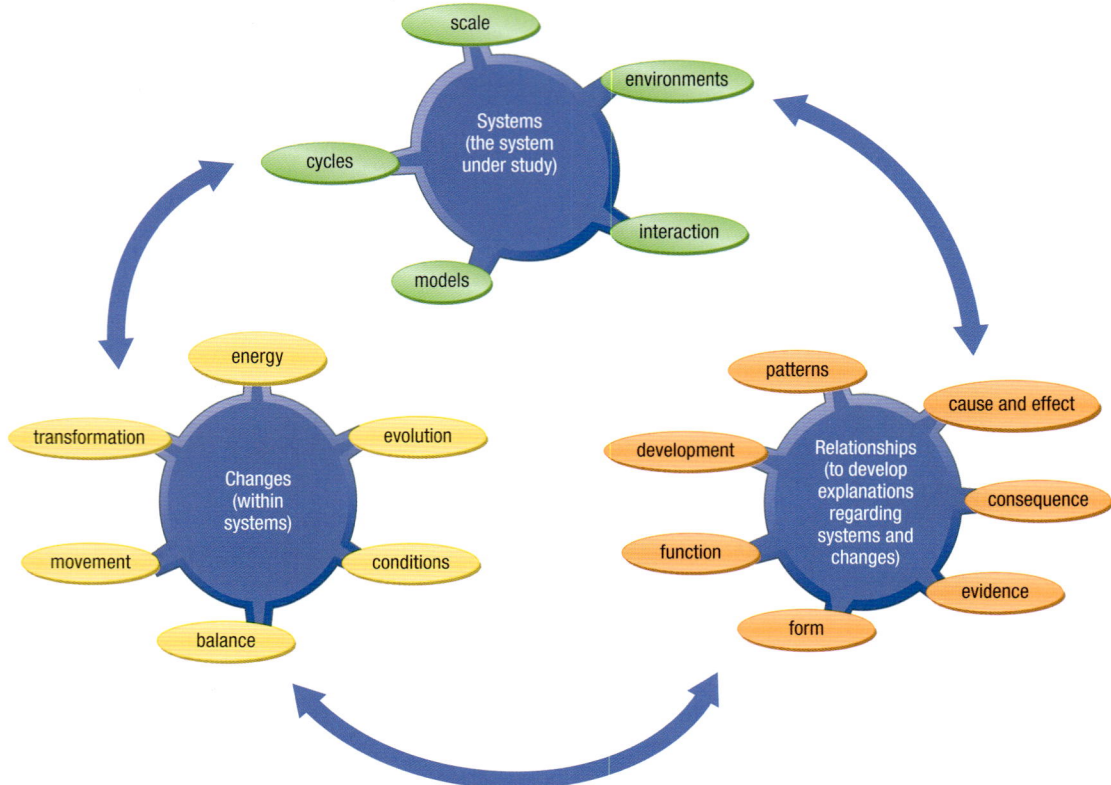

Glossary

acceleration an increase in speed over a period of time
acid a substance that tastes sour, reacts with bases and has a pH of less than 7
acid rain rain containing dissolved chemicals that form an acid
acid–base reaction any reaction between an acid and a base
accurate (of information) exactly correct; free of error
adaptation a change to a characteristic over time to enable a living thing to successfully live in its natural habitat
air resistance a force exerted by air that resists (opposes) the movement of objects through the air (also known as drag force)
alkali a base that can dissolve in water
alkaline solution a solution with a pH greater than 7
ammeter an instrument used to measure electric current in a circuit
ampere (amp) the SI unit for measuring electric current
anaerobic without oxygen
anode the negative terminal of a battery
anomaly a result that is very different from or inconsistent with the other results of an experiment
animal a complex multicellular organism that gets its nutrition by consuming other organisms
anode the negative terminal on a battery
antibiotic a substance that kills bacteria
aquaculture the farming of freshwater or saltwater organisms
archaebacteria simple micro-organisms that live in extreme environments

assessment criteria reference points against which something can be assessed
attract pull towards
aurora lighting effect caused when solar particles are drawn to the Earth's magnetic poles
axis an imaginary line running through a planet around which it rotates

bacteria simple micro-organisms
balanced forces forces that have a net zero effect on an object when they are all applied simultaneously
base a substance that tastes bitter, reacts with acids and, if soluble (alkali), has a pH greater than 7
binomial having two names
biodiversity all the differences within and between living things
biological weathering the breakdown of rocks by plant and tree roots
boiling point the temperature at which a liquid turns into a gas
boundary the region where two tectonic plates meet
buffer a protective barrier between two things
buoyancy force an upward force exerted by a liquid on an object placed in or on the liquid

caloric theory an incorrect theory that said heat was a substance that entered another substance as it heated
carbonic acid an acid formed when carbon dioxide bubbles into water
cartographer a person who makes maps
cathode the positive terminal of a battery
change of state a change from one state (solid, liquid or gas) to another

chemical weathering the breakdown of rocks into clay as a result of slow reactions with water
class a set of similar organisms within a phylum
classify sort things into groups on the basis of their similarities
climate change any long-term change to weather patterns
compass an instrument with a magnetised needle that points to magnetic north and south
compress press together into less space
concentrated containing a large amount of a substance dissolved in water
concentration the proportion of a given substance that is contained within another substance
concept a big idea
condensation formation of liquid water when gaseous water loses energy and changes into a liquid state
conductor substance in which electrons move around easily and transmit electrical energy
consumer an organism that eats other organisms
contact force a force between objects that are touching each other
control variable a variable that is kept constant in an investigation
convergent boundary the region where two tectonic plates come together, or collide
core the innermost layer of the Earth
corrosive can do irreversible damage to another substance on contact
crust the hard outer layer of the Earth, which is approximately 40 kilometres thick
crystal a multi-sided solid mineral that has an ordered arrangement of atoms

cyanobacteria a type of one-celled organism, sometimes called blue-green algae, which obtains its energy through photosynthesis
cytoplasmic streaming the movement of cytoplasm within a living cell

decay rotting or decomposition of organic matter caused by bacteria and fungi
deceleration a decrease in speed over a period of time
dense of a high density (see *density*)
density the quantity of mass contained per unit of volume
dependent variable the variable that is measured in an investigation
descriptive name also known as the species name
dichotomous key a chart used to assist scientists to classify living things, presenting two choices at every level
diffusion the spread of particles through random motion from regions of higher concentration to regions of lower concentration
dilute containing a small amount of a substance dissolved in water
discharge loss or removal of built-up electrostatic charge
divergent boundary the region where two tectonic plates move apart from each other, allowing magma to ooze up and create new crust
DNA the genetic material found inside cells
domain (mini-magnet) the smallest part of a magnet that still shows magnetic properties
down fine, fluffy feathers under the exterior feathers; young birds often only have down feathers

ecosystem the combination of all the living organisms and all the non-living parts, such as water, soil, rocks, air and wind, that make up a particular environment
electric circuit a closed loop in which electricity travels
electric current the rate of flow of electrons past a certain point in the circuit
electromagnet iron with electrical wire coiled around it that becomes magnetic when an electric current is running through the coil
electrostatic force a force between objects that have an electrical charge
equilibrium a situation where the forces acting on an object are balanced
era a division of time on the geologic scale
erosion the process by which rocks are worn away by the action of water, glaciers, winds and waves
eubacteria simple micro-organisms
evaporation the conversion of liquid water into its vapour form below its boiling point
evidence information that proves or demonstrates the truth of a statement
expansion a process by which the amount of space taken up by matter is increased
experimental data information that is collected from measurements taken during an experiment

fair test a scientific investigation in which only one variable is changed at a time
family a set of similar organisms within an order
feature a characteristic, for example, relating to how an organism is built, how it behaves and how it functions
fertile able to produce offspring
field the region where a force is experienced
field line an invisible line of magnetic attraction, visible when you map a magnetic field with iron filings
fluid a substance whose molecules move freely past one another and which will take on the shape of its container; the collective name for liquids and gases
food chain a diagram that shows who eats whom in an ecosystem
food web a complex diagram that shows all the feeding interactions within an ecosystem
force a push or pull
force of attraction a force between objects that pulls them closer together
force of repulsion a force between objects that pushes them away from one another
formative assessment assessment carried out in such a way as to help students improve their learning
fossil the remains or impression of a dead organism found in sedimentary rocks
freezing point the temperature at which a liquid turns into a solid
frictional force a force that opposes the motion of an object when it is in contact with another surface
fungus (plural: fungi) a complex multicellular organism that gains its nutrition by absorbing the decayed remains of other organisms

genus set of similar organisms within a family
global context a description of interesting and globally relevant contexts for students' learning; one of six in the MYP framework
glucose the simple sugar produced during photosynthesis
gravitational force a force of attraction between two objects that weigh something, such as the force exerted on you by the Earth

host an organism in or on which a parasite lives and obtains its nutrients
hotspot an area where a large plume of magma reaches from the mantle up to the crust, forming volcanoes
humidity the level of water vapour in the air
hypothesis a prediction of a probable outcome of an investigation that is based on observation, knowledge or research

igneous rock a type of rock that forms when molten rock is cooled
independent variable the variable that is changed in an investigation
indicator a substance that changes colour at different pH values
infertile unable to produce offspring
inner core the dense, solid centre of the Earth that contains iron and nickel
insulation material that prevents or reduces the transfer of heat, electricity or sound
insulator substance in which electrons do not move easily
investigation a special method scientists use to answer research questions about the world around us
isobar a line on a weather map that connects areas of similar air pressure

keystone species a species that has a large effect on its environment relative to the size and number of the species
kinetic (energy) the energy of movement
kingdom a set of similar living things

line of best fit a line on a scatter plot or line graph that best expresses the trend shown in the plotted points
living takes in food, gets rid of waste and is able to reproduce

magma molten rock that collects under the Earth's crust
magnet an object that is able to attract certain materials
magnetic field the region over which a magnet can affect objects
magnetic force a force of attraction or repulsion between a magnet and another object
magnetic levitation a method by which an object is made to hover above a surface using a magnetic field
magnetic north pole/south pole the natural poles of the Earth's magnetic field, which compasses point to
magnetite (lodestone) a magnetic mineral found in nature; a type of iron ore
magnify increase the apparent size of something
mangrove a woody plant that lives between the sea and the land in a mangrove swamp ecosystem
mantle the layer of the Earth directly underneath the crust
matter the 'stuff' of which the world is made; has mass and occupies space
mean a type of average
melting point the temperature at which a solid becomes a liquid
metamorphic rock a type of rock that has been changed by high temperatures and pressures
micro-organism a small living thing, only able to be seen with a microscope
mineral a solid substance that occurs naturally, does not contain any matter derived from living organisms, and has a definite chemical composition and an ordered internal structure
misconception incorrect idea about science
model an idea that is used to explain patterns and predict data
moulting the annual shedding of feathers to replace damaged and old feathers

moving particle theory a model used to describe the behaviour of solids, liquids and gases in terms of how fast the particles move
MRI (magnetic resonance imaging) a medical technique that uses electromagnets to take images of the tissues of the body
multicellular made up of more than one cell
mutualism a relationship between two living things in which both organisms benefit

nanomagnet a very small magnet, which measures only a few nanometres across
neodymium a rare earth element used in making powerful permanent magnets
neutral pH 7, neither acidic nor basic
neutralise add a base to an acid in the right proportions, or vice versa, to result in a neutral pH of 7
newton the SI unit that measures force; 1 N will accelerate a mass of 1 kg at a rate of 1 m/s^2
non-contact force a force that acts on an object without touching it; for example, magnetism and gravity
non-living not satisfying the criteria for living
non-science ideas, beliefs or information that cannot be confirmed by scientific investigation

open ecosystem an ecosystem that organisms can freely enter or leave to move to another ecosystem
order a set of similar organisms within a class
organism a living thing
outer core the layer of the Earth under the mantle that contains molten rock; the only liquid layer of the Earth.

parasite an organism that lives on or inside another living organism to obtain its needs, and weakens the host

parasite–host relationship the relationship between two organisms when one consumes part of the other without killing it
period time division on the geologic scale, shorter than an era
permanent magnet a magnet that always stays magnetic
pesticide a chemical spray used to kill insects and other organisms harmful to farming
pH scale a scale for measuring the acidity of a solution: the more acidic the solution, the lower the pH most solutions have a pH between 1 and 14
photosynthesis a chemical process used by plants, in which they take in water, carbon dioxide and sunlight and convert them to food (sugar), releasing oxygen
phylum (plural: phyla) a set of similar organisms within a kingdom
physical weathering the breakdown of rocks by physical means, such as wind, water, roots or temperature extremes
plant a complex multicellular organism that makes its own simple sugars by the process of photosynthesis
plasma the fourth state of matter; is most similar to gas; found in stars (such as our Sun), televisions and extremely hot flames
pneumatophore a type of aerial root used by mangroves to absorb oxygen
porous rock a type of rock that water can penetrate
precise consistent with (close to) other measurements of the same variable
predator an organism that kills and eats other organisms
predator–prey relationship the relationship between two organisms when a large consumer eats a smaller consumer

preening grooming, cleaning and maintaining feathers
pressure a force applied to a surface; measured in pascals (Pa)
prey an organism that is eaten by a predator
producer an organism that produces its own simple sugars through photosynthesis
prop root a branching root that arises from the trunk and provides support
protist one of a wide range of organisms that don't fit into any of the other five kingdoms
pseudoscience a claim that is presented as scientific but has not been, or cannot be, confirmed by scientific investigation
PYP transdisciplinary theme one of six themes that bridge various subject areas and provide the framework for learning in the IB Primary Years Programme

range the difference between the largest and the smallest values of the independent variable
relationship interaction between living things
repel push away from; push something away
resultant force the sum of all forces acting on an object; sometimes called the net force
rift a large break in the crust of the Earth
rock cycle the cycle of formation and decomposition of the three types of rock – igneous, sedimentary and metamorphic – that explains how they are related to each other

safety flame the yellow flame of a Bunsen burner that is easily seen; the cooler flame obtained with the air holes closed

scanning electron microscope a microscope that produces a three-dimensional image of the object it is magnifying
scientific method the careful and logical way scientists ask and answer questions by experimentation
sedimentary rock a type of rock that is formed from weathering and erosion of rocks, the fragments of which are then deposited in layers and compacted
shaft the strong central rib of a feather
solar nebula a giant cloud of dust and gas that might eventually form a solar system
soluble able to dissolve in other substances
solution liquid consisting of a solute uniformly distributed in a solvent
species a group of similar organisms that are able to mate with one another and produce fertile offspring
speed the ratio of the distance that an object travels to the time taken to travel that distance
static electricity the build-up of electrical charge on a surface
stimulus (plural: stimuli) an external action that produces a response
subduction the movement of denser oceanic crust under lighter continental crust at a convergent plate boundary
sublimation the process by which a solid changes quickly to a gas state, or vice versa, without becoming liquid
superconducting magnet a type of electromagnet that must be chilled to extremely low temperatures (colder than outer space)
sustainability capacity to maintain the diversity and health of a biological system

tectonic plates the large sections into which the Earth's crust is split

temporary magnet a magnet that only attracts things when it is next to a permanent magnet

transform boundary the region where two tectonic plates grind past each other, causing earthquakes

trend the general direction of change in data; can be used to predict future events

tsunami a long, high sea wave caused by an underwater earthquake

unbalanced forces forces that have a net non-zero effect on an object when they are all applied simultaneously

universal indicator a mixture of different indicators that displays a range of colours when added to solutions of different pHs

valid describes an experiment in which the variables are controlled (fair test), and you are measuring what you think you are measuring

vane the long flat surface of a feather

vapour a substance in a gaseous state

variable a factor of an investigation that can be changed

voltage a measure of the pressure moving electrons in an electric current

weathering the natural process of breaking down solid rock

Index

A

acceleration 116, 117
accuracy (results) 13
acetic acid 63
acid-base reactions 74–6
acid lakes 75
acid rain 62, 63–4, 71, 74, 159
acidic soils 70, 71
acidity 66–8
acids 62, 63, 67, 72–3
air pressure 96–7
air resistance 112–15
alkalinity 66–8
alkalis 65, 66, 67
ammeters 125
ampere 125
anaerobic environments 33
animal kingdom 30, 36
animalcules 28
anode 124
antacids 65, 74
antibiotics 58
aquaculture 58
archaebacteria kingdom 30, 33
Aristotle 37
assessment criteria, MYP Science 14–15, 167–8
asteroids 146
ATL (Approaches to Learning) skills and skill clusters 21, 165–6
atmospheric composition 147
atoms 120
attraction 110, 111
auroras 137
average speed 118

B

bacteria 28, 29, 30, 33
baking soda and vinegar reaction 74
balanced forces 114, 115
bases 62, 65–6, 72–3
batteries 124, 129
beaks 50–1
bicycle helmets 100, 109
bicycle tyres 107
Big Bang 146
big ideas in science 15–16
bimetallic strips 91, 93
binomial system of naming living things 39–40
biodiversity 57, 58
biological weathering 160
birds 50, 54
    beaks 50–1
    feathers 51–3
    use of thermals 92
bleach 65
boiling point 84, 85
brown algae 32
Bunsen burner usage 76–7
buoyancy force 111–14
burning of fossil fuels 63, 159

C

caloric theory 94
car tyres 108
carbon dioxide 53, 88
carbonic acid 62
cathode 124
caustic soda 65, 66, 72
cell complexity 30, 33
cells 30, 31, 33
ceramic magnets 133
change in motion 116–19
changes of state 84–8, 89
charges
    on atomic particles 120
    and electrostatic forces 110
    and transfer of electrons 120
chemical weathering 159
circuit diagrams 124, 127, 128, 129–31
circuit symbols 124
citric acid 62, 63
class 39
classification
    dichotomous keys 31–2
    kingdoms 30, 32–6
    Linnaeus' naming system 39–40
    living world 26, 28–9
    seven levels of 39
    timeline 37–8
cleaner wrasse 56
climate change 58, 91
clothes drying 87
clouds 89, 97
coal-fired power stations 63, 75
collecting and presenting data 11
collisions in sports 108–11
column graphs 12
common names 40
compass needle 136
compressibility 80, 81, 83
concentrated acids and bases 72–3
concentration (particles) 95
concepts, use of 15–16
conceptual framework, MYP Sciences 171–4
conclusion (investigations) 12, 169
condensation 88
conductors 123
consumers 53, 54, 59
contact forces 101, 106
continental crust 152
continental drift 151
continents 150, 151
control variables 10
convection currents 149
convergent boundaries 152
core 149
corrosive chemicals 72
crust 149, 151
cyanobacteria 147
cytoplasmic streaming 28

D

deceleration 116, 117
decomposers 59
density 80, 81
dental plaque 28, 29
dependent variable 10
descriptive names 40
dichotomous keys 31–2
diffusion 95–6
dilute acids and bases 72–3

discharge 110
distance-time graphs 118–1
divergent boundaries 152
DNA sequencing 37
domains 137
downy feathers (down) 51
drag force 112
dry ice 88

E

Earth 102, 103
   changing 146–8
   early atmosphere 147
   formation 146, 147, 155
   geologic time 147–8
   magnetic poles 136, 137
   rock formations 144–5, 146
   structure 149–50
earthquakes 153, 154
Earth's axis 146
Earth's magnetic field 136–7
ecosystems 56
   mangrove 56–9
   tundra 59
electric current 123, 124, 125, 128–9
electrical circuits 124
   drawing 124
   models 125
   parallel circuits 126, 127–9
   series circuits 126, 127–9
   showing voltages 129–31
   see also circuit diagrams
electricity 120, 123
electromagnets 138–9
electrons 120, 123, 124, 125
electrostatic forces 110
endangered species 42
energy in the environment 53, 54
environmental sustainability 57
equilibrium 114
erosion 156, 160–2
eubacteria kingdom 30, 33
evaluation (investigation) 13, 170
evaporation 86, 87
evidence 5
expansion 90, 93
   gases 92, 93

   liquids 91–2, 93
   and moving particle theory 90, 93
   solids 91
experimental data 11
experiments see scientific investigations

F

fair test 10, 13
family 39
feathers 51–3
fertile offspring 40
field 101
field lines 135, 136
fish habitat 58
flexible magnets 133, 134
fluids 81
fold mountains 152–3
food chains 54, 57
food webs 57, 59
force of attraction 134
force or repulsion 133
forces 101
   air resistance 112–15
   balanced and unbalanced 114–19
   buoyancy 111–14
   in collisions 108–11
   electrostatic 110
   frictional 106–10
   gravitational 101–7
   magnetic 111
   resultant 115, 116, 117
formative assessment 15
fossils 147, 150
freeze-thaw cycle 158
freezing point 84
friction in sports 107–10
frictional forces 106–10
fungi kingdom 30, 34, 35

G

gardening 70
gases 81
   diffusion 95
   expansion 92, 93
   kinetic theory 82
   particles in 82, 83

genus 39, 40
geologic time scale 147–8
global contexts 17, 18–19
global warming 92
glossary 175–9
glucose 53
gneiss 157
gravitational field 101, 102, 146
gravitational forces (gravity) 101–7, 111, 114
gummy bear challenge 8–13

H

Haeckel, Ernst 37
helmets 100, 108, 109
herons 50, 55, 56
high pressure 97
Himalayas 153
history of science 5
hosts 55
hot-air ballooning 92
hot-water systems 91, 92
hotspots 154
humidity 86
hypothesis 9–10, 169

I

ibis 50, 51, 54, 55
ice skates 107
igneous rocks 156, 157
independent variables 10
indicators 66–7, 68–9
Indonesian Island Arc 152
infertile offspring 41
inner core 149
insulation 51, 108
insulators 123
isobars 97

J

jam-making 70
Jansen, Zacharias 37
Jupiter 103

K

keystone species 59
kinetic energy 94
kinetic theory 82–3
kingdoms 30, 32–6, 39

L

Large Hadron Collider 141
leaves, dichotomous key 32
lemmings 59
lightning 110
lime 66, 71, 74, 75
limestone 74, 156, 159
line of best fit 11
line graphs 12
Linnaeus, Carolus 30, 37
    naming system 39–40
liquids 81
    diffusion 95
    expansion 91–2, 93
    kinetic theory 82
    particles in 82, 83
litmus paper 67
living things
    kingdoms 30, 32–6
    versus non-living 26–8
living world, classifying 26, 28–9
low pressure 97

M

Maglev trains 139–40
magma 155, 157
magnetic fields 132, 135–7, 138
magnetic forces 111, 132
magnetic levitation 140
magnetic north pole 136, 137
magnetic poles 134, 135–6
magnetic resonance imaging (MRI)
    machines 139, 140
magnetic south pole 136, 137
magnetite 133
magnets 120, 132–7
    Earth as a giant magnet 136–7
    electromagnets 138–9
    future of 141

    materials 133
    permanent 137
    temporary 137, 138
    uses for 139–41
mangrove ecosystems 56–7
    threats to 58–9
mangrove swamps 46, 47, 50–1
    birds of the 50–3, 54
    food chains 54
    food webs 57
    interactions in 53–6
mangroves 46, 48
    adaptations 48–50
    distribution 47
    and humans 47, 58
mantle 149, 152
marble 63, 157
mass 102–5
matter, states of 80–1
mean 11
medicine, magnets use 139
melting point 84, 85
metamorphic rocks 157
method (investigation) 10–11, 169
micro-organisms 28, 30
microscopes 28, 29
Mid-Atlantic Ridge 151, 152, 153, 154
Millennium Development Goals
    19, 57
mind maps 16
minerals 149
misconceptions in science 17
mobile phones
    dichotomous key 31
    recycling 26
    sorting 25
models 80, 125
Moon 102, 103, 146
moulds 34, 35
moulting 52
movement of objects 116–19
moving particle theory 80, 82–3
    and air pressure 96
    and diffusion 95
    and expansion 90, 93
    and temperature 94
multicellular organisms 35, 36
mushrooms 30, 34
mutualism 56

MYP Science
    assessment criteria 14–15, 167–8
    ATL skills and skill clusters 21, 165–6
    conceptual framework 171–4
    key and related concepts 17
    use of global contexts 18–19

N

naming system (Linnaeus) 39–40
nanomagnets 140–1
neodymium magnets 133
neutral (pH) 66
neutralisation reactions 74–6
neutrons 120
new species 41
new technologies 2–3
Newton, Sir Isaac 5
newtons 101
nitrogen oxide 63, 159
non-contact forces 101, 110, 111
non-science 6
nucleus 120

O

oceanic crust 152
onion skin 31
open ecosystems 56
order 39
outer core 149
outliers 12
over-cropping 71
oxygen 49

P

Pangaea 150–1
parachutes 112
parallel circuits 126, 127–8
paramecium 31
parasites 55
parasite–host relationship 55
particles
    in a gas 83
    in a liquid 82, 83
    in a solid 82, 83

pendulums 4
permanent magnets 137
pesticides 58
pH, applications 70–1
pH scale 66–8
photosynthesis 35, 53, 54, 147
phylum 39
physical weathering 158
pie graphs 12
plant kingdom 30, 35
plants, photosynthesis 35, 53, 54
plasma 81
plate boundaries 152–3, 154
plate tectonics 150–5
pneumatophores 49, 58
poles of a magnet 133–4
pollution 58, 62, 159
porous rocks 158
potential difference *see* voltage
precision (results) 13
predators 55, 59
predator–prey relationship 55
preening 51
pressure 96–7
prey 55
primary consumers 54
producers 53, 54
prop roots 49
protective helmets 100, 108, 109
protist kingdom 30, 32
protons 120
protozoa 32
pseudoscience 6
PYP transdisciplinary themes 17

Q

quartzite 157

R

railway tracks 91
rain 97
ramps 103–7
range 10
Ray, John 37
recycling 26
red cabbage indicator 68–9
repulsion 110, 111

research question 8–9, 169
resultant forces 115, 116, 117
results (investigations) 12, 169
Richter scale 154
rifts 152
Ring of Fire 154
rock cycle 145, 155–7

S

safety considerations, acids and bases 72–3
safety flame 76
safety gear, in challenging sports 100, 104
safety helmets 100, 108, 109
salt tolerance of plants 48
San Andreas Fault 153
sandstone 156
scanning electron microscope 37
science, how does it work? 5
science education 7, 15–17
scientific claims 6
scientific discoveries 2–3
scientific investigations 5, 7
    guidance on carrying out and writing up 169–70
    practice investigation 8–13
scientific method 7–13
scientific names 39, 40
scientists 3, 4, 5, 20
scuba divers 111, 112
sea level rising 58, 91, 92
seafloor spreading 151
seat belts 108
secondary consumers 54
sedimentary rocks 156
series circuits 126, 127–8
single cells 31, 33
skateboarders 104
skiers 104, 107, 112
skis 107
slate 157
snowboarders 104
sodium bicarbonate 73
sodium hydroxide 65, 66, 72
soil acidity 70, 71
soil erosion 160
solar nebulae 146

solar system 146
solids 80
    expansion 91
    kinetic theory 82
    particles in 82, 83
sorting
    natural world 26–7
    things 24–5
species 39, 40–1, 42
speed 118–1
sport
    collisions in 108–11
    friction in 107–10
    ramps in 104
    safety gear 100, 104, 108, 109
states of matter 80–1
static electricity 110
steam 85
strong acids and bases 72–3
subduction zones 154
sublimation 88
sulfur dioxide 63, 75, 159
Sun 102, 103
superconducting magnets 141
superheroes 6
surfboards 107
sweating 86
swimmers 111
swimming pools 70

T

tectonic plates 151–2, 154
temperature, and moving particle theory 94
temporary magnets 137, 138
thermals 92
thermometers 94
think, pair, share activity 16, 17
tinea 34
title (investigation) 169
transform boundaries 153
transform faults 153
transportation, magnet use 139
trends 12
tsunamis 154–5
tug-of-war 114, 115
tundra ecosystem 59
tyres 107, 108

U

unbalanced forces 114, 115
    and movement of objects 116–19
    and resultant force 115, 116, 117
universal indicator 67

V

validity 13, 170
van Leeuwenhoek, Antoni 28

variables 10, 169
volcanoes 152, 153, 154
voltage 129–31
voltmeters 129
von Linné, Carl *see* Linnaeus, Carolus

W

water authorities, pH monitoring 70–1
water droplets 89
water vapour 86, 89, 97
weather
    and air pressure 97
    and changes of state 89
weather maps 97
weathering 156, 157–60
Wegener, Alfred 150–1
weight 102, 103
wind 97

Y

yeast 34

NOTES

NOTES

NOTES

NOTES

NOTES

NOTES